THE HOPE FACTOR

THE HOPE FACTOR
ENGAGING THE CHURCH IN THE HIV/AIDS CRISIS

**Edited by Tetsunao Yamamori,
David Dageforde, and Tina Bruner**

Authentic
MEDIA

Published in partnership with World Vision Press

The Hope Factor: Engaging the Church in the HIV/AIDS Crisis

Copyright © 2003 by Tetsunao Yamamori, David Dageforde, and Tina Bruner

ISBN: 1-932805-11-7

09 08 07 06 05 04   9 8 7 6 5 4 3 2 1
Published by Authentic Media
129 Mobilization Drive, Waynesboro, GA 30830 USA www.authenticbooks.com
and 9 Holdom Avenue, Bletchley, Milton Keynes, Bucks, MK1 1QR, UK

Published in partnership with World Vision
34834 Weyerhauser Way South, P.O. Box 9716, Federal Way, WA 98063 USA
www.worldvision.org

Cover design: Paul Lewis

Printed in United States of America

Dear Reader,

World Vision invites you to share your response to the
message of this book by writing to World Vision Press at
worldvisionpress@worldvision.org or by calling 800-777-7752.

For information about other World Vision Press publications,
visit us at www.worldvision.org/worldvisionpress.

CONTENTS

Part Three: Biblical Reflections

Appendixes

FOREWORD

In the fourteenth century, the Black Death struck Europe, wiping out a third of the population. Early in the twentieth century, influenza killed 30 million people in Europe, Asia, Australia, and the Americas. Today, a new and terrible epidemic is ravaging Africa. If nothing is done, an estimated 55 million Africans will die an early death from AIDS by 2020.

But for the first time in a decade, the number of new AIDS cases is declining in sub-Saharan Africa. *The Boston Globe* speculated that this might be due to better efforts at prevention.

Of course it is, and the reason for this good news is the abstinence-first program aggressively promoted by the government of Uganda. There the infection rate—because of abstinence—has fallen from 30 to 10 percent in the last ten years. Studies show that Ugandans are taking fewer sexual partners and are practicing fidelity. Now other African countries are beginning to implement the same model, zealously advocated by Trans World Radio and others, and it's paying off.

Never before has a plague been stopped. But this one can be. President Bush recently gathered a dozen leaders at the White House for a discussion of his extraordinary $15 billion AIDS initiative. At that meeting, Franklin Graham, Theodore Cardinal McCarrick, and I applauded the president's leadership. Let us remember that great nations prove they are great, not merely through the might of their armies, but through the mercy of their hearts. Let's put politics aside and unite to fight this great plague of the twenty-first century—taking mercy on "the least of these."

So I am delighted to introduce and commend this fine book, which reviews so much Christian thinking and practice on the ground. It draws on the extensive experience of Christians in medical missions who are on the front line engaging in warfare against this terrible disease. It offers models of good practice and will encourage and refocus practitioners fighting AIDS in the field as well as spur the giving and prayers of Christians in the West.

AIDS presents us with a challenge that is as unique in its scope as it is disastrous for so many individuals, their families, and their communities. Christians have an equal opportunity to rise to the occasion—under God. Ted Yamamori and his colleagues have provided a tool that will help us combat this fearful scourge with courage and with skill In doing so, we'll not only be engaged in Christian compassion, we'll be making a powerful witness, showing the world that God's ways—abstinence and monogamy—are not only morally right but provide the answer that works.

Charles W. Colson
Chairman
Prison Fellowship Ministries and The Wilberforce Forum

PREFACE

The enormity of the global AIDS pandemic threatens to overwhelm us. More than 3 million people died of AIDS last year—about 8,000 per day—and another 5 million were infected with the pernicious HIV virus. Globally, nearly 40 million are infected, and an estimated 23 million more have already died. And the numbers are growing.

Particularly hard hit is the continent of Africa. On medical mission trips all over the continent, I have seen first hand how HIV/AIDS is decimating an entire generation of people.

I have vivid memories of the Kibera slum in Nairobi, Kenya. With a population of over 750 thousand, one out of five in the population is HIV-positive. As I walked the crowded pathways flanked by shanties built of sheet metal and sticks, I was amazed that everyone I saw seemed to be either a child or very old. The disease was wiping out the generation in between—the parents, teachers, police, health workers, and farmers. In other words, the economic providers.

This pattern is appearing all over the world. Poor countries are confronted with a disease-laden cycle that is destroying entire societies. How do we even begin to address a problem of this scale and magnitude? The first challenge is to understand the complex nature of this disease. The HIV/AIDS epidemic embodies immense medical, economic, and behavioral challenges. If we are to succeed, we must attack it in all these dimensions. The second challenge is to accept the fact that we must win this war. Failure cannot be an option.

In my experience, the countries with the greatest success in combating the spread of the HIV virus have used a combination of political leadership, financial support, technical competence, and comprehensive national plans.

Furthermore, in every case where I have seen progress in this war of wars, a key weapon in the arsenal has been the work of religious and other community-based organizations.

The essays shared in *The Hope Factor* reflect the growing understanding of the critical role religious organizations play in AIDS-ravaged communities. Churches build their programs on the moral imperative to help those in need. That simple principle guides church leaders, inspires workers, and motivates donors. In many poor countries, local religious organizations are the most committed, the most trusted, and the most effective force for education and change. In far too many places, they are the only such force.

This book describes some of the ways religious groups can be powerful agents for change in the HIV/AIDS crisis. Taken together, the essays provide a religious paradigm for effective participation in the war against global HIV/AIDS. I am heartened by the ideas and values shared in these pages, for they reflect a growing understanding of what is possible.

Faced with the enormity of the challenges ahead, one is tempted to say that there is too much to do, more than man is capable of. As Christians, we gain power from confronting the seemingly impossible. Our faith sustains us. It gives us hope. It empowers us to forge ahead. And it is our Lord who calls us to minister to the "least of these," faithfully following his call to bind up the wounds of the poor and oppressed, the orphan, and the widow. We are to be God's hands and feet to a broken world. We remember John's words: "let us not love with words or tongue, but with actions and in truth" (1 John 3:18).

The authors of these essays bear witness to this call to love in action. They tell real life stories about what believing brothers and sisters are doing to bring hope and light to some of the world's bleakest and darkest places. May they inform and inspire us all.

Undoubtedly, the days ahead will be challenging and difficult. Millions more will die before we get the disease under control. However, to be successful we must remain committed to a vision of a future without

AIDS. I know these essays will inspire us to remain steadfast in our aims to ease the burden of AIDS, so that we can continue combating the disease and spreading justice and peace throughout our global community.

Senator William H. Frist, M.D.
Majority Leader
United States Senate

EDITORS AND CONTRIBUTORS

Tetsunao Yamamori (book coeditor, introduction) is the international director of the Lausanne Committee for World Evangelization and president emeritus of Food for the Hungry International. Currently he is senior research fellow at the Center for Religion and Civic Culture, University of Southern California, and adjunct professor of sociology, Arizona State University. He was born and educated in Japan and earned a Ph.D. from Duke University. He has authored, coauthored, and edited two dozen books. He was responsible for convening the "Church and the HIV/AIDS Crisis" consultation, held as part of the Global Missions Health Conference sponsored by Southeast Christian Church, Louisville, Kentucky, on November 6, 2003.

David Dageforde (book coeditor, conclusion) practiced as an interventional cardiologist for 23 years before changing his focus to now direct the annual medical missions conference held each year in Louisville, Kentucky. This conference, the Global Missions Health Conference, began in 1996 and is the largest such conference in the United States. He serves on the Board of Directors of SOZO International and Project MedSend. David graduated from the Indiana University School of Medicine and received his postgraduate training in medicine at Baylor College of Medicine and his cardiology training at Georgetown University in Washington, D.C.

Tina Bruner (book coeditor, conclusion) is missions director at Southeast Christian Church, Louisville, Kentucky. Tina oversees all the missionary programs and activities of Southeast Christian Church. The church annually sends more than 1,000 of its members on short-term mission trips. The church also sponsors the Global Missions Health

Conference, held annually since 1996. Tina has assumed the presidency of SOZO International, a not-for-profit organization specializing in strengthening communities through transformational development. Tina often serves as a consultant to other churches on developing volunteers and staff members.

Roger Drew (chapter 1) is a medical graduate with 20 years experience of working in health and development in the United Kingdom and internationally. Dr. Drew has particular skills in analytic review, training, and communications, with a particular interest in issues relating to HIV/AIDS, children, and young people. He is an independent consultant in health and development issues. Previously he worked in Zimbabwe for 10 years as the medical superintendent of a mission hospital and as the projects director of the country's largest AIDS service organization.

Milton Amayun (chapter 2) is senior HIV/AIDS program representative of World Vision International. A family physician, Amayun holds a master's of public health from Harvard University, a bachelor's degree in zoology, and a doctor of medicine degree from the University of the Philippines. He has in-depth training and experience with child survival and maternal health, public health programs in humanitarian emergencies, and HIV/AIDS.

For more than two decades, Amayun has designed, implemented, and supervised various health programs in many frontline locations around the world, including the Indo-Chinese refugee crisis in Thailand, famine in Somalia, post-Pol Pot recovery in Cambodia, famine and internal displacement in Ethiopia, drought in West Africa, and the Balkan wars in Europe.

Gracia Violeta Ross (chapter 3) is vice president of VIDA (an association providing integral support for people living with HIV), coordinator for Voces VIHvas (Women and children living with HIV in Bolivia), and she is a reference person for REDLA (Latin American network of people living with HIV). She is organizing a mission called "Neither do I condemn you . . ." with people from churches in La Paz that presents the gospel to people living with HIV and AIDS in Bolivia.

Igho Ofotokun (chapter 4) is a clinical investigator in HIV/AIDS research and an assistant professor of medicine at Emory University School of Medicine. His research is focused on sex-related differences in the effects of the antiretroviral drugs. Dr. Ofotokun was raised in a small town in the delta region of Nigeria and attended Baptist elementary and high schools. He received his undergraduate degree in pharmacology at the University of Benin School of Medical Sciences. He did his residency in internal medicine at the University of Michigan, where he received further training in infectious diseases with an emphasis on HIV/AIDS. His HIV/AIDS clinical research continued at the University of Kentucky for two years as a faculty member before taking the current assignment at Emory University.

Deborah Dortzbach (chapter 5) is director of international HIV/AIDS programs for World Relief International and resides in Nairobi, Kenya. She has assisted churches in addressing the AIDS crisis since 1988. She holds two master's degrees in public health from Emory University and a bachelor's degree in nursing from Columbia University. Mrs. Dortzbach and her husband, Karl, have been missionaries for 20 years with Mission to the World. Their book, *Kidnapped*, chronicles God's faithfulness during Mrs. Dortzbach's experience of being held hostage for 26 days by the Eritrean Liberation Front.

Edward C. Green (chapter 6) is senior research scientist at the Center for Population and Development Studies, Harvard University, and a member of the Presidential Advisory Council for HIV/AIDS. He holds a Ph.D. in anthropology from The Catholic University of America. He has worked for over 25 years in developing countries, serving as an advisor to the ministries of health in both Mozambique and Swaziland. He is the author of some 250 articles, books, book chapters, conference papers, and commissioned reports. His most recent book is *Rethinking AIDS Prevention* (2003).

Mary Tyler (chapter 7) is a registered nurse, a midwife health visitor, and a trainer in public health with many years of experience in the United Kingdom, Germany, Switzerland, and Uganda. Since 1985 she has worked in Uganda with Save the Children Fund/U.K., seconded to Uganda's Ministry of Health, and with Food for the Hungry International working on the AIDS Awareness Project. Her chapter first appeared in Tetsunao Yamamori, et al (eds.), *Serving with the Poor in Africa* (Monrovia, CA: World Vision Resources, 1996). Reprinted by permission of World Vision Resources.

Kathy A. McCarty (chapter 8) is a registered nurse with B.S.N. and M.S.N. degrees from the University of California, San Francisco. She served as a minister of missions for Sebastopol Christian Church in California with an extended assignment at Chidamoyo Christian Hospital in Karoi, Zimbabwe, as clinical officer and matron. Her chapter first appeared in Tetsunao Yamamori, et al (eds.), *Serving with the Poor in Africa* (Monrovia, CA: World Vision Resources, 1996). Reprinted by permission of World Vision Resources.

Florence Muindi and Leigh Anne Dageforde (chapter 9). Born in Kenya, Dr. Muindi graduated from the University of Nairobi Medical School. She also holds an M.P.H. degree and has been trained in Switzerland and Belgium in specialized public health interventions. Drawing from her experiences working with governments and nongovernmental organizations, she has served for seven years in cross-cultural medical missions work with CMF International in Ethiopia. Leigh Anne Dageforde was a senior mathematics major at Wheaton College at the time of this writing. While at Wheaton, Leigh Anne served on Wheaton's "Missions in Focus" cabinet and traveled to Africa five times. During the summer of 2003, she and Dr. Muindi investigated how churches in Ethiopia were responding to the HIV/AIDS crisis. Leigh Anne is due to enter Vanderbilt University School of Medicine in the fall of 2004.

Paul Kennel (chapter 10) has served as the president of World Concern since 1995. He joined World Concern in 1982, serving as manager for Malaysia, then as Southeast Asia manager, and as Asia director, when he helped develop HIV/AIDS programs in Thailand and India. Paul's international career began in Vietnam during the war. His relief work included running a large children's hospital. Later, Paul assisted with disaster relief and community development in Central America, India, and Bangladesh with the Mennonite Central Committee and the Lutheran World Federation. Paul has a master's degree in international administration from the School of International Training in Vermont and an MBA from Lausanne University in Switzerland.

Vinod Shah and *Mathew Santosh Thomas* (chapter 11). Dr. Shah is a pediatric surgeon who has been executive director of Emmanuel Hospital Association (EHA) for the last seven years. He comes from a business family in West India. He has been trained at Christian Medical College in Vellore, South India. A strategic thinker, he has brought to EHA a strong track record in hospital management and innovative community health care. He has published several journal articles on medical mission ethics. EHA has extensive HIV/AIDS programs in India. Coauthor Mathew Santosh Thomas works with Dr. Shah.

Peter Meadows (chapter 12) has been on the cutting edge of communication in the churches of the United Kingdom for 25-plus years. As a writer, speaker, strategic thinker, cultural commentator, and activist, he is recognized as one of the U.K.'s leading laymen. He is currently head of church action for World Vision U.K. He is co-founder of Europe's largest annual interchurch Bible-teaching event, Spring Harvest. He founded the U.K.'s first Christian radio station, which serves London's 16 million people. He also co-founded the U.K.'s largest evangelical relief agency, Tear Fund. Mr. Meadows has authored several books, including *Pressure Points, Beyond Belief,* and *Rich Thinking About the World's Poor.*

E. Anne Peterson (chapter 13) was appointed by President George W. Bush to be the assistant administrator of the Global Health Bureau of the U.S. Agency for International Development, where she manages over $2 billion in international health programs. She represents the United States on the board of the Global Fund to Fight AIDS, Turberculosis and Malaria, as well as the Global Alliance for Vaccines and Immunization. Previously, she served as Commissioner of Health in Virginia and has consulted for the Centers for Disease Control and Prevention, as well as the World Health Organization. For six years, she worked as a medical missionary in Kenya and Zimbabwe. Anne obtained her M.D. from the Mayo Medical School and her M.P.H. and Preventive Medicine residency from Emory University.

Dick Day (chapter 14) is co-founder and executive director of Sub-Saharan Africa Family Enrichment (SAFE). He and his wife have lived in Blantyre, Malawi, for the last 14 years. He serves as professor at the University of Malawi. He co-authored two books: *Why Wait? What You Need to Know About the Teen Sexuality Crisis* and *How To Be A Hero To Your Kids*. He is also the series editor and a contributing writer for the biblically based 8-year curriculum dealing with abstinence, life skills, and character development.

Ken Isaacs (chapter 15) is international director of projects for Samaritan's Purse. He served as project director for "Prescription for Hope," an unprecedented global conference on the Christian response to HIV/AIDS, held in February, 2002, in Washington, D.C. He joined Samaritan's Purse in 1988 after beginning his missions career in Ethiopia, where he designed and developed water programs and emergency relief efforts. He has traveled to more than 120 countries and has led major international relief projects in Somalia, Bosnia, Rwanda, Sudan, Honduras, Kosovo, Mozambique, El Salvador, Afghanistan, and most recently, Iraq.

Dorothy Brewster-Lee (chapter 16) is a medical doctor. She has been coordinator of the International Health Ministries Office of Presbyterian Church USA since 1998. Prior to coming to the Presbyterian Center in Louisville, Kentucky, Dorothy and her husband, Dr. Derrick Matthews, were Presbyterian mission co-workers in Cameroon. Dorothy is a pediatrician. For four years she served as the coordinator of an HIV/AIDS program at an inner city health program in the USA. Dorothy is a graduate of the Howard University School of Medicine in Washington, D.C., and holds an M.P.H. degree from Johns Hopkins University in Baltimore, Maryland.

Andrew Tomkins (chapter 17) is director of the Centre for International Child Health at the Institute of Child Health, University College, London, United Kingdom. Professor Tomkins is responsible for managing a program of research and postgraduate teaching in child health in developing countries, which is conducted in association with universities and governments in Africa and Asia. Professor Tomkins' research group is currently developing ways of reducing transmission of HIV from mothers to infants. He is chairman of the Technical Advisory Group on Nutrition and HIV of the World Health Organization and is advisor to UNICEF, the World Bank, and DFID (U.K.). He is vice chairman of Tear Fund U.K. After qualifying in medicine in London and doing postgraduate training in infectious disease and nutrition, Professor Tomkins and his family lived in West Africa working with the Medical Research Council in Nigeria and Gambia.

Randall L. Hoag (chapter 18) is president of Food for the Hungry International (FHI). After graduating from the University of Washington with a B.A., Randy, now with a C.P.A., began his career as a staff accountant for the public accounting firm of Raines and Co. In the early 1980s, he felt called to join FHI to serve as a volunteer in Bolivia during a famine. Since then, he has held various positions from country directorship in Bolivia to vice president and executive vice president, and finally, in 2001, he was selected to become the president of an international relief and development organization serving in over 40 countries. He now holds an M.A. in organizational leadership from Regent University and a doctorate in humane letters from Hope International University.

John Piper (chapter 19) is senior pastor of Bethlehem Baptist Church in Minneapolis and the head of Desiring God Ministries. He has authored numerous best-selling books, including *Desiring God, Future Grace,* and *A Hunger for God.* He is a graduate of Wheaton College, Fuller Theological Seminary, and the University of Munich (Dr. Theol.). "Guilt, Grace, and the Global AIDS Crisis" (December 4, 2002) is found on http://desiringgod.org/library/fresh_words/2002/120402.html. Reprinted by permission of the author.

Richard Stearns (chapter 20) is president of World Vision in charge of U.S. operations. He brings nearly 25 years of corporate experience to his role. Before joining World Vision in 1998, he was president of various companies, including Parker Brothers Games and Lenox Inc. At World Vision, he has seen a 70 percent revenue increase. He has also been a catalyst for World Vision's efforts to turn the tide on the AIDS pandemic and has worked energetically to engage the Christian community across America, challenging them to respond with compassion and commitment to this great humanitarian crisis of our time. He holds a bachelor's degree from Cornell University in neurobiology and a master's in business administration from the Wharton School of the University of Pennsylvania. His chapter is adapted from a speech to supporters attending the World Vision Forum, "Widows and Orphans—the Hidden Faces of AIDS," on May 18, 2002, in New York City. Reprinted by permission of the author.

Tom Correll (chapter 21) is missions pastor at Wooddale Church in Eden Prairie, Minnesota. Prior to joining the staff of Wooddale Church, he spent more than 25 years in the computer industry working for the Control Data Corporation and later for a small telecommunications firm. Tom is a 1965 graduate of the University of Michigan with a B.S. in mathematics. In the 1970s, while a resident of South Africa, he began a theology degree at the University of South Africa. He received a master's of divinity degree from Bethel Seminary in St. Paul, Minnesota, in 2000. He is coordinator of the Africa AIDS Initiative, mobilizing megachurches of North America to partner with churches in Africa, to combat HIV/AIDS.

Dan Fountain (chapter 22) was a medical missionary in the Democratic Republic of Congo for 35 years. He served as surgeon, educator, and community health leader. He developed an approach to caring for the whole person. He spearheaded an evangelical team of educators to work in churches, schools, and population centers to combat the spread of HIV. He is currently an assistant professor at King College in Tennessee and director of the Global Health Care masters degree program. He is the author of numerous books in English and French on community health, primary health care, and care for the whole person. He holds M.D. and M.P.H. degrees.

Ken Casey (chapter 23) is the special representative to the World Vision International president for the HIV/AIDS HOPE Initiative. In this role, Ken is providing leadership to the global mobilization of resources and program capacity to address the growing pandemic of HIV/AIDS. The HOPE Initiative was first announced by World Vision International President Dean Hirsch on December 1, 2000. Ken was appointed to lead the Initiative in March 2001.

Tokunboh Adeyemo (chapter 24) was born to a wealthy Muslim family in Nigeria. Following his conversion in 1966, he abandoned his partisan political ambition in order to train for Christian ministry, in particular, and service for humanity, in general. His spiritual transformation gave him a global perspective deriving from his understanding of the kingdom of God. He holds an M.Div. from Talbot Theological Seminary, Biola University, and a doctorate from Dallas Theological Seminary. He later did postdoctoral research at Aberdeen University in Scotland. Dr. Adeyemo has written a number of books, including *The Making of a Servant of God* and *Is Africa Cursed?* Since 1978 until recently, he was general secretary of the Association of Evangelicals in Africa. Since 1980, he has been chairman of the International Council of World Evangelical Alliance. His HIV/AIDS-related work has been extensive through churches in Africa and UNAIDS, a United Nations organization focused on AIDS issues.

Doug Priest (Appendix A) was named general director of Christian Missionary Fellowship in 1995. He has been an affiliated member of CMF for 25 years. As a missionary child, he graduated from Good Shepherd School in Ethiopia. After graduating from Northwest Christian College and the University of Oregon, Doug was approved by CMF for missionary service. He has served churches in Oregon and California. He obtained his M.A. in missiology and his Ph.D. in intercultural studies from Fuller Theological Seminary. He and his wife, Robyn, have served as missionaries in Kenya and Singapore. Doug has authored *Doing Theology with the Maasai* and edited *Unto the Uttermost* and *The Gospel Unhindered*.

Evvy Hay Campbell (Appendix B) is an associate professor of missions and intercultural studies at Wheaton College Graduate School, where she has worked for eight years. She served two terms with the Wesleyan Church at Kamakwie Hospital in Sierra Leone, West Africa, and for nine years as director of international health with MAP International, a Christian relief and development organization. She has served as editor of the AERDO Occasional Papers Series, *Ethical Issues in Health-Related Missions*, and *The Church's Response to the Challenge of AIDS/HIV: A Guideline for Education and Policy Development*. She holds a Ph.D. from Michigan State University.

Michael J. Kane (Appendix C) is founder and president of Voice For Humanity, Inc. (VFH), a Kentucky-based 501C-3 not-for-profit technology company. He is a highly skilled international business executive and entrepreneur. He has provided leadership in Fortune

500 organizations, small private businesses, and high-risk startups. His international management experience spans Europe, Asia, South America, and the Middle East. Most recently he was president and chief executive officer of Galtronics, Ltd. He held a senior executive position with Lexmark International, traveling extensively abroad. He holds a Ph.D. in international management from the University of South Carolina. For five years, Dr. Kane taught at the University of Kentucky Graduate School of Business and Economics.

INTRODUCTION

You have probably never heard of Elukwatini, South Africa.[1] Most people haven't. This township of 30,000 people near Swaziland has a high unemployment rate. For a variety of reasons, including the poor economy, many people in the town turn to theft and prostitution to make ends meet. Aside from the moral guilt that accompanies such choices, people there have received something else. Three years ago, Elukwatini had South Africa's third-highest HIV/AIDS infection rate. This makes it one of the world's worst killing fields for AIDS. The country and the continent are so strongly in the grip of this merciless disease.

Lying on a pile of old blankets on a cold, mud-packed floor in Elukwatini, an emaciated woman looks off into space as she says, "I have been so bad in my lifetime that God could never forgive me—God will never forgive me." A single tear rolls down her face.

Yet there is hope in Elukwatini, and in Africa. With the woman is Busi Mdamba, the wife of the pastor of the Elukwatini Nhlazatshe Baptist Church. Busi encourages her to eat and prays with her. The church has trained others to help. In all, twelve women from the church's Baptist Women's Association Home-based Care Unit, wearing their easily recognizable red shirts, wash the sick, administer medicines, and do evangelism. It is a hard calling.

After one AIDS patient, a man, died, Mdamba told *Christianity Today*, "Sometimes our efforts seem so worthless, especially when people die without knowing God. But when a patient like this dies, we are sad because he is like family, but we are also joyful in his recent decision to follow Jesus Christ."

To those of us in the West, whose main exposure to AIDS has been through the media, Busi and the women who work with her in all-but-forgotten Elukwatini may seem exceptional. Thank God, they are becoming less and less so, as more and more Christians around the world take up the burden of caring for people affected by HIV/AIDS.

Of course, right off the bat we have to acknowledge that Christians have not always been the first to volunteer. In the West, AIDS (Acquired Immune Deficiency Syndrome) had been strongly associated with homosexual behavior. Comparatively few Christians had the disease. In the non-Western world, HIV (Human Immune-deficiency Virus) was mostly a problem of heterosexuals. Those becoming sick largely were those engaging in premarital sex, adultery, serial monogamy, and drug abuse. It was all too easy to write off the victims as simply under God's wrath, "receiving in themselves the due penalty for their error."[2] Many Christians had little compassion for AIDS sufferers, and many were afraid.

But there are problems with this approach. First, many of the victims—wives of faithless husbands, newborns during birth—are getting the disease through no fault of their own. Second, the number of children orphaned by AIDS are burgeoning, and they need help, not lectures. Third, AIDS is beginning to turn up in church people. Fourth, the disease is beginning to devastate not only families, but also neighborhoods, towns, and nations. The need is simply too great to turn away.

Misconceptions of the Crisis

Inspired by Jesus' teaching,[3] example,[4] and sober words of warning,[5] Christians and churches have started ministering in the midst of the pandemic. In fact, we have quickly made ourselves indispensable. But we must confront three common assumptions and the paucity of "best practice" models that impede our fight against HIV/AIDS.

1. *HIV/AIDS statistics are confusing and numbing.* Statistics are quoted frequently between the covers of this book. You encounter them in newspapers, magazines, radio, and television. The numbers are indeed numbing. Here are some helpful guidelines in dealing with HIV/AIDS statistics.

- Take careful note of the dates and sources for the reported figures.

- Regard global statistics provided by the United Nations AIDS organization and World Health Organization as generally reliable.

- Consider figures given by national governments as likely to be lower than is truly the case.

Some overzealous—frankly, irresponsible—writers in some publications project the crisis as so horrendous that people simply tend to tune it out. The situation is bad enough without exaggerations. People have told me, "They are just trying to scare us by giving us big numbers." Responsible persons engaged in the fight against HIV/AIDS handle statistics with care because statistics represent people. Responsible HIV/AIDS specialists do not use statistics as a scare tactic.

2. *One person can do little.* On the contrary, history is replete with the stories of lone individuals who make a difference. Peter Meadows (chapter 12) and others in this book write about some of them. One person can do a lot to help those whose lives have been rocked by HIV/AIDS.

Here is an apocryphal story that nonetheless points out an important lesson. Leo Tolstoy (1828–1910), the Russian novelist and social critic, met a beggar one morning. Embarrassed that he had no money to give, Tolstoy said to the beggar: "I'm sorry, my brother, I have no money." And he began walking away. Barely audibly, the beggar called after him: "Thank you." Tolstoy turned around and told him: "I didn't give you anything." The beggar replied: "But you called me *brother*."

In Africa and elsewhere, AIDS-inflicted people are dying alone, often abandoned by their own families. Can we not, at least, be a brother or sister to them? Can Western churches demonstrate love and compassion?

In the mid-1980s, when I was president of Food for the Hungry International, I often accompanied Ugandan young people who were challenging other young people with the message of abstinence (in a project Mary Tyler describes in chapter 7). The adults (mostly women) in the churches were recruited and trained to visit AIDS patients and their families. I visited at length with grandparents who were caring for grandchildren whose parents had died of AIDS. I came to learn about the agony of people infected by HIV/AIDS but also of those affected by it. My own commitment to the fight was born then.

3. *The church has forfeited its moral authority and has little to offer.* This is a painful indictment against the church, but it is not the whole truth. Edward C. Green (chapter 6) has been at the forefront of research in examining how faith-based organizations in Africa have contributed to AIDS prevention. Tom Correll (chapter 21) tells how the "Africa AIDS Initiative" coalition came into being. Its mission is to engage North American churches to join with African churches in collaborative initiatives that transform communities devastated by AIDS.

While the church has gone through a period of disorientation, it has gradually strengthened its response. Indeed, the church has taken a leadership role in many African countries. It works closely with governments, intergovernmental agencies, and other nongovernmental organizations. The church has a very special contribution to make in advocating the ABC approach.[6] Several chapters in this book touch on it.

However, heated debates are occurring in journals, magazines, and conferences on whether to use antiretroviral (ARV) drugs or the ABC approach. Proponents of ARV treatment (contra Green and others) say ABC doesn't work. Several chapters in this book examine the complex issues related to ARV treatment. The church needs to think carefully about its own involvement. ARV treatment has a definite place in easing the suffering of the infected and retarding the spread of HIV from mothers to their babies.

I believe the church, by exercising its moral authority, must speak out boldly on ABC. It must lead in this crisis. It must give hope to the hopeless—those languishing alone. It must use the HIV/AIDS crisis to demonstrate the love of Christ in caring for AIDS sufferers and their family members with whatever means available. The church has not forfeited its moral authority and has much to offer.

Indeed, the church and Christian organizations have been helping for some time now. But while there are many good programs out there, research documenting them is lacking. We desperately need in-depth ethnographic research to describe best practice models. There will be more good programs emerging in the future. We must carefully sketch the best practice examples to guide those already working to alleviate this crisis as well as those contemplating doing so.

This volume distills the presentations of some of the world's top minds and hearts at a consultation aimed at maximizing churches' effectiveness. In November 2003, some 200 delegates gathered at Southeast Christian Church in Louisville, Kentucky, for a meeting called "The Church and the HIV/AIDS Crisis: Providing Leadership and Hope." It was held before Southeast Christian's annual Global Missions Health Conference. Most of the chapters in this book come from those two events and are shared here for wider distribution.

This is a handbook showing how we in the Western church can come alongside and help people impacted by AIDS. Academicians, pastors, AIDS patients, and doctors from around the world share hard-won insights that will help you and your church or organization make a difference in practical ways.

There is a lot of technical material in this book, but you don't need to master every detail to implement effective and compassionate ministries. But if you need to understand epidemiology, the history of the disease in certain countries, and other matters, they are here, along with lots of notes and references you can use for further exploration. Also, you don't have to read the chapters in order to glean insights, although there is a certain logic to how we have arranged the presentations. For ease of use, the book is divided into several sections.

Part One, "Understanding the HIV/AIDS Crisis," provides current statistics and trends (chapter 1), the link between HIV/AIDS and other diseases among the poor such as tuberculosis (chapter 2), the painful experiences of someone who has the disease (chapter 3), a look at the vulnerability of Nigeria (chapter 4), and an examination of the church's role in Africa (chapter 5).

Part Two, "Crisis Interventions," explores how faith-based organizations have helped fight the pandemic (chapter 6); how Christians and others have responded in Uganda (chapter 7), Zimbabwe (chapter 8), Ethiopia (chapter 9), Thailand (chapter 10), India (chapter 11), and the United Kingdom (chapter 12); how one person has been confronting AIDS (chapter 13). Part Two also provides information on biblically based resources on marriage and sex (chapter 14), a call for deeper involvement of Christian aid agencies (chapter 15), a Christian approach in treating patients (chapter 16), Christian interventions (chapter 17), and a prescription for improving prevention efforts (chapter 18).

Part Three, "Biblical Reflections," offers a moral call to action from John Piper (chapter 19), a look at how AIDS affects women and orphans (chapter 20), a call for church action (chapter 21), an examination of the link between AIDS and a society's worldview (chapter 22), a look at HIV/AIDS in light of Scripture (chapter 23), and a focus on the church's strategic role (chapter 24).

David Dageforde, M.D., and Tina Bruner, coeditors of this volume, offer a concluding challenge. The appendixes provide some advice on church involvement, further reading, and information technology.

As I close my introduction, I wish to thank Southeast Christian Church for its enthusiastic support of the consultation. The staff and volunteers of its Missions Department were superb in welcoming all of us and meeting our needs. The church contributed money, as did World Concern and Food for the Hungry International, to bring resource people to the meeting and to make the publication of this book possible.

Two of the busiest men I know are Chuck Colson of Prison Fellowship and The Wilberforce Forum and Bill Frist, M.D., majority leader of the United States Senate. I am grateful for their contributions to this volume.

My thanks also go to Stan Guthrie of *Christianity Today* for his editorial assistance.

I commend the following pages to you. May they help us respond with appropriate biblical passion, as the Christians in Elukwatini have done, to the plague of our time.

Notes

1. Sue Sprenkle, "Dying Alone: Baptist women seek out and care for ashamed, abandoned AIDS patients," Christianity Today, July 9, 2001, p. 22. I have reworked some of this article for the introduction.

2. Romans 1:27 ESV.

3. Luke 10.

4. John 4.

5. Matthew 25.

6. A stands for abstinence until marriage, B for being faithful within marriage, and C for condom use when A and B have failed.

PART ONE

UNDERSTANDING THE HIV/AIDS CRISIS

THE CURRENT STATUS OF THE HIV/AIDS CRISIS

Ophelia and Catherine's Stories[1]

Ophelia was born in Zimbabwe in 1970. Only 17, she married and had three children. She found out that she was HIV-positive when her third child became ill and died. Ophelia blamed her husband for infecting her, although he denied being HIV-positive. She separated from him and went to live with her relatives. However, her parents found out she was HIV-positive when they read the child's death certificate. They reacted very negatively, screaming and shouting at her. As a result, her neighbours found out that she was HIV-positive. Because of the stigma, she stayed inside, afraid to come out. She felt very isolated.

Catherine was born in 1971. She lives in Mutendere, a crowded residential part of Lusaka, Zambia. "In 1991, when I was 20 years old, I was living in the house of a preacher. I became sick and had an HIV test, which was positive. I went to the preacher's house and told him what had happened. Over a short period of time, he became more and more unfriendly. He said that he feared catching the disease from me and said that it was embarrassing for him to share a home with me. Later, they chased me out of the house. I went to my sister's house, but her husband felt the same way as the priest and insisted that I couldn't stay."

The Issue

HIV/AIDS has made a dramatic entry on to the world stage. First recognized in 1981, it has gone from being a medical curiosity, affecting certain groups of people in a few countries, to a global epidemic, or pandemic.

Not all countries are affected equally. HIV/AIDS particularly affects poorer regions, e.g., sub-Saharan Africa, India, and southeast Asia. In fact, the wide-ranging nature of factors leading to its spread, its linkage to poverty, and the severity of its impact mean that HIV/AIDS is not only a health problem, but also a development problem.

What is the Response?

Despite the severity of the HIV/AIDS pandemic, all is not gloom and doom. Very imaginative efforts have been launched the world over to fight the spread of the virus and to provide care and support for those that have already been infected and affected. In some countries (e.g., Uganda and Thailand), these efforts have produced reductions in HIV infection rates. We have learned many important lessons about what works and what does not.

About 14 thousand people get infected with HIV every day[2] . . . but what does that mean? What do they look like? What are their hopes and aspirations? We must remember that behind every statistic are people like Ophelia and Catherine—real people, real families, real communities. Many people responding to HIV/AIDS do so because the disease has touched them or someone close to them. Perhaps this is why you are involved (or would like to become involved).

How Severe is the HIV/AIDS Epidemic?

HIV/AIDS is arguably the worst health problem facing the world. UNAIDS/WHO estimated in December 2003 that 34–46 million people were living with the virus. Of these, 4.2–5.8 million had been infected in the previous year. Approximately 10 men, women, and children were infected with HIV every minute in 2003. More than 23 million people have lost their lives to the virus, an estimated 2.5–3.5 million in the last year alone.

Figure 1: Estimated Number of Adults and Children Newly-Infected with HIV/AIDS During 2003

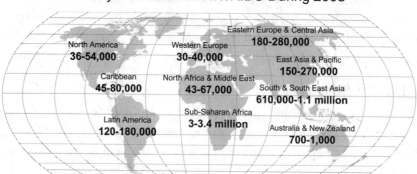

However, the problem does not affect all countries equally. Poorer countries and communities are bearing the brunt. Sub-Saharan Africa continues to be the most severely affected area. Fifty-nine to 71 percent of all new infections in 2003 occurred there. In some countries in the region, HIV prevalence in adults exceeded 25 percent. South Africa has surpassed India with the largest number of people living with HIV/AIDS. The epidemic is spreading most rapidly in Asia, particularly in China and India, and also in countries of the former Soviet Union. Approximately 20 percent of all new infections occur in Asia.

HIV/AIDS spreads in different ways in different parts of the world. In rich countries, it spreads largely through homosexual intercourse, injecting drug use, and blood transfusions. In poor countries, particularly in sub-Saharan Africa, it spreads primarily through heterosexual intercourse and from mother to baby. However, in Asia homosexual intercourse and injecting drug use have also been significant routes of transmission.

Globally, most infections have occurred through heterosexual intercourse, although in Europe and North America, the epidemic has mainly affected men. Worldwide, approximately 50 percent of all people living with HIV/AIDS are women.

HIV/AIDS has a profound effect on societies. It strikes predominantly at the sexually active, who are also the main providers of food, income, and care. It increases the vulnerability of children and older people. HIV/AIDS is much more than simply a health problem. Its scale and nature mean that it is already having severe social and economic effects on the world's poorest countries. In addition, conditions within these communities (e.g., poverty, low status of women, underdevelopment) have accelerated the virus's spread. As a result, HIV/AIDS is also a key development issue.

What Has Been Done?

There has been a wide range of responses to the epidemic in developing countries, particularly in sub-Saharan Africa. South Africa, Uganda, Zambia, and Ethiopia have all reported achieving reductions in prevalence levels among young people. We will take a look at these responses under three headings: prevention, care and support, and treatment.

1. Prevention

Many organizations have been involved in HIV prevention, including governments and both international and local nongovernmental organizations. In the past, these largely focused on providing correct information about HIV/AIDS to increase awareness and knowledge of the disease, leading to safer sexual practices such as abstinence, condom use, and mutual faithfulness.

However, organizations discovered a number of problems with this approach. First, using negative, fear-based messages and images (e.g., "AIDS kills") increased the stigma and discrimination of people living with HIV/AIDS. Second, an increase in knowledge was not always accompanied by a change in behavior. Third, controversies exist within Christian and other faith-based communities over the relative emphasis to be placed on different messages, particularly in relation to condoms. Fourth, this approach failed to fully consider the major influence on behavior exerted by peer pressure, culture, and community norms.

2. Care and Support

Many countries sought to provide wards and services for people with HIV/AIDS. However, in sub-Saharan Africa, significant problems accompanied this approach. Available services were simply overwhelmed. In addition, this approach contributed to increased stigma. A response focused on narrow medical and health needs often overlooked broader social, emotional, nutritional, and spiritual needs. Also, there was often a feeling that nothing could be done for people with HIV/AIDS because there was no cure.

In response, many organizations established teams of professional people to provide care and support to people in their own homes. However, this approach had significant problems, including high cost and low coverage. Organizations began to have doubts about the sustainability of this approach. They also wondered about the quality of services offered by teams that often spent more time traveling than with people. In addition, such approaches often had a narrow focus on medical and health needs. They risked creating dependency and stifling the emergence of the community's own responses.

3. Treatment

One of the most dramatic developments in recent years has been the emergence of antiretroviral drugs, which have proved extremely effective in extending the lives of people with HIV/AIDS in developed countries. These drugs have also proved to be effective in preventing the transmission of HIV from mother to child. However, they have not been introduced widely in developing countries, largely because of their cost. People with HIV/AIDS in developing countries want these drugs, which have begun to be used in those countries, particularly to prevent transmission from mother to child. Thankfully, prices have fallen dramatically in recent years. For example, the cost of treating one per person per year was estimated at over $10,000 in 2000. Today it is between $200 and $1,000. However, these prices are still too high for most people in poor countries.

Principles for Good Practice

"Good practice" refers to the principles underlying activities that have been shown to work. As mentioned earlier, many countries have practical experience of effective HIV/AIDS interventions. Based on these, UNAIDS has identified certain principles of good practice, including integrating prevention and care activities, working to reduce vulnerability to infection, and alleviating the epidemic's social and economic impact.

By following these principles, we can make a positive contribution in the lives of hurting people.

Notes

1. Ophelia's story is based on a case study in HIV counselling in Zimbabwe: Krabbendam, A.A., Kuijper, B., Wolffers, I.N., Drew, R.: AIDS Care, Vol. 10, Supplement 1, 1998, pp. S25–S37. Catherine's story is based on a presentation made by Catherine Nyirenda at the XI International Conference on AIDS, Vancouver, July 7–12, 1996. The full text of that presentation is available on http://www.undp.org/hiv/publications/issues/english/issue22e.htm.

2. This estimate is based on figures in the UNAID/WHO publication AIDS Epidemic Update, December 2003, available from http://www.unaids.org/en/Resources/Publications/Corporate+publications/AIDS+epidemic+update+-+December+2003.asp

CHAPTER 2
MILTON B. AMAYUN

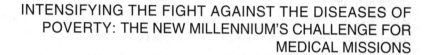

INTENSIFYING THE FIGHT AGAINST THE DISEASES OF POVERTY: THE NEW MILLENNIUM'S CHALLENGE FOR MEDICAL MISSIONS

"Poor people will only be able to emerge from poverty if they enjoy better health. Health should be at the heart of our struggle for sustainable development."

Gro-Harlem Brundtland, M.D., M.P.H. Director-General
World Health Organization (1998–2003)

In 2001, nearly two-thirds of all deaths among children and young adults (0–44 years) in Africa and Southeast Asia were due to seven diseases: AIDS, malaria, tuberculosis, diarrheal diseases, measles, acute respiratory infections, and maternal/perinatal conditions. The combined death toll from AIDS, TB, and malaria alone was roughly 6 million for the year, including infants, young children, mothers, and fathers in their productive years of life.[1]

Table 1: Major Causes of Death in Children and Young Adults, 0–44 years Africa and Southeast Asia, 2001

Disease	Proportion of Deaths	Population Affected
AIDS	13%	Mostly young adults
Maternal and Perinatal Conditions	11%	Mothers and infants
Acute Respiratory Infections	9%	Mostly children, 0-5 years
Diarrheal Diseases	9%	Mostly children, 0-5 years
Malaria	6%	Mostly children, 0-5 years
Measles	5%	Mostly children, 0-5 years
TB	4%	Mostly young adults, often associated with AIDS
All other conditions	43%	All ages combined; includes non-infectious diseases
Total	100%	

Death is only one part of the story. For every death, many more victims of each disease suffer debilitating consequences or become carriers of the infection, often for the rest of their lives. As carriers, they become the reservoir of infection for a new generation of victims. Some become impoverished due to a combination of the high costs of treatment and care, and the missed opportunities at becoming productive adults. This vicious cycle occurs worldwide: the poor are unhealthy, and they stay unhealthy because they do not have the resources to rid themselves of common illnesses. And because they are unhealthy, they are unlikely to be able to lift themselves out of poverty.

Each death also represents a loss of life, each one precious in the sight of God. To family members, losing a loved one means emotional and psychological suffering. For many children losing their parents, it means a life of being an orphan—including the economic, social, and psychological dislocation that being an orphan represents. For AIDS, and to a lesser extent TB, they also face the stigma of being associated with a close loved one dying of the disease.

The seven top diseases listed above are all preventable, and mostly infectious. Today, we have the knowledge to prevent them, the medicines to treat them, and the technology to deliver both treatment and prevention. What we lack are the resources and the political will to finish the task. We have a lot to learn from the successful efforts at reducing child mortality and morbidity of the two previous decades. But as the above table shows, we have not yet reached our goal. Child survival and safe motherhood programs have saved many children and mothers, but we still have numerous pockets of need. Acute respiratory infections, measles, and malaria still afflict and kill millions of young children in the developing world.

Focusing on AIDS, TB, and Malaria

The combined total number of victims AIDS, TB, and malaria is estimated to be as high as 2.5 billion, and new cases are added each year. The numbers are unacceptable. They will continue to rise without intensified and concerted global action.

Table 2: AIDS, TB, and Malaria
Basic information, 2002

Disease	Deaths/year	New Cases/year	Total affected	% in Third World
HIV/AIDS	3.1 million	5.3 million	42 million	90%
TB	1.9 million	8.8 million	2 billion	84%
Malaria	1 million	300 million	300 million	99%
Totals	6 million	315 million	2.3 billion	95%

HIV/AIDS: AIDS is caused by the human immune-deficiency virus, which is transmitted through sexual contact, blood transfusions, skin-piercing instruments, and from mother to child. From the early 1980s, when the first cases were detected, to the end of 2002, the total number of deaths due to HIV/AIDS has reached 25 million. In addition, a total of 42 million are living with the virus, 3.2 million of them children under 15 years. Of the 39 million adults infected, roughly half are women. More than 90 percent of all AIDS deaths and new infections have occurred in developing countries, mostly in sub-Saharan Africa and South Asia. In only a few countries has the number of HIV/AIDS cases been stabilized or reduced. Statistical models indicate that unless drastic measures stabilize current rates of infection, by 2020, AIDS will have caused more deaths than any other epidemic disease in history.

Apart from the additional disease burden and the resultant socioeconomic dislocation on communities and whole countries, part of the lingering impact of AIDS includes the care and nurture of orphans, estimated to be more than 15 million today. Current estimates indicate that there could be as many as 40 million orphans due to HIV/AIDS by the year 2010. This number does not include those who are caring for parents who are chronically ill due to HIV/AIDS.

TB: Tuberculosis is caused by the tubercle bacillus, *mycobacterium tuberculosis;* it infects various organs of the body, but the pulmonary form is prevalent. TB is a droplet infection: the bacillus is transported through the air through close contact with someone with an active infection. There are about 2 billion carriers of the TB bacillus worldwide, and each year 8.8 million of them develop active TB. Of those who have active TB, 1.9 million die of the disease each year. The majority of TB cases are adults between 15 and 54 years, mostly poor people in developing countries. Unless current programs are intensified and expanded, experts estimate that nearly a billion people will become carriers of the TB bacillus, 200 million will develop active TB, and 35 million will die of the disease by the year 2020.

Increasing the challenge for public health professionals, people living with HIV/AIDS are several times more likely to develop active TB because of their depressed immune systems. In sub-Saharan Africa, TB has become a very common immediate cause of death for AIDS patients. Today, an estimated 10 million-plus people have HIV-TB co-infections.

Malaria: The malaria parasite causes malaria, which is transmitted through mosquito bites. The most virulent strain, *falciparum malaria*, may infect the brain, a common immediate cause of death. Malaria kills more than a million people a year, mostly young children under five in sub-Saharan Africa. This translates to nearly 3 thousand child deaths per day. In addition, hundreds of millions of people in malaria-endemic zones survive one or more bouts of fever due to malaria annually.

In malaria-endemic countries, women—especially pregnant women—face increased risk of contracting malaria, and suffering from its most important consequences, including miscarriages, stillborn babies, and maternal anemia. Babies born to mothers with malaria often have low birth weight, potentially leading to impaired development in infancy and early childhood.

Tools and Resources to Control AIDS, TB, and Malaria

Effective tools to prevent AIDS, TB, and malaria have been available to health professionals for decades. For TB and malaria, we know the medicines that cure them. We have the antibiotics that cure the opportunistic infections associated with AIDS, and we are constantly developing drugs to prolong the lives of persons with HIV/AIDS. Yet only 25 percent of those who need those medicines or tools for prevention have access to them.

Table 3: Available Tools for Prevention and Treatment: AIDS, TB, and Malaria

Disease	Prevention	Treatment/Care
HIV/AIDS	ABC (Abstinence, Being Faithful, Condoms) strategy Safe blood transfusions Voluntary counseling and testing Clean needles for injections Treatment of sexually transmitted infections Prevention of mother-to-child transmission	Anti-retrovirals Essential drugs for opportunistic infections (including TB) and palliative care Good nutrition
TB	BCG vaccine for children	Sputum smears for detection Anti-TB drugs
Malaria	Insecticide-treated nets Insecticides for vector control Intermittent prophylaxis	Blood smear examinations and dipstick diagnosis Combined malaria therapy

HIV/AIDS: The interventions that prevent HIV/AIDS are well known, and several national programs have been effective. In Uganda, for example, the ABC (Abstain, Be Faithful, and use Condoms if A and B fail) strategy is credited for the reduction of the country's HIV/AIDS prevalence that was at one time among the highest in Africa. Between 1991 and 2000, the HIV/AIDS prevalence among pregnant mothers visiting Uganda's sentinel antenatal clinics has been cut by two-thirds. Other countries, such as Thailand, have focused on the use of condoms among high-risk groups, such as prostitutes and military recruits. Most countries now have facilities to test donated blood.

In high-prevalence countries, the push has been for expanded voluntary counseling, as well as testing and prevention of mother-to-child transmission. Many pregnant mothers are unaware of their infection and unknowingly pass the virus to their infants during delivery. In Eastern Europe, where high levels of intravenous drug use fuel the epidemic, needle exchange programs are having differing levels of success.

The cornerstone of treatment of HIV/AIDS is the control of the proliferation of the virus in the patient and the treatment of opportunistic infections, coupled with positive living and good nutrition. The use of several drugs (anti-retrovirals or ARVs) to control the virus is called anti-retroviral therapy or highly active anti-retroviral therapy (HAART). No medicines have been developed yet to eradicate the virus within a person, but many people living with HIV/AIDS and who are on anti-retroviral therapy can lead close-to-normal lives for two decades.

The main obstacles to widespread prevention and treatment/care of HIV/AIDS are still enormous: stigma, lack of testing facilities, the prohibitive costs of treatment, and compliance with the regimens that include several pills or tablets that need to be taken three times daily. Each of these obstacles is being addressed. Researchers are developing combination drugs that will only need to be taken once a day, for example.

TB: More than half a century ago, TB was a global scourge, claiming many deaths even in the industrialized world. But since 1944, the TB death toll in developed countries has been reduced through a combination of better hygiene and mass treatment of known cases. Today, we have the medicines to cure TB. With active case detection and careful adherence to the six-month drug treatment regime, nearly 100 percent of cases of pulmonary TB can be cured. Even multiple-drug resistant TB cases are becoming more curable with second-line drugs.

Diagnosing TB has also become easier. Chest x-rays used to be the cornerstone of TB diagnosis. Now, sputum microscopy has enabled health professionals to confirm the presence of TB bacilli at an affordable cost and with ease and accuracy.

The acceptance of the Directly-Observed Therapy, Short-Term (DOTS) as a global strategy has improved TB control. It involves microscopy for accurate diagnosis, regular and uninterrupted drug supply of the most effective drugs in the national protocol, standardized and rigorous record-keeping and reporting, directly observed treatment for six to eight months, and political commitment and resources to ensure sustainability.

Malaria: Years ago, malaria control mainly occurred through the destruction of the laying and hatching sites of mosquitoes. Anti-malarial drugs and mosquito nets are now seen as more critical. Sleeping under an insecticide-treated mosquito net is an effective, affordable, and easily implemented way to prevent malaria in young children and pregnant mothers. Mosquito nets can last up to four years and may need to be re-treated with insecticide only every six months.

The principal problem in malaria control has been the growing resistance of the malaria parasite to common treatments, such as chloroquine. Fortunately, new drugs using an old Chinese remedy, artemisinin, have been developed. These derivatives are effective and affordable. Drug companies are marketing them worldwide.

Costs: Until recently, the cost of the supplies and drugs to diagnose and treat AIDS, TB, and malaria has been the highest hurdle. National programs simply did not have enough money. The following table, however, shows that effective cure and prevention are within the means of all countries, even the least developed nations, *if* donor countries provide some assistance. Globally, scaled-up programs of prevention and treatment cost between US$11–12 billion annually ($9.2 billion for HIV/AIDS, $1–1.5 billion for TB, and $1 billion for malaria). Unfortunately, only about a quarter of the needed amount is currently available.

Table 4: Examples of Effective Interventions and Costs: AIDS, TB, and Malaria

Disease	Intervention	Estimated Cost	Remarks
AIDS	Abstinence	Free	Balanced ABC approach is known to have reduced Uganda's AIDS prevalence by two-thirds
	Being Faithful	Free	
	Condoms	US$14 for year's supply	
	ARV/HAART	US$350 for one year	Can prolong life for years
TB	DOTS: Multidrug therapy	US$10 for six-month treatment	Cure rate up to 95%
Malaria	Anti-malarials	US$0.12 per tablet	Cure rate up to 95%
	Insecticide-treated nets	US$4 per net	

Strategies and Programs for the Millennium

Controlling AIDS, TB, and malaria is one emphasis of the international community's Millennium Development Goals. It has the support of nearly all governments and many multilateral organizations.

The mainstream multilateral development assistance agencies (United Nations Development Program, the World Health Organization, the World Bank, UNAIDS), bilateral donors (United States Agency for International Development, European Union, Canadian International Development Agency), and the private sector (the Gates Foundation) have developed common Millennium Development Goal targets with a 2010 deadline. Those related to the diseases of poverty are:

> *HIV/AIDS*: to reduce the number of newly infected young people (15–24 years) by 25 percent.
>
> *TB*: to halve TB deaths and prevalence.
>
> *Malaria*: to reduce the malaria disease burden by 50 percent.

To ensure momentum for the above goals, several global partnerships have been created, including, but not limited to, the following:

- *International Partnerships against AIDS in Africa (IPAA)* is a coalition of the United Nations, African governments, civil society organizations, and the private sector to curtail the spread of AIDS and mitigate its impact through scaled up and sustained national responses. It has the full support of UNAIDS and WHO, and seeks to ensure that national AIDS strategic plans are reviewed, run, and financed.

- *Stop TB Initiative* assists countries with large TB disease burdens to promote DOTS as a universal strategy to control TB. In addition to the 2010 commitment above, it has the following supplementary commitments:

  - By 2005, 70 percent of people with infectious TB will be diagnosed, with 85 percent of those people cured.

- By 2050, the global incidence of TB will be less than one in 1 million people.

- *Roll Back Malaria* was launched by WHO, the United Nations Children's Fund, the United Nations Development Project, and the World Bank in 1998 to increase the political commitment of countries. In addition to the commitment for 2010, the targets of Roll Back Malaria include:

  - By 2005, 60 percent of those suffering from malaria will have prompt access to and are able to use correct, affordable, and appropriate treatment within 24 hours of the onset of symptoms.
  - By 2005, 60 percent of those at risk of malaria, particularly pregnant women and children under 5, will benefit from insecticide-treated nets and other accessible and affordable interventions.

- The *Global Fund to fight AIDS, TB and Malaria* is a public-private partnership outside the UN system to manage the resources needed to scale up interventions to fight AIDS, TB, and malaria. In three years it has distributed more than US$1.5 billion to programs in 92 countries.

- *Massive Effort Campaign* is an advocacy network to catalyze global commitment to fight the diseases of poverty.

- *Global TB Drug Facility* and the *Global Alliance for TB Drug Development* seek to ensure that TB drugs are available to programs that need them and that affordable new drugs are developed.

- *International AIDS Vaccine Initiative* is the lead agency in the research, development, field testing, and approval of a vaccine to prevent HIV/AIDS.

The Way Forward

Experiences from the four years since the earlier initiatives began have provided many lessons for public health professionals. Lives are being saved, but our goals are still far from being attained. Below are some recommendations for those of us engaged in Christian medical missions:

- Target the diseases of the poor to achieve the greatest impact on health.

- Work with and through existing programs and partnerships for efficiency, effectiveness, and appropriateness.

- Improve the access of the poor to proven interventions; involve them in designing programs.

- Establish new and effective mechanisms to maximize the access of the poor to life-saving interventions.

- Create independent monitoring and evaluation systems to verify progress and impact.

- Encourage transparency, equity, and compassion in government stewardship of health resources.

- Link health efforts with poverty reduction and other efforts in development.

- Master collaboration with other stakeholders, be they government, other civil society organizations, or the private sector.

- Build local and national capacity for sustainability.

- Increase political action to ensure that the benefits of globalization reach the poor.

For More Information

The websites of many organizations and agencies have very helpful information on the diseases of poverty. The most significant ones include the following:

1. Global Fund to Fight AIDS, TB, and Malaria: www.theglobalfund.org

2. Global Health Council: www.globalhealth.org

3. International Union Against TB and Lung Diseases: www.iuatld.org

4. Massive Effort Campaign: www.massiveeffort.org

5. Roll Back Malaria: www.rbm.org

6. UNAIDS: www.unaids.org

7. UNDP: www.undp.org

8. World Bank: www.worldbank.org

9. World Health Organization: www.who.org

For a distinctively Christian perspective, the following may be helpful:

10. Christian Connections for International Health: www.ccih.org

11. World Vision International: www.wvi.org

Notes

1. The sources of data used in this paper included many documents from the following: Global Fund to fight AIDS, TB and Malaria, Massive Effort Campaign against the Diseases of Poverty, UNAIDS, World Health Organization, and World Vision International. For more information, see the list of websites included at the end of this chapter.

"I HAVE AIDS":
A TESTIMONY OF A PASTOR'S DAUGHTER

In Spanish my name means *grace*. My parents named me Gracia to reflect God's grace, the unmerited favor of God that enables human beings to be saved. This essay shows how I received the grace of God.

Dual Life

I was born to a Protestant family. My father is a pastor, and both my parents have founded churches in Bolivia. I grew up in the church. For a while, our church was based in my garage, because we did not have a place to meet. I went to Sunday school, where I learned about Abraham, Joseph, and Jesus. I also heard about Samson and his mistake involving a woman who did not belong to God's people.

At school my classmates used to tease me about my name, saying, "Gracias, Gracia." I continually had to explain to people about the grace of God and that I was a Christian. As a child, I was not ready to do this with every person I met. Therefore, I decided to use my second name, Violeta, which means *violet*. This name was easier to remember and did not prompt so many questions.

As I grew older I began living a dual life, which in one sense reflected my two identities. Within the church I was Gracia, living a "good" life as the daughter of pastor. Gracia went to church every Sunday, performing for the benefit of other people. Violeta, however, was a rebellious teenager doing her will and ignoring God's commandments. As Violeta I did all the things Gracia was not allowed to do. As Violeta I did not belong to God's family at all. I was playing with God and the flesh at the same time. I was not aware of the great risk I was taking.

Bitterness

This history of rebellion started with my incapacity to forgive and the bitterness I let grow in my heart. I was not able to forgive my older sister when she became engaged to a boy I used to like. I began to think all Christians were fakes. I needed to feel loved by someone to show my sister that I did not need the boy to whom she had become engaged. I began dating boys outside the church—lots of boys.

I was looking for love, for someone to take care of me, to understand me, to be loyal, to never lie, to support me, to be faithful, to speak the truth. I was looking for a man to supply what only God has, so I never found it. Men realized I needed love and took advantage of my need. Men can love, but they will ask a price for it. They will ask for your body, for your integrity. They will ask for the temple of the Holy Spirit. They asked for my body, and I gave it.

Though I kept going to church every Sunday, my heart was far from God. I went to the university to study anthropology. I began to drink alcohol, smoke marijuana, and use other drugs.

My family suffered much during this time. They could not understand the decisions I was making. My mother and father tried to rescue me. They locked the doors so that I could not escape. They prayed for long nights when I did not come home. They denied me access to the telephone. Finally, they begged me to change and to remember God, but I became more rebellious each time they talked to me.

A Life Far from God

I knew about the severe risk of getting pregnant outside of marriage, but I did not know about the risk of contracting AIDS. One Saturday night I sneaked out to a party without my parents' knowledge. After a time of dancing and drinking, I had no money for a taxi home, and I was drunk. As I walked home alone, I did not realize that two men were following me. They hit me and took me to an alley, where they raped me.

I felt my heart was being destroyed. As a child of God, I thought that my heavenly Father had a duty to protect me. I told my older sister about what had happened, but not my parents. I did not want to see them suffer. Traumatized, I did not want any man near me. However, even this experience did not bring about real repentance. I thought that nothing worse could happen now, and I had lost everything, so I did not change my lifestyle.

In March 2000 I went to a small town to do research for my thesis about small loans for micro enterprises. There an insect bit me, and the bite got infected. Quickly I became very tired. I started having nosebleeds. My family and I thought I had contracted malaria, which is common in that part of the world. I went to a laboratory to get tested. My older sister told the staff to test me for HIV as well.

My HIV test came back positive. Believe it or not, I was shocked. I had not had as many sexual experiences as most of my school friends. I saw myself as simply a girl from university discovering her sexuality. I never injected drugs, and I was not a sex worker.

How would I tell my parents? What was going to happen to me? When was I going to die? How could I face people and their prejudices about AIDS? How could I ever tell people from church that I was HIV-positive?

I cried for a very long time. Finally, one day my sister told me that I had to tell my parents. But how could I? We had never even talked about sexuality. The thought of telling them tortured me for many months. They would probably throw me out of the house. I decided that if my parents rejected me, life would not be worth living. However, I could bear the burden no longer. One day while staying with a friend I wrote a letter to my parents. My sister brought it to them.

A week later I saw their astonished, questioning, tear-stained faces. They couldn't understand why this had happened to their daughter. Nevertheless, my family did not reject me. In fact, they received me with open arms. They told me they did not want to know what had happened. They just wanted to be with me until the last day. The Bible says:

As a father has compassion on his children, so the Lord has compassion on those who fear him.[1]

I began to understand that this display of love was a reflection of God's love in my family. This love was just one of the gifts that God had prepared for me.

"Let the bones you have crushed rejoice . . ."[2]

In my anguish, I earnestly started looking for God—and I found him. He gave me freedom from blame and shame. I found peace, forgiveness, and hope. My Heavenly Father consoled me with strength to go on and promises of eternal life:

> Even though I walk through the valley of the shadow of death, I will fear no evil for you are with me.[3]

The Lord has used different Christian brothers and sisters to replace the pain in my heart with health and consolation. He has shown me that nothing can separate me from his incomparable love, neither all the evil I had committed, nor the virus, nor death:

> No, in all these things we are more than conquerors through him who loved us. For I am convinced that neither death nor life, neither angels nor demons, neither the present nor the future, nor any powers, neither height nor depth, nor anything else in all creation, will be able to separate us from the love of God that is in Christ Jesus our Lord.[4]

Not even AIDS can separate me from the love of God. The sacrifice Jesus made on the cross was enough to save me and enough to forgive my sins and those of people living with HIV. The Lord is faithful to me even though I was unfaithful. He had a mission for my life, even one based on my mistakes.

"Jesus reached out his hand and touched the man . . ."[5]

I become reconciled with God, as Hezekiah did.[6] I humbled myself in God's presence, repented of my sins, asked for forgiveness, and gave God my broken life. The Lord forgave me, restored me, and healed my body, soul, and spirit.

No longer the same person, I started to study the Bible again. I needed to find out what God demanded of me.

In all this I discovered how privileged I am among those living with HIV. I have family members who support me instead of judging me or discriminating against me. I am healthy, I am alive, and I have eternal life. I have met other people living with HIV and AIDS. The pain in their souls and bodies is terrible. They die alone, abandoned by their own families, without a glimmer of hope.

The Lord told me to volunteer among these people. As I began, I wanted to find out what God said about illnesses such as AIDS and discovered that judging is only for God. I had to put aside my prejudices if I really wanted to work with sex workers, homosexuals, and others with the illness.

I was impressed by Jesus' attitude among people with leprosy. The society and synagogues of that day treated lepers with physical, social, and symbolic discrimination. However, Jesus touched them, ate[7] with them, and healed them, physically and spiritually:

A man with leprosy came to him and begged him on his knees, "If you are willing, you can make me clean." Filled with compassion, Jesus reached out his hand and touched the man. "I am willing," he said. "Be clean !"[8]

"He has given us new birth into a living hope . . ."[9]

I decided it was not important to know how much time I would live. Each day, however many were left, would be for God's glory.

The Lord had prepared a mission of hope for persons living with HIV and AIDS based on my worst mistakes. His mercy and grace covered my broken promises and failures. Rather than rejecting me, he used my experiences to help me console other suffering people.

Praise be to the God and Father of our Lord Jesus Christ! In his great mercy he has given us new birth into a living hope through the resurrection of Jesus Christ from the dead.[10]

I know from my own experience that God has a living hope for persons with HIV and AIDS. Although most people will judge us, the divine response provides forgiveness and living hope.

Together with others, I have founded a self-help group for people living with HIV and AIDS. We work as volunteers in prevention, advocacy, and assistance for the ill. We provide information for families, community-based organizations, and the government. The Lord has blessed us. The Pan American Health Organization has highlighted our work as effective. More importantly, God has used us to bring hope to suffering people.

"The AIDS crisis is the harvest God gave us"[11]

We have also been messengers to Bolivian evangelical churches. In September 2002 I met Leah Mutala at the Conference on Integral Mission and HIV/AIDS held by the Micah Network in Chiang Mai, Thailand. Leah is a volunteer who takes care of AIDS orphans in Africa. She widened my perspective still further by teaching that God defends the widow and the orphan and is a Father to the fatherless.[12] HIV/AIDS has left millions of children without their parents in Africa. We need to reach out to them. However, the most important thing Leah taught me is that "the AIDS crisis is the harvest God gave us":

> Do you not say, "Four months more and then the harvest"? I tell you, open your eyes and look at the fields! They are ripe for harvest.[13]

This is the message I received for evangelical churches:

> Let's open our eyes and see; the harvest is ready.
> The AIDS crisis is the harvest God gave us.
> We will reap for eternal life.

"I will not die but live, and will proclaim what the Lord has done"[14]

I don't worry any more about how long will I live. Whenever I die, I will be with my Heavenly Father for eternity. The time God has given me I will use to proclaim the wonders he has done in my life and the way his great love and mercy reached me. God has taught me the meaning of my name—*Gracia*—in my own flesh.

This church that I love.

God had even more beautiful things prepared for me. My family and I did not tell the local church where my father pastors about my condition. We were afraid we might be kicked out. People in Bolivia can ignorantly discriminate against people with HIV. We prayed a lot, but we did not really trust God in this area. Sometimes my fear was bigger than my need to confess my sin.

However, as a public speaker on HIV and AIDS for the community-based organization REDBOL (Bolivian Network of People Living with HIV/AIDS), I am on television all the time. We knew it was impossible to keep the secret about my HIV status. The moment I started speaking about it to the church one Sunday, I could not stop crying. I was so ashamed for causing pain to my father and the rest of the family and for being a bad testimony for my church.

Yet God had prepared loving church members for us. They have supported us continually since learning of my HIV status. My dear brothers and sisters pray for me every week, asking God that I be healed. They support my speeches with prayer and my family with words of hope. I love this church. It is a gift from God.

Today

My viral load (number of viruses in the blood) is 15,000 copies/ml.[15] Currently I do not take any antiretroviral medicines, which cost US$1,500 per month. (Few people in Bolivia can afford this.) So the virus reproduces itself every 37 hours in my body, and medically I am getting weaker every day. But I hang on to the fact that God supports me, that he freely gives me his inexhaustible grace.

> "My grace is sufficient for you, for my power is made perfect in weakness." Therefore I will boast all the more gladly about my weaknesses, so that Christ's power may rest on me. That is why, for Christ's sake, I delight in weaknesses, in insults, in hardships, in persecutions, in difficulties. For when I am weak, then I am strong.[16]

Notes

1. Psalm 103:13.
2. Psalm 51:8b.
3. Psalm 23:4
4. Romans 8:37–39.
5. Mark 1:41b.
6. 2 Kings 20.
7. "While he was in Bethany, reclining at the table in the home of a man known as Simon the Leper . . ." Mark 14:3.
8. Mark 1:40–41.
9. 1 Peter 1:3b.
10. 1 Peter 1:3.
11. Leah Mutala, Zimbawe 2002.
12. Psalm 68:5; 146:9.
13. John 4:35.
14. Psalm 118:17.
15. A person living with HIV can die with over a million copies/ml.
16. 2 Corinthians 12:9–10.

THE EMERGING AIDS CATASTROPHE IN NIGERIA

The impact of the AIDS epidemic in Africa was initially concentrated in the southern and central parts of the continent. However, reports from other regions indicate that the relatively low prevalence rates reported for Nigeria and other countries in the 1980s and early 1990s are now being shadowed by more rapid patterns of growth.[1] The situation in Nigeria has become particularly worrisome because it is the most populous country in the world that has crossed the critical 5 percent prevalence threshold. This means it has a critical mass of HIV-infected individuals from whom the infection can rapidly spread both within the country and to neighboring countries[2].

Nigeria therefore is at risk for the explosive phase of the AIDS epidemic, and many investigators both within and outside of the country fear that the next wave of the AIDS epidemic is likely to hit hard in Nigeria if nothing is done.

Current Statistics

We have obtained current statistics on the prevalence of HIV infection mainly from prenatal clinics, patients with sexually transmitted diseases (STDs), patients with tuberculosis, and female prostitutes across the country.[2] Results from these surveys conducted by the Nigerian Federal Ministry of Health (FMOH) and partly funded by the United States Agency for International Development have estimated the prevalence of HIV infection in Nigeria to be 5.8 percent.

About 3.47 million adults between ages 15–49 are believed to be HIV-infected in the country, making Nigeria the fourth most critical case-country in the world, contributing 8 percent of global infections and 11.6 percent of the African HIV burden. The cumulative death toll from AIDS-related illnesses is estimated at 1.4 million, resulting in over 1 million AIDS orphans in a country that lacks resources, infrastructure, and programs for orphans, many of whom are themselves HIV-infected.[3]

HIV infection rates in Nigeria vary across communities and states and across age groups and by risk behavior. The age group mostly affected is 20–24 years (8.1 percent). Rates are substantially higher in some high-risk groups, such as female sex workers (34.3 percent). The HIV rate among commercial blood donors has reached an alarming 11 percent. The North Central zone, consisting of Benue, Federal Capital Territory, Niger, Nasarawa, Plateau, Kwara, and Kogi states, has the highest rate of 9.5 percent. The lowest rate of 3.6 was reported for the North East zone consisting of Zamfara, Sokoto, Kano, Kastina, Kaduna, and Kebbi states (see Tables 1 and 2). Although prevalence is reported to be highest in large cities such as Lagos (6.7 percent), Abuja (8 percent), Port Harcourt (9.3 percent), Kaduna (11.6 percent), and Markurdi (16.8 percent), infection is by no means restricted to these urban areas.[4]

Table 1: HIV Prevalence Rates by Region

Geopolitical Zone	Median HIV Sero-prevalence (percent)	Hot Spot State and Median HIV Sero-Prevalence (percent)	Sero-prevalence Rate Among Youth In Zone (20-24) (percent)	Prevalence Rate Among ANC Attendees in Hot Spot State (percent)
South East	5.2	Ebonyi (9.3)	8.4	11.1
South West	3.5	Lagos (6.7)	4.2	4.7
North West	3.2	Kaduna (11.6)	4.5	15.0
North Central	7.0	Benue (16.8)	9.5	21.0
North East	4.5	Taraba (5.5)	3.6	7.0
South South	5.2	Akwa Ibom (12.5)	6.8	13.3

Source: National AIDS/STD Control Program/FMOH, 1999

Table 2: HIV Prevalence Rates by States, 2001

State	HIV Prevalence (percent)	Estimated HIV infections	State	HIV Prevalence (percent)	Estimated HIV Infections
Abia	3.3	34,335	Kano	3.8	299,197
Adamawa	4.5	57,149	Katsina	3.5	76,544
Akwa Ibom	10.7	122,169	Kebbi	4.0	56,884
Anambra	6.5	134,325	Kogi	5.7	88,385
Bauchi	6.8	114,288	Kwara	4.3	45,779
Bayelsa	7.2	49,935	Lagos	3.5	70,171
Benue	13.5	245,066	Nasarawa	8.1	49,275
Borno	4.5	62,140	Niger	4.5	55,383
Cross River	8.0	93.582	Ogun	3.5	58,480
Delta	5.8	125,842	Ondo	6.7	92,875
Ebonyi	6.2	51,901	Osun	4.3	52,125
Edo	5.7	54,828	Oyo	4.2	79,561
Ekiti	3.2	31,326	Plateau	8.5	82,076
Enugu	5.2	51,639	Rivers	7.7	163,233
FCT	10.2	7,127	Sokoto	2.8	45,229
Gombe	8.2	103,620	Taraba	6.2	60,460
Imo	4.3	79,865	Yobe	3.5	24,280
Jigawa	1.8	47,043	Zamfara	3.5	32,162
Kaduna	5.6	199,723	Total	5.8	3,470,000

Source: National AIDS/STD Control Program/FMOH, 2001

The current burden of HIV infection in Nigeria is definitely a source of concern. But even more worrisome is the rate of its spread. According to the sentinel survey report of prenatal clinics, the average national HIV prevalence rate rose from 1.8 percent in 1991, to 3.8 percent in 1995, to 5.4 percent in 1999, and 5.8 percent in 2001. Within one decade (1991–2001), the prevalence of HIV infection in Nigeria increased by over 300 percent. Among sex workers in Lagos, HIV prevalence rose from 2 percent in 1989, to 12 percent in 1991, representing a sixfold increase; and by 1996, up to 70 percent of sex workers screened tested positive for HIV.[5]

In a report of the National HIV/AIDS database project conducted by the Nigerian Institute of Medical Research (NIMR), the median annual HIV infection rates, based on data from 379 laboratory facilities in the six geopolitical zones of the country, increased from 2.28 percent in 1989 to 13.25 percent in 1999 (see Figure 1).[6] This change represents a sixfold increase in the national median infection rates in laboratory facilities. Although these were samples from individuals who came to the health care system (and therefore are expected to have higher rates of disease), nevertheless, the higher prevalence rates in the NIMR report compared to the sentinel survey suggests the current national prevalence of HIV infection based on the sentinel survey is underestimated.

Figure 1: Median HIV Seropositivity Rate in Nigeria 1989–1999

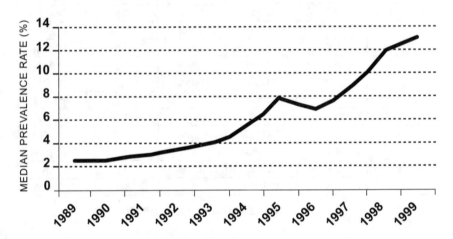

Source: NIMR HIV/AIDS Technical Report.

Future Fears

This trend of exponential increases in the rates of AIDS cases has raised a lot of concern among policy makers in Nigeria and the international community. A recent report by the Intelligence Community Assessment team of the United States listed Nigeria along with Ethiopia, China, Russia, and India as the five countries anticipated to suffer from explosive increases in AIDS cases.[7] Nigeria has a population of over 115 million people and an annual growth rate of 2.9 percent. Many experts predict an overwhelming outbreak of this epidemic within the next decade.

Should an AIDS epidemic of the proportion seen in other parts of Africa—with rates as high as 25–35 percent—occur here, about 10–15 million adults will be affected, resulting in annual AIDS-related deaths of close to 2 million. This will be catastrophic for a nation such as Nigeria, where poverty is endemic, cities are crowded, illiteracy is high, and health care infrastructure is rudimentary.

In addition, an epidemic of this magnitude will provide a huge reservoir of HIV infection for surrounding countries and beyond. The economic impact will be immeasurable, as young adults will be most affected, communicable diseases such as tuberculosis will spread unabated, and morbidity and mortality will surpass records for any one infectious disease in the history of any nation. There are indications that an AIDS epidemic of this magnitude is imminent in Nigeria. Besides the increasing rate of AIDS cases in overpopulated cities and towns, many of the factors that favor the spread of the virus abound in the countryside, where most Nigerians live. People in rural communities have limited knowledge of the AIDS virus and how it passes from person to person.

Reasons for Infection

The transmission of HIV occurs through multiple routes: heterosexual intercourse, homosexual intercourse, intravenous drug use, transfusion of contaminated blood products, transmission from mother to newborn, breast feeding, occupational exposure to infected body fluid, and unsafe medical practices, such as the use of non-sterile injections and medical devices.

Unlike in developed countries where a greater proportion of HIV infection is acquired through homosexual activities and intravenous drug use, more than 90 percent of HIV infection in Nigeria and many other African nations comes through heterosexual intercourse.[8] HIV infection rates among Africans strongly follow patterns of sexual behavior and those of other sexually transmitted diseases. Children under 14, who are generally not sexually active, have very low infection rates.[9] These observations suggest the current trend of rising HIV infection in the country is largely from the sexual behavior and practices of Nigerians.

Traditionally, many cultures in Nigeria uphold the sanctity of marriage and sexual relationships. Although polygamy is part of some African societies, sex outside of marriage has been strongly frowned upon and chastity among young unmarried women prized. Over the past three to four decades, however, there has been marked deviation from these traditional values. Young men and women are becoming sexually active at an increasingly early age, premarital sex is common, divorce rates are rising, and extramarital affairs are rampant.

In the 1999 health survey and demographic report by the National Population Commission,[10] more than 16 percent of teenage females polled reported first sexual intercourse by age 15, and nearly half (49.4 percent) of young women ages 20 to 24 reported first sex by age 18. On the other hand, 8.3 percent of teenage males reported first sex by age 15, while 36.3 percent of males ages 20 to 24 reported first sexual intercourse by age 18. Among sexually experienced teens, over 13 percent of women and over 27 percent of men reported exchanging money, gifts, or favors for sex in the previous 12 months.

In another survey of 440 Nigerian secondary school students with a mean age of 17.6, Fawole et al[11] reported over 30 percent were sexually active, the average age of first sexual experience was 16 years, and 67.6 percent of male and 32.4 percent of female students who were sexually active had multiple partners. Oronsaye and colleague[12] also reported sexual intercourse before age 16 in 55 percent of secondary school girls in a large Nigerian city.

In a country where the HIV prevalence rate is already greater than 5 percent, sexual permissiveness of this magnitude among young people (who are also more likely to engage in high-risk sexual practices that can enhance HIV transmission) raises a huge concern. These findings also indicate that young women are more likely to experience sex earlier than young men, thus suggesting that young women are sexually involved with older and more experienced men with higher rates of HIV infection. This may partly explain the growing rate of HIV infection among women in Nigeria and other African countries.

Laxity in sexual moral standards does not appear to be limited to the younger age group. Sexual permissiveness among older and married individuals in many communities is occurring in Nigeria. In one study[13] among adults, 60 percent of sexually active respondents had at least two partners, 18 percent reported a history of sex with prostitutes, while 25 percent admitted to having at least one sexually transmitted disease (STD). Another study of five Nigerian towns[14] reported extramarital sexual relations among 54 percent of men and 39 percent of women. Eighteen percent of the men and 11 percent of the women had engaged in sex in the previous week. While this pattern of sexual behavior is not unique to Nigerians, in the context of high HIV infection rates in many towns and villages, it threatens to significantly escalate the AIDS epidemic.

Another factor contributing to the exponential rise of HIV infection in Nigeria is the high prevalence of STDs. The relationship between STDs and HIV transmission is well established. Genital ulcers and inflammation that result from STDs such as gonorrhea, syphilis, genital herpes, etc., compromise the protection the genital mucosal barrier against HIV transmission. The presence of STDs also increases the recruitment of co-receptors (CCR5 and CXCR4) to the genital mucosal. These co-receptors facilitate entry of HIV into the genital cells when an individual is exposed. In addition, co-infection of HIV and STDs increases HIV viral load and the shedding of HIV in the genital organs of both men and women. As a result, individuals with HIV and STD co-infection have high concentrations of HIV in their genital secretions and are therefore highly infectious.

With all these facts, it is not surprising that the prevalence of STDs is high in many cities and villages. Equally worrisome is the fact that many of these STDs remain untreated or unrecognized because of the poor health care infrastructure and lack of access to health care by many, particularly women in rural areas. The prevalence of STDs varies across the country. Estimates range from as low as 6 percent to as high as 40 percent among sexually active adults.

In a large study[15] of reproductive tract infections among 868 adolescent girls in rural Nigeria, 82.4 percent reported vaginal discharge, though few sought treatment. At the time of the study, 8.2 percent had chlamydial infections, and 6.6 percent had trichomoniasis. Over 6 percent of women under age 17 had documented STDs, and, overall, 16.5 percent had documented STDs. Other studies in Nigeria have estimated the incidence of Trichomonas to be 24.8–37.6 percent, gonorrhea 7.5–26.7 percent, syphilis 3.06–5.1 percent, and Chlamydia 5.3–18.3 percent.[16] It is likely that these STDs have contributed to the current HIV crisis in Nigeria. If these STDs are not identified, and treated, they have the potential to tremendously escalate the AIDS epidemic in Nigeria and the surrounding regions.

A salient trend often overlooked is the higher HIV prevalence rate among women, especially those of childbearing age. The proportion of women with HIV infection is highest in African countries (see Figure 2 and note 1). Many factors may account for this. First, women in Nigeria are at a disadvantage in negotiating safe sex, compared with males. Second, because of differences in the anatomy of the female and male genital organs, the transmission of HIV from a man to his female partner is twofold more efficient than from a woman to a male partner. Third, women are more likely than men to harbor STDs with no symptoms. Thus, they are more susceptible to HIV infection.

Since a greater proportion of HIV infection in Nigeria comes through heterosexual transmission, we expect that HIV prevalence rates among women will continue to increase faster than among men. This trend has grave consequences, because HIV can be transmitted from mother to child both at delivery and during breast-feeding. Transmission of HIV from mother to newborn is estimated at 20–30 percent in the absence of antiretroviral drugs. The HIV transmission rate through breast-feeding can be as high as 15 percent. Consequently, since only very few Nigerian women have access to antiretroviral treatment during pregnancy, at least one in every four newborns to HIV-positive mothers is at risk of infection. A significant number of breast-fed infants will acquire the infection from their mothers. This again is another threat that has the potential to create a perpetual cycle of escalating AIDS cases that will rapidly tip the balance toward catastrophe.

Figure 2: Sex Distribution of HIV Infections, End 2002

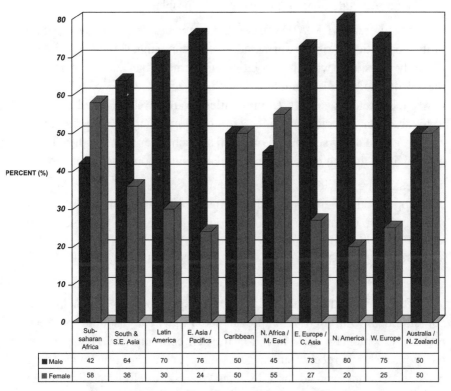

	Sub-saharan Africa	South & S.E. Asia	Latin America	E. Asia / Pacifics	Caribbean	N. Africa / M. East	E. Europe / C. Asia	N. America	W. Europe	Australia / N. Zealand
■ Male	42	64	70	76	50	45	73	80	75	50
■ Female	58	36	30	24	50	55	27	20	25	50

Source: Adapted from UNAIDS/WHO database on HIV/AIDS 2002

Recommendations

Unsafe medical practices—including using poorly sterilized medical instruments, recycling injection needles and syringes, and transfusing blood products without appropriate screening for blood-borne pathogens—constitute a serious problem with health care delivery in Nigeria. Poorly trained personnel, even quacks, use non-sterile techniques that spread infection, including HIV. For example, while the HIV prevalence among commercial blood donors is as high as 11 percent, many health care centers lack adequate blood screening facilities. The World Health Organization estimates that 2.4 percent of HIV transmission in Africa is due to unsafe medical practices.[17] In a recent report, Gisselquist, et al[18] attributed over 40 percent of HIV infection in Africa to unsafe medical practices. While this may be an overstatement, it underscores the problem.

An aggressive HIV/AIDS prevention campaign targeting every strata of the population at risk is warranted. Such a campaign should be directed not only at people who live in cities and large urban areas but also at the uneducated rural communities with no access to radio, television, newspapers, and magazines. Communities should be encouraged to return to the tradition of practicing safe sex. Young men and women should be encouraged to delay sexual activity until a much older age, and the culture of sex within the context of a marital relationship should be promoted.

Health care providers at all levels should receive training to recognize and appropriately treat sexually transmitted infections. Authorities must limit the transfusion of blood products as much as possible. They should screen blood products for HIV and other blood pathogens before transfusion. They should not use poorly sterilized medical equipment, needles, and syringes.

Officials should make HIV screening programs available in communities with high HIV prevalence rates. They should promote routine screening for HIV infection in such communities. HIV-positive individuals should receive support, treatment, and counseling on avoiding behavior that may spread the infection. We need to eliminate the stigma people living with HIV in both urban and rural communities face.

We need to place greater emphasis on women's health. HIV prevention programs should include mandatory HIV screening for pregnant women. All pregnant women who test positive for HIV should receive counseling and antiretroviral therapy to reduce the risk of transmission to newborns. We should offer alternatives to breast-feeding to mothers with newborn infants whenever possible.

Nigeria is a nation of strategic importance by virtue of her population, resources, and regional leadership role. An AIDS epidemic of the magnitude that has occurred in other parts of the continent will be devastating in Nigeria. Such a massive outbreak will provide a huge reservoir for spreading the AIDS virus within the country and beyond. It will destabilize the economy by weakening the work force, overwhelming the fragile health care infrastructure, creating a public health menace, and compromising national security and political stability. Steps need to be urgently taken to reverse the increasing spread of HIV in Nigeria. Yet the spread of HIV is preventable. With these measures, we can begin to make a difference.

Notes

1. AIDS epidemic update—December 2002 [Joint United Nations Programme on HIV/AIDS (UNAIDS)]. December 2002. Available at: http://www.unaids.org/epidemic_update/report_dec02/index.html

2. National AIDS/HIV/STD Control Programme, 2002. The 2001 National HIV/Syphilis Sentinel Survey among Pregnant Women attending Ante-natal Clinic in Nigeria. National AIDS/STD Control Programme. The Federal Ministry of Health, Department of Public Health, December, Technical Report.

National AIDS/STD Control Programme (Federal Ministry of Health). 1999 HIV/Syphilis Sentinel Sero-prevalence survey in Nigeria. Technical Report.

National AIDS/STD Control Programme (Federal Ministry of Health). 1997 HIV/Syphilis Sentinel Sero-prevalence Survey in Nigeria. Technical Report.

National AIDS/STD Control Programme (Federal Ministry of Health). 1995 HIV/Syphilis Sentinel Sero-prevalence Survey in Nigeria. Technical Report.

3. See note 1.

4. E. Esu-Williams, C. Mulanga-Kabeya, H. Takena, et al. "Seroprevalence of HIV-1, HIV-2, and HIV-1 group O in Nigeria: evidence for a growing increase of HIV infection." J Acquir Immune Defic Syndr Hum Retrovirol 1997 Nov. 1; 16 (3):204–10.

5. M.N. Ani and S.M. Agwale, "Human Immunodeficiency Virus Infection in Nigeria." Braz J Infect Dis 1998 Jun; 2(3):143–159.

6. Nigerian Institute of Medical Research (NIMR) HIV-AIDS Technical report, 2002.

7. National Intelligence Council ICA 2002-04D. The Next Wave of HIV/AIDS: Nigeria, Ethiopia, Russia, India, and China Prepared under the auspices of David F. Gordon, formerly National Intelligence Officer for Economics and Global Issues. Additional copies of this assessment can be downloaded from the NIC public website at www.odci.gov/nic or obtained from Karen Monaghan, Acting National Intelligence Officer for Economics and Global Issues.

8. K. M.De Kock, E. Ekpini, E. Gnaore, et al, "The public health implications of AIDS research in Africa." JAMA 1994; 6:481–6.

9. See note 1.

10. National Population Commission. Nigeria Demographic and Health Survey 1999. Abuja, Nigeria: The Commission, 2000.

11. I.O. Fawole, M.C. Asuzu, S.O. Oduntan, W.R. Brieger, "A school-based AIDS education programme for secondary school students in Nigeria: a review of effectiveness." Health Educ Res 1999 Oct; 14 (5):675–83.

12. A.U. Oronsaye and G.I. Odiase, "Attitude toward abortion and contraception among Nigeria secondary school girls." International Journal of Gynecology and Obstretrics. 1983; 21:423–426.

13. B.A. Olayinka and A.A. Osho, "Changes in attitude, sexual behaviour and the risk of HIV/AIDS transmission in southwest Nigeria." East Afr Med J 1997 Sep; 74 (9):554–60.

14. U.C. Isiugo-Abanihe, "Extramarital relations and perceptions of HIV/AIDS in Nigeria." Health Transit Rev 1994 Oct; 4(2):111–25.

15. L. Brabin, et al, "Reproductive tract infections and abortion among adolescent girls in rural Nigeria." Lancet 1995; 345:300–304.

16. N.M. Otuonye, D.K. Olukoya, N.N. Odunukwe, E.O. Idigbe, M.N. Udeaja, M. Bamidele, J.I. Onyewuchie, C.T. Oparaugu, O.S. Ayelari, B. Oyekunle, "HIV association with conventional STDS (sexual transmitted diseases) in Lagos State, Nigeria." West Afr J Med 2002 Apr–Jun; 21 (2):153–6.

C.I. Ogbonna, I.B. Ogbonna, A.A. Ogbonna, J.C. Anosike, "Studies on the incidence of Trichomonas vaginalis amongst pregnant women in Jos area of Plateau State, Nigeria." Angew Parasitol 1991 Nov, 32 (4):198–204.

F.E. Okonofua, R.C. Snow, G.A. Alemnji, A. Okoruwa, C.O. Ijaware, "Serological and clinical correlates of gonorrhoea and syphilis in fertile and infertile Nigerian women." Genitourin Med 1997 Jun, 73 (3):194–7.

A.O. Oyelese, M.C. Asuzu, A.O. Osoba, "Pattern of reactive serological tests for syphilis in different population groups attending the University College Hospital Ibadan (1976–1985)." Afr J Med Med Sci 1990 Sep; 19 (3):163–6.

P.C. Gini, W.O. Chukudebelu, A.N. Njoku-Obi, "Antenatal screening for syphilis at the University of Nigeria Teaching Hospital, Enugu, Nigeria—a six year survey." Int J Gynaecol Obstet 1989 Aug; 29 (4):321–4.

A.O. Osoba, "Sero-epidemiological study of Lymphogranuloma venereum in Western Nigeria." Afr J Med Med Sci 1977 Sep; 6 (3):125–32.

17. D. Gisselquist, J.J. Potterat, S. Stuart Brody, F. Vachon, "Let it be sexual: how health care transmission of AIDS in Africa was ignored." International Journal of STD & AIDS 2003; 14: 148–61.

D. Gisselquist and J.J. Potterat, "Heterosexual transmission of HIV in Africa: an empiric estimate." International Journal of STD & AIDS 2003; 14: 162–73.

18. See note 1.

GROWING GLOOM, GROWING GRACE:
PERVASIVE CONSEQUENCES OF THE CRISIS

My name is Elizabeth, and I am 11 years old. I live in
Kenya with my mother and two brothers. My father died of
AIDS two years ago. My mother also has AIDS.

When my father died, my uncles came and took all our
property. Now it is difficult to get money for school fees.

If my father were alive, I would be the happiest girl in the
whole world.

Elizabeth's story is not over. She will yet face the death of her
mother, confusion about what to tell people who claim AIDS is a curse
from generation to generation, stigma and rejection, the loss of household
income, the threat of stopping school, and the reality of no evening meal
or morning breakfast.

Elizabeth is one of the hundreds of millions of people affected by our
global AIDS crisis. What future will she have? What global impact can
we expect? What is our responsibility to respond today and to prepare for
tomorrow?

We know a lot about AIDS . . . too much to be comfortable or
complacent, too much to wait to respond. But we do not yet know what
it will mean for Elizabeth or us as Christians put by God himself into the
crucible of this crisis.

In the Family

Elizabeth's home is destroyed. She has no father and soon no mother. Members of her extended family, the traditional caretakers in crisis, are not helping. Much contributes to the fracture of her family.

We have known about many of these issues for a long time, but we have turned away to keep our hands from getting dirty and kept on preaching. Many of us contribute to this crisis. We don't talk about sex in church. We don't welcome homosexuals to the hospitality of our homes. We don't turn off sexually explicit language in pop songs or popular television shows. We don't support our youth in making wise choices about sexual debut. We don't guard our marriages enough.

The consequences include ever-deepening acceptance of sexual fulfillment apart from marriage and the risk of AIDS through billions of sexual acts across our globe.

AIDS rips through our families in Africa, exposing the worst of our hidden lives. Some traditions had value at one time, like the Levitical law essentially practiced as given in ancient times by Moses and lived in the life of Ruth and Boaz. Inheriting the wife after the death of a family member for the purpose of protecting, nurturing, and extending to the next generation is still practiced in some African cultures. When practiced in the context of selfish desire to gain property, or abuse through sexual greed, the consequence may be death. Children suffer the most.

Facing the demands of life today, many married couples are separated for long periods. Employment, education, the search for survival, or something more may become a harbinger of destruction rather than economic gain. HIV hides for years as it spreads among couples, married or not.

Family disruption begins long before the effects of the virus erupt on the skin or in the lungs of one family member. Sexual freedom outside marriage destroys the essence of family trust and commitment and even the coping capacity to face hard days ahead.

Our families wrestle with these consequences. Many faithful spouses tremble with fear over an unfaithful spouse. Many parents face the likelihood of leaving their children orphaned. Many grandparents care for all their children's children. This gloom shrouds much of family life in Africa today.

Yet I know a faithful Christian wife in Maputo, Mozambique. She was HIV-positive and faced the reality of one day dying of AIDS herself. Yet she cared lovingly not only for her husband, but her husband's girlfriend and baby, all of whom were HIV-positive.

In the Church

Our churches cannot cope adequately. We are burying people many days of the week, and our pastors are sometimes more busy with the affairs of death than with the affairs of life. What toll will this take on tomorrow's church?

We already see creeping evidence. False doctrine fans this AIDS crisis. Preachers pound pulpits and public address systems proclaiming healing for those who pray hard enough. It is not uncommon for wives, petrified of husbands' passing the virus on their marriage bed, to believe that God will protect them night after night because they are believers. Seldom is there open discussion about unfaithfulness, fear, or suspicion. These false beliefs are killing the church.

To other church leaders, solutions are simple. Get rid of the curse. In every way AIDS acts like a traditional curse with no cure, coming like a thief at night, attacking strong persons in the prime of life, and passing from generation to generation. To many, the Bible seems to support such belief.

However, while Leviticus is explicit about the existence of sicknesses with no cure, burdened African Christians have little time to examine the Scriptures and consider the claims of Christ who challenged curses forever and embraced those who were outcast in society because of them.

Our churches are overwhelmed. Many thousands in Africa are pouring life into homes affected by AIDS as they care for families. They are not only visiting the sick but also are scrubbing homes, carrying water and firewood, bathing bodies burning with fever, singing, praying, and sharing the Word. When all is said and done, and parents are buried, the children are picked up and also cared for along with failing grandparents no longer supported by their children in whom they invested retirement security.

The toll on caregivers is far-reaching. There is no glory in cleaning up diarrhea, sometimes without water. There is no redemption in hard work for persons who end up dying anyway. There can be no sense of satisfaction for a life saved from AIDS. Too often, what is left is another family member still to die, or another mouth still to feed.

In the Community

While the many in Africa dying of AIDS represent a tragedy, it is only part of the pain. Those not dying are consumed by giving daily care for the sick, dying, and orphaned.

AIDS ripples through every sector of society. Who will teach, if the teachers are dying faster than they are being replaced? Who will guide the plane safely to the ground, if governments do not keep up with training new controllers? Who will work the fields and bring in the season's crops for the family to sell for school fees? Who will run the business when the father and sons leave it behind? Where will you go for medical treatment when the beds are 60 percent occupied by patients with AIDS and tuberculosis? Who protects the streets when 50 percent or more of the police and army forces are infected?[1]

Households are strangled by expenditures related to AIDS and the depletion of workforce capacity and resources. Preparing for this is critical for families and communities.

This means admitting, first, that AIDS is in a family and that it is fatal. This remains a tremendous hurdle for many families. It forces people to accept vulnerability, to deal with stigma and possibly rejection, to communicate openly about hard issues, and to make difficult decisions about how to handle resources. Without taking this step, however, many families dive into destitution, from which it may take generations to recover.

Eighty percent of Africans depend on small-scale agriculture for food and income. Up to 60 to 70 percent of some large-scale farms have lost workers due to HIV/AIDS.[2] This drives up food prices and increases the economic burden of households.

A study in Zimbabwe in 1999 showed that AIDS deaths in households caused maize production to fall by 61 percent, in addition to other losses, such as cattle owned.[3] In Zambia, homes where a chronically ill person lived planted up to 53 percent less food than other homes.[4]

Our world must prepare for much more famine and hunger in Africa, not from drought, but from the reality that families cannot work their fields. When family food producers are dying and family consumers are caring for them, who are left to garden?

Conflict is also part of our world. In Africa, most of the countries with the highest rate of AIDS also experience internal conflict. In Rwanda, 24 percent of women in the capital city going to prenatal clinics were HIV-positive in 1995.[5] Armed men—whether police, military, or militia—are known to spread AIDS. In many countries, the highest rate of AIDS is clustered around military, police, and immigration posts.

AIDS also contributes to conflict. How does one decide in a community who gets antiretroviral (ARVs) drugs to prolong lives up to 10 years or more—and who does not? In Kenya alone, only five thousand HIV-positive persons of more than one million who are eligible will receive ARVs. Inequality, unequal access, poor development, and sheer desperation, all resulting from AIDS, fuel irrational choices to fight for people's rights.

With global debt, conflict, and poor infrastructures, AIDS is one more dilemma for Africa. But it may be the one with most pervasive consequences that will drive communities and families into deeper poverty, with little opportunity to climb out for two or three generations.

These pervasive consequences belong to all of us. We Christians, living in every culture, need to take our global responsibility to be watchmen on the wall to our youth, beacons of light to wayfarer truck drivers and their girlfriends, friends to homosexuals and users of injecting drugs, physicians for broken hearts and marriages, and nurses binding the wounds of Kaposi's sarcoma and herpes.

If we fail to act now, our children will face a world without peace, a human catastrophe unparalleled in history, and a conscience that cannot cope with the scale of suffering from children growing up without parents or parental guidance.

Minimizing Impact

How can we minimize these consequences? We first must recognize that just as the failure is collective, so are the answers. Until we all admit our failure to act, our failure to be the family God designed us to be, we cannot work together to address these consequences.

Second, we must recognize that today no one has to get AIDS. Prevention works. We know following God's design for sex in marriage not only works to prevent AIDS, but also to secure families in healthy and lasting relationships. We must model more, speak more, listen more, nurture our marriages more, and prepare our youth more. Our homes should be laboratories where youth test their questions about growing up, and confirm their commitment to save the gift of sex until God gives them a lifelong mate. Our homes should be havens of trust and sexual purity.

Preparing for consequences also means preparing families for loss. Who will care for the children? How can we guard family cohesion and keep children together with extended family? How can dying parents prepare their children for their death?

Death from AIDS is usually slow. Children are often primary caregivers of dying parents. How can they be prepared for the emotional and physical trauma of caring for a dying parent? How can children cope with caring for children after both parents die?

Safety Nets

Here are some suggestions for developing safety nets to catch these consequences and minimize them.

1. *We must promote truth—all of it.* AIDS has no cure. We groan in the weak shells of our physical bodies and yearn for the day there is a cure.

Yet, we live in Christ even as we die in our bodies. Death is not a mystery to God; to his children, it is a fulfillment. We must not demand answers from God, as if he conforms to our plans. We can expect him to fulfill his own plans for our lives. Christ promises his power in his presence, not power in conformity to our demands for healing.

The condom is not the best answer for AIDS. But the condom can help. This issue remains a very divisive one for many Christians. We sometimes spend more time discussing how bad this piece of latex is than how to prevent the need for it and how to care for those left behind because it was not used. Abstinence and continued faithfulness between marriage partners is the best solution and needs constant promotion and support.

It is also true that many people choose to live a life of heavy risk and participate in sex apart from marriage. Using a condom may save this person's life and children from being orphaned. Individuals who do not obey God's law need their lives to change, their thinking and will to obey. We must think of preserving life and bringing people to new life before we expect obedience.

2. *Youth need youth-friendly services in the church and hope for the future.* Youth need role models and someone to listen, not just preach to them. Youth need instruction before they reach puberty and face peer challenges. Churches have vital roles to play in openness about God's gift of sex and man's role in protecting it.

3. *All churches must be a safety net for the sick and orphaned, both young and old.* The safety net needs to be strong and tethered to secure footings, and it needs to hold those who are caught in the consequences. World Relief and others support a movement for church-based orphan support known as "Every Church, Every Orphan."

God commands every church to help orphans, regardless of the breadth of resources. God endows each church member with gifts to be used in the body of Christ. To fulfill this call, church members can discover how to help elderly persons left alone or young children now in the care of elderly grandparents.

4. *Churches must prepare for the crisis.* We need leadership that looks ahead and prepares policies to ensure that people are not stigmatized but loved, youth are not stepped over but involved, and pastors are not ignorant about AIDS but active in counseling, preaching, and pastoral care.

No matter what the tradition, spiritually or culturally, we need to follow the biblical example of addressing all aspects of life, including sexuality, in open and contextual ways. Our children's lives depend on how we address the AIDS crisis publicly.

We may need to create denominational policies that enable pastors and wives to stay together in pastorates or education institutions rather than face long separations. We can develop curricula to teach church leaders in formal and informal Bible classes. We need biblically based sex education that begins at age 8 and celebrates preserving God's gift of sex until marriage. We can support youth clubs that actively encourage one another in making wise choices and that become involved in outreach ministries to care for families with AIDS.

We can enhance our marriages through better premarital preparation and better nurture after marriage. We can use our church facilities for multipurpose functions to train caregivers for AIDS or support after school tutoring for orphans. We need diaconal outreach through financial contributions, food and clothing, and securing homes for children so that they are not placed in impersonal institutions.

Growing Grace

We cannot absorb more gloom as a global church. We must absorb more of God's grace growing in us.

The tragedy of AIDS should increase our resolve to strengthen what is good and change what is wrong in our relationships. Those relationships involve the most intimate nature of our being in sexual union, and it involves the most social way—how we relate to each other in community. There are many ways God is using this crisis to challenge his people and provide his guidance and grace. We need to see God in this crisis in a fresh and transforming way. Here are some suggestions.

1. God's call in my life

Relationships have to begin with the individual. Before we can impact others' behavior or attitude, we must examine our own.

AIDS is in the church, and we can no longer speak as if we were immune to the devastation. We are threatened as a global Christian community. While many pew-warmers are not bedroom defilers, none of us can claim purity in our thought life, hearts, or actions.

Few of us have the attitude of Jesus with the woman caught in adultery. Some of us seek shelter from shame for our expressions of sexual freedoms. Others prepare to throw stones but are halted by Jesus' words challenging our self-righteous thoughts and behaviors. At the cross we all stand before Jesus as sin-positive, needing a Savior. We have nothing to give apart from him, and we have everything to gain through him.

This crisis opens wide the bedroom door of our hearts. This crisis clearly forces self-examination of Christ's words, "He who is without sin, cast the first stone." How different, then, is our response when we throw out our righteousness and throw on Christ's humility and acceptance of people where they are. In the context of this epidemic, we all are called to serious reflection, conviction, confession, reconciliation, and action.

The consequences of these reflections and confessions before God will astound our world. No more will a pastor in the urban slums of Nairobi shout from his loudspeaker that those struggling with AIDS are fourth-generation witches. No longer will a church in China fear posting a red banner proclaiming that people with AIDS are welcome. No longer will there be 10-year-old children in Rwanda who do not understand God's gift of sexuality and the importance of protecting it. No longer will our church elders live double lives with girlfriends in the cities and wives in the country.

2. God's call in my church

What is the consequence of the local church heeding God's call?

For Mars Hill Community Church in Michigan, it meant stepping out of a comfortable Midwest existence and walking side-by-side on a street march with community members bearing no resemblance except a common concern for AIDS. As reports of AIDS in Africa swept away the church community, church members realized they could find and love people dying of AIDS at their back door.

Rwanda, just a few short years after the genocide and war left the country bleeding and grieving, faces today a more sustained and deadly struggle with HIV/AIDS. Many children are orphaned twice, once from the war and now from AIDS. Churches gathered in 1997 and again in 1998 determined not to let another crisis engulf them. They spoke boldly and committed to changing "belief to action and apathy to care."[6]

They didn't stop with words. Through training in workshops and guidance in integrating HIV/AIDS programs into their churches with World Relief Rwanda's HIV/AIDS program, *Mobilizing for Life*, churches slowly opened their doors. Pastors led the way to the community around them and welcomed people with AIDS inside. Now more than 250 support groups for persons living with AIDS meet inside churches throughout Rwanda. Suspicion and fear are replaced with counseling and love.

This prompted Pastor Ngedahayo in Kigali to report, "AIDS was not understood in the same way by everyone in the church, but they are changing. AIDS is not the equivalent of adultery. Our church members know how to welcome a person with AIDS into the church as a human being. We have created an Association of People Living with AIDS. They meet once a week, and we give them spiritual help, and once a month we can give them food. This reduces their complexes. We see them change in front of our eyes. Our spiritual counselors are there for them."[7]

In Malawi, young people not only learn about God's way for building friendships, they develop dramas about AIDS to present in open markets and then visit families with AIDS to carry firewood or build latrines. These youth are making wise choices to protect their virginity, to prepare themselves for the blessing and responsibility of lifelong commitment in marriage, and to minister to people hurting in their communities. Caring for people dying from AIDS is not only a ministry; it is a powerful motivator to avoid AIDS. One pervasive consequence of the AIDS crisis is a generation of youth prepared to say no to premarital sex.

Chrub was dying of AIDS when I saw her shriveled on her wooden platform bed in the space under her traditional stilt house in Phnom Penh, Cambodia. She had slept in many beds before, perfuming them with enticement for men on brothel row. Her long, black hair was matted now and her gaunt eyes and prominent cheeks only hinted of beauty lost long ago.

"I just want to die alone," she said as church members greeted her, brought her a cool drink, and stroked her forehead.

"No, no," her Christian friends said. "We are here to be with you. Jesus is here with you. You will not die alone."

Church members from True Way of Life Church, a small but growing church in the neighborhood, found Chrub. Her mother and friends had abandoned her, and she was living with her grandmother. They visited often and shared what they had, including the peace Jesus gives for forgiveness of sin and eternal fellowship with God. Chrub became a member of God's family.

Just as we reached church for the Sunday afternoon service, we learned that Chrub had left us for her eternal home. Church members leaped to action and nailed together her coffin, bought a flower wreath, prepared a Christian memorial service for that very afternoon, and prepared for her cremation that night. As the body entered the flames of the crematorium, her grandmother confessed Jesus as her Savior for the first time and shouted, "I'll see you in heaven!"

AIDS is creating the opportunity for the small minority of Christians in Asian countries to introduce Jesus to neighbors and relatives. Some churches are burgeoning with response. Most new members are energetic soul-winners, but not on streets. They are found in cluster Bible studies and prayer groups as they lay on mats and are carried into church services. While the virus has not left from their bodies, the fear of death has.

Few would choose this wretched epidemic as the catalyst for an evangelistic revival. But God has never stopped at anything—not death nor life, angels nor rulers, things of today nor things of tomorrow, powers of viruses, nor the height and depth of despair, nor anything else in all of creation—to keep us from his redemptive love.

3. God's call in Africa to Asia

Spinning out of tragedy may come one of the greatest missionary movements of the new century. Africa has what the world needs: many

Christians, and experience in a Christian response to one of history's deadliest epidemics. How will God use this kingdom resource?

We can only imagine. Perhaps our lifetime will give glimpses of bold African Christians vaulting barriers of race and language to take the gospel to a continent nearly devoid of church—Asia. The HIV/AIDS epidemic fans across heavily populated communities in Asia at a disturbing pace, insidiously wrecking bodies over years of healthy living and active sharing of blood, sexual fluids, and breast milk.

China braces for what UNAIDS calls a "titanic peril" should the AIDS epidemic grab a foothold as it has in Africa, India, and Cambodia. With her 1.3 billion people and rapid escalation of modernity—replete with divorcing of cultural norms and exploitation of sexual freedoms— China will rival the devastation of family and community, culture, and development of Africa.

"God sent you here," exclaimed a woman from a church in Hunan Province, China, as she showed me her notebook scribbled with characters. "Look at all I have learned. I came back to bring my daughter to hear about AIDS, too."

Following a teaching in another church, a late middle-aged woman stayed behind to ask, "My husband is unfaithful and brings me sexually transmitted disease. Do you think I should divorce him?"

"For how long has he been unfaithful?" we ask, trying to assess her risk.

"Twenty years."

Can Africa do something? Does Asia also have to die? What can we give that billions of dollars and the scrutiny of 20,000 scientists meeting every two years at the International AIDS Conference have not yet given?

Pressing Ahead

As a global family, we press ahead to face the pervasive consequences of the global AIDS crisis—more fractured families, more orphans, more hunger, and more unemployment. To meet these challenges, we must strengthen people not programs, direct people into movements not projects, and share ideas and resources, not possess them.

As the gloom grows, so does grace, the kind of grace God asked Hosea to dramatically give and prophesy about—for days such as ours.

"Then the Lord said to me, 'Go, show your love to your wife again, though she is loved by another and is an adulteress. Love her as the Lord loves'" (Hosea 3:1).

Notes

1. United Nations, "UNAIDS Fact Sheet: AIDS as a Security Issue (Geneva: UNAIDS, January 7, 2002).

2. United Nations, "UNAIDS Fact Sheet: HIV/AIDS and Food Security" (Geneva: UNAIDS, September, 2003).

3. Lori Bollinger and John Stover, The Economic Impact of AIDS (The Futures Group Int., 1999).

4. See note 2.

5. United Nations, "UNAIDS Fact Sheet: HIV/AIDS and Conflict" (Geneva: UNAIDS, January 8, 2003).

6. Church Legal Representatives Declaration, Kigali, Rwanda, November 1, 1998.

7. Jean Kagubare, Lilian Wambua, Gwendolyn Lusi, *Mobilizing for Life HIV/AIDS Project Final Evaluation*, Kigali, Rwanda, August–September, 2003, p. 9.

PART TWO

CRISIS INTERVENTIONS

HOW FAITH-BASED ORGANIZATIONS HAVE CONTRIBUTED TO AIDS PREVENTION

During the early years of the HIV/AIDS pandemic, many people who worked in HIV/AIDS prevention thought of religious leaders and organizations as naturally antagonistic to what they were trying to accomplish. In many minds, the stereotypical religious leader was a conservative moralist who disapproved of any form of sexual behavior outside of marriage, to say nothing of non-standard sexual practices. They were also thought or known to disapprove of what was seen as the "only solution" to HIV infection, i.e., condoms. Some religious leaders "have also added to the misery of people living with HIV by condemning them as 'wrong-doers' or 'sinners,' thus contributing to the stigma to which they were already subjected from other sections of society."[1] Organized religion was also seen as an impediment to sex education in schools. A UNAIDS report put it this way:

> Perhaps the greatest obstacle to AIDS prevention activities in many countries has been opposition, or even just the fear of opposition, from religious authorities. The tendency for religious leaders to prescribe abstinence and mutual monogamy in the face of overwhelming evidence that these behaviours are not always the norm has been seen in almost every corner of the world. The fear of offending powerful religious constituencies has created gridlock in some national governments, and for good reason. Conservative lobbies have shown that they can obstruct everything from family life education to condom promotion if they choose.[2]

These dated and stereotypic generalizations miss the point that many faith-based organizations (FBOs) have been working patiently, compassionately, and effectively, for a number of years in AIDS mitigation, specifically in: (1) care, support, and counseling of people living with HIV/AIDS, including care of AIDS orphans and income-generation projects for such people and their dependants; and (2) HIV/AIDS prevention.

There have been workshops and seminars for leaders of a variety of Christian, Muslim, Hindu, Buddhist, and other FBOs. These efforts often have resulted in programs aimed at both followers of the religion and others in local communities. Further, these efforts generally demonstrate the ability of FBOs to bring AIDS support and education to communities not being reached by government campaigns, often using creative educational approaches. Part of the challenge now is for health workers to overcome their own biases against working with FBOs.

> Activists in HIV/AIDS prevention need to purge themselves of their own prejudices and negative attitude towards religious institutions and engage them as partners in breaking the silence.[3]

Recent evaluations have shown that FBOs can have considerable impact in prevention and care. This should not be surprising. An introductory note from an FBO that works internationally describes accurately the potential role of religious organizations:

> RBIs [religious-based initiatives] are pivotal to the success of prevention and care efforts in Latin America as well as globally. Churches are found in nearly all communities in the region and wield a significant level of cultural, political, social, educational and economic influence. The Church can be viewed as the largest, most stable and most extensively dispersed nongovernmental organization in any country. Churches are respected within communities, and most have existing resources, structures and systems upon which to build. They possess the human, physical, technical and financial resources needed to support and implement small and large-scale initiatives. They can undertake these actions in a very cost-effective manner, due to their ability to leverage volunteer and other resources with minimal effort.

Unfortunately, the resources, capabilities and potential of the Church are considerably neglected or untapped, and it has not been considered part of the solution and/or a driving force in the fight against HIV/AIDS.[4]

Indeed, faith-based organizations are often the *only* genuine nongovernmental organizations in many rural parts of poor countries, or at least the strongest and most influential. FBOs are able to mobilize people and resources and are able to reach rural or isolated areas because of their vast organizational networks. They have strong, expansive infrastructures and a good understanding of local social and cultural patterns. Many FBOs have long worked in health care as well as related areas such as education.

There are more than 1,000 faith-based hospitals in sub-Saharan Africa alone. The number of religious schools may be uncountable. In all parts of the world, FBOs have the power to mobilize large numbers of volunteers to contribute to worthy causes. In addition, those who work with or volunteer their efforts through an FBO tend to be motivated by faith, idealism, and compassion rather than merely by salary or career prospects. These can be powerful and sustaining motivators when working under extremely difficult conditions with the sick and dying.

Faith-based organizations can be very influential in timely policy debates concerning the legal, ethical, and moral issues surrounding AIDS and human rights.[5] They can be influential in the debate over introduction of sex education, reproductive health, AIDS, and sexually transmitted diseases (STDs) in schools—and at what level this can occur. In fact, religious leaders and FBOs can be more than merely influential, since they provide a substantial proportion of primary and secondary education in many less-developed countries.

This chapter will focus on FBO contribution to AIDS prevention, since this has been the most controversial area of FBO involvement in AIDS. I will present evidence to show that when governments asked FBOs to become involved in AIDS prevention in resource-poor countries, they had considerable impact. Moreover, what they promoted as the best way to avoid HIV infection, namely marital faithfulness and abstinence, has turned out to be just what is needed to bring down HIV infection rates at the population or national level.[6]

The Need for Paradigm Change

Mounting evidence shows that the global model of AIDS prevention, designed by Western experts, has been largely ineffective in Africa. The model is based on risk-reduction or "remedies" interventions (condoms, or treating sexually transmissible infections with drugs), rather than on risk avoidance (mutual monogamy, abstinence, or delaying the age of first sexual activity). This dichotomy is imperfect because reduction in number of sexual partners would have to be classified as risk reduction, not avoidance. The remedies-based global model does not promote partner reduction, nor even address multi-partner sex.

John Richens proposed the term *primary behavior change* to denote fundamental changes in sexual behavior, including partner reduction, that do not rely on devices or drugs. He, I, and a very few others have suggested treating AIDS as a behavioral issue that calls for behavioral solutions, although not to the exclusion of risk reduction remedies. The dominant paradigm treats AIDS as a medical problem requiring medical solutions. Yet AIDS is largely a behavioral problem requiring a behavioral solution. Primary behavior change deals with the problem itself, getting at what is needed for primary prevention, while the medical model deals with symptoms.

If we consider the simple ABC approach to AIDS prevention, to which lip service has long been paid (Abstain, Be faithful, use Condoms if A and B fail), it is clear that most prevention resources have gone to condom promotion, and more recently, to the treatment of the curable sexually transmitted infections. Few in public health circles really believed—or even believe nowadays—that programs promoting abstinence, fidelity or monogamy, or even reduction in number of sexual partners would pay off in significant behavioral change. My own view changed when I evaluated HIV prevention programs in Uganda and Jamaica and conducted a national survey of behavioral change in the Dominican Republic.

Here I present findings from several countries that seem to best illustrate the positive impact of faith-based organizations. We will see a pattern of behavioral changes compatible with the prevention strategies favored by FBOs, as well as data showing stabilization and reduction in national HIV infection rates. In each of these countries, the governments asked FBOs to become involved in AIDS prevention from the beginning of their national responses to AIDS.[7]

Uganda

Uganda has had the most dramatic decline in HIV infection rates. HIV prevalence declined from 21.1 percent to 6.1 percent among pregnant women between 1991 and 2000. In 1987, the major religious organizations in Uganda (Catholic, Anglican, Muslim) became significantly involved in AIDS prevention, with modest funding from the World Health Organization, through the Ministry of Health.[8]

By 1992, the United States Agency for International Development decided to allocate funds for FBOs to work in prevention, but on each FBO's own terms. The FBOs stated clearly that they wished to promote fidelity and abstinence rather than condoms. At the time, many working in HIV/AIDS prevention thought that fidelity and abstinence promotion would have few if any measurable results. However, Uganda's President Museveni strongly favored this approach. Museveni is credited with being the most activist African head of state in addressing the AIDS crisis. Museveni stated his views in a speech to the First AIDS Congress in East and Central Africa:[9]

> Sex is not a manifestation of a biological drive; it is socially directed . . . I have been emphasizing a return to our time-tested cultural practices that emphasized fidelity and condemned premarital and extramarital sex. I believe that the best response to the threat of AIDS and other STDs is to reaffirm publicly and forthrightly the respect and responsibility every person owes to his or her neighbor.

As for condoms, Museveni said in the same speech:

> Just as we were offered the "magic bullet" in the early 1940s, we are now being offered the condom for "safe sex.". . . I feel that condoms have a role to play as a means of protection, especially in

couples who are HIV-positive, but they cannot become the main means of stemming the tide of AIDS.[10]

After 1991, we have seen a downward trend in HIV infection rates in Uganda; in fact, the rate of new infection (incidence) actually peaked in about 1989. There are also studies showing a significant decrease in casual sex. Looking at all age groups, 41 percent of males had more than one sex partner in 1989, and this figure was probably higher earlier in the 1980s.[11] This figure declined to 21 percent by 1995. For females, the decline was from 23 percent to 9 percent. Furthermore, the proportion of males reporting three or more sex partners fell from 15 percent to 3 percent between 1989 and 1995.[12]

Decline in infection rates was greatest among the 15–19 age group, the very group that was targeted with the abstinence or *delay* message. This is also the group where behavior changed the most, and the earliest. The proportion of young males age 15–24 reporting premarital sex decreased from 60 percent in 1989 to 23 percent in 1995. For females, the decline was from 53 percent to 16 percent. Decrease in sexual activity among females is particularly important because of the increased biological, social, and economic vulnerability of young females.

Some reports continue to claim that the world's great success story in AIDS prevention, Uganda, owes its achievement to condoms, but this is not true.[13] Only about 6 percent of Ugandans reported using a condom during last sex with any type of partner, according to the U.S.-funded Demographic and Health Survey. However, condom use has become quite high among those who need condoms most, namely those relatively few still having multiple partners. The ABC approach recognizes that some people cannot or will not avoid risky sex, and so they need to reduce their risk with condoms.

If sizable numbers of men and women reduce their number of sexual partners, can this have significant impact on HIV infection rates? Recent studies that have modeled the impact of different behavior changes, including condom use, suggest that reduction in number of partners can have great impact on averting HIV infections—in fact, greater than either condom use or treatment of sexually transmitted diseases.[14]

How has involvement of faith-based organizations impacted behavior in Uganda? To cite one example, the Anglican Church of Uganda implemented the CHUSA project, an AIDS prevention program aimed at youth, in Sunday schools and primary schools. The project trained 96 diocesan trainers and 5,702 community health educators and had sensitized 736,218 members of the community by 1995. CHUSA clients reporting two or more sexual partners declined from *86 percent to 29 percent* between 1989 and 1995.[15]

As noted, FBOs were involved in AIDS prevention from the very start. There has always been a bishop on the national AIDS commission. And over time, the number of religious leaders and groups involved in AIDS prevention has expanded. In 1998, I reviewed the evidence for HIV decline and behavioral change evidence in Uganda for the World Bank. Reviewing district work plans between 1995–98, and interviewing key people, I estimated that an average of 150 religious leaders (ministers, deacons, imams, and so on) were being trained in each of Uganda's 45 districts *per year*, resulting in some 6,750 religious leaders trained in HIV/AIDS annually. Even if there may have been over-reporting of training, if we reduce figures by a third, there would still be 4,500 trained per year since 1995. "Training" here refers to religious leaders being educated about AIDS and what they can do to help prevent it, usually in brief workshops. Those trained then become peer educators and group leaders, talking to others in their religious groups or broader communities.

Taken altogether, the foregoing suggests that religious organizations and other more conservative opinion leaders in Uganda (e.g., school authorities, traditional healers, and local political leaders such as chiefs) that have advocated abstinence and fidelity have had a significant impact on the overall decline in infection rates.

Senegal

Senegal was one of the first countries in Africa to acknowledge HIV/AIDS and to begin implementing significant HIV/AIDS prevention and control programs. Like Uganda, according to the U.S. Bureau of the Census (BUCEN), "Senegal has been a success story, as the government has managed to keep the epidemic from getting out of control."[16] According to UNAIDS, Senegal currently has one of the lowest HIV seroprevalence rates in sub-Saharan Africa, and it appears to be stable at 1 percent or less of the general population.[17]

Sittirai attributes Senegal's ability to keep the infection rate low first to the relatively late age of sexual debut, and then by reductions in numbers of partners.[18] In 2001, a Ministry of Health study in Dakar of never-married females conducted by Family Health International, with funding from USAID and the U.S. Centers for Disease Control and Prevention, found that only 4.1 percent of those in a random sample were having sex.[19] Of that 4.1 percent, more than half reported having just one partner.[20] According to Senegal demographic and health surveys, the average age of sexual debut among young Senegalese women (aged 15 to 24) rose from 17.5 in 1992/93 to 18.8 in 1997.[21] This suggests that people have been responding to the *delay* message.

Sittirai also credits increased condom use and "apparently quite effective" sexually transmitted infection control. A UNAIDS study found significant declines in sexually transmitted disease among women between 1991 and 1996. Chlamydia fell from 11.7 percent to 6.1 percent; gonorrhea from 2.9 percent to 0.9 percent; and syphilis from 7.5 percent to 4.4 percent.[22]

Politicians in Senegal were quick to move against the epidemic, once HIV/AIDS cases appeared in the latter 1980s. President Abdou Diouf acknowledged the presence of AIDS and began to implement a vigorous national AIDS prevention and control program in 1987. Unlike Uganda, Senegal had only a few cases of HIV at this time.[23] Religious leaders were slower.

> During the first stages of the AIDS epidemic the majority of religious (leaders) condemned those infected with the virus, calling the illness a divine curse. This attitude made AIDS shameful and a positive diagnosis difficult. Religion systematically condemned certain modes of prevention as well as certain individual and group behavior.[24]

This perspective changed quickly, however, within this nation with a 93 percent Muslim population. In dialogue with the government, Muslim

FBOs became involved in HIV/AIDS prevention early in the epidemic. A conservative Muslim organization, Jamra, approached the national AIDS program in 1989 to discuss prevention strategies.[25] Following initial disagreement over whether FBOs should promote condoms, the Senegalese government conducted a survey of Muslim and Christian leaders to better define a role for them in HIV/AIDS mitigation. The survey found that religious leaders needed and wanted more information about HIV/AIDS, so that they in turn could educate their respective religious communities. In response,

> educational materials were designed to meet the needs of religious leaders. They focused in part on testimonials from people living with AIDS—the human face of the epidemic, often hidden where prevalence remains low. Training sessions about HIV were organized for Imams and teachers of Arabic, and brochures were produced to help them disseminate information. AIDS became a regular topic in Friday sermons in mosques throughout Senegal, and senior religious figures addressed the issue on television and radio.[26]

A Catholic organization, SIDA (AIDS) Service, became involved in prevention as well as in counseling and psychosocial support. In 1996, every bishop in Senegal attended a meeting on AIDS prevention. Participants agreed that AIDS prevention was an important national priority.[27] The following year, Senegal hosted the First International Colloquium on AIDS and Religion in Dakar. Approximately 250 persons from 33 countries attended, including Muslim, Christian, and Buddhist religious leaders and health ministers from five African countries.[28] The effect on Senegalese religious leaders of all faiths seems to have been to empower them "to act freely in the promotion of prevention strategies."[29]

A 2001 *Los Angeles Times* article described the role of FBOs and religious leaders in Senegal:

> Conservative Islamic leaders are supporting AIDS prevention activities. Imams have started making AIDS a regular topic in Friday sermons throughout Senegal, where more than 90 percent of the population is Muslim. While the religious leaders insist that they encourage abstinence over the use of condoms, they

acknowledge the importance of dispelling myths about the disease, such as the common theory that AIDS is a curse or a punishment by God.[30]

In addition to the contribution of FBOs, many other levels of Senegalese society joined in the discussion, and by 1995, 200 nongovernmental organizations were responding, as were women's groups with about half a million members. The government included teaching about HIV prevention when introducing sex education in schools. Parallel efforts reached out to young people who were not in school.[31]

Some may argue that sexual behavior in Senegal is conservative, and that pre-existing norms and values rather than interventions have kept infection rates low. This interpretation, however, does not explain why HIV infection rates have risen in countries neighboring Senegal, countries with similar marital and sexual practices, as well as similar religious profiles. Further, skeptics cannot argue that behavioral change, followed by seroprevalence stability or decline, developed from seeing so much death everywhere, since national HIV prevalence never exceeded about 1 percent. In fact, the evidence suggests that Senegalese, despite their very low HIV infection rates, have come to feel personally at risk of HIV infection, due probably to effective AIDS education. The highest proportion, 39 percent, of African women who perceive their risk of getting AIDS as "great" is in Senegal.[32]

Senegal and Uganda stand out in Africa as countries where the governments supported HIV/AIDS prevention efforts boldly and strongly at a relatively early stage. This support has made a major difference and has allowed prevention programs to have maximum effect. Perhaps one of the factors inhibiting such a government response elsewhere in Africa and in other parts of the world is fear of a negative reaction from religious authorities. This argues for involving religious leaders and FBOs as early as possible.

Other Examples

We also have evidence of HIV prevalence decline among young people as well as patterns of decline in premarital and multipartner sexual activity among youth in Zambia.[33] Pending the results of current research, anecdotal evidence suggests that Christian FBOs, which are very influential, have been involved in AIDS prevention.

In the Caribbean, FBOs have been very involved in two countries where HIV prevalence has stabilized or actually declined. Studies have shown that there has been less casual sex as well as increased condom use in Jamaica and the Dominican Republic.[34]

Conclusion

Of course, it is very difficult to attribute behavioral change in Uganda, Senegal, or elsewhere to any one strategy, or any combination of specific interventions, whether from FBOs or other organizations. It is very hard to control confounding variables. In any case, few studies have looked specifically at the impact of FBOs. Indeed, very few countries have even supported major, national-level, faith-based initiatives in AIDS prevention. It is not surprising that national and international HIV/AIDS donor organizations have not recognized the contribution of faith-based organizations, at least outside the countries discussed in this chapter. Yet there is now enough suggestive evidence to encourage FBOs to play greater roles in HIV/AIDS prevention, and for donor organizations such as USAID, the World Bank, and UNAIDS to support more faith-based initiatives.

Here are the key points to remember from this chapter:

- FBOs are in the best position of any group to promote fidelity and abstinence; this is their *comparative advantage* over other organizations. The behavioral changes they encourage are partner reduction and delay of first sexual experience, to use the language of public health.

- These behavioral changes tend to be widely overlooked. Yet we have highly suggestive evidence from a handful of countries that have experienced national-level success in reducing HIV infection rates that these changes do occur when promoted, and that—according to recent epidemiological modeling studies—such behavioral changes can have major impact on HIV prevalence rates. Preliminary yet published findings from the USAID-funded ABC study show clearly that national HIV prevalence does not decline without primary behavior change; it does not occur by condom use alone.

- Religious organizations ought to receive more support in doing what they do best—promoting fidelity and abstinence. If FBOs also want to promote condom use, fine. But they should not be forced to do so. There is now a new congressional amendment to the President's HIV/AIDS Initiative that codifies the principle that FBOs should not be forced to prevent AIDS in ways that are incompatible with their religious beliefs and values. And as of this writing, most United States AIDS prevention funds for international programs continue to go to condom social marketing and similar programs. Yet there are (still) very few programs directed at partner reduction and delay of sexual debut among youth. Some FBOs, such as World Vision, have adopted the prevention called ABc ("Big A and B, little c.")

- Very little international funding has gone to FBOs for AIDS prevention programs. There have been few evaluations of FBO AIDS prevention programs (probably because most such programs rely on the FBOs' own funds); and existing results have often remained unpublished. FBOs remain largely untapped in the global fight against AIDS. There is a chance through the president's HIV/AIDS Initiative to redress this.

Many of us in public health become very wary at the sound of language such as *abstinence* and *fidelity* (Uganda actually used "chastity" in earlier years). It sounds judgmental, moralistic. But it's hard to argue with success, "Abstain and Be Faithful" is the primary approach that Uganda took in its early period of national response to AIDS, whether we agree with this approach or not.

And, interestingly, there is probably less stigma associated with AIDS in Uganda than in virtually any other African country. In fact, there is less stigma and more empowerment of women. The latter has actually been partly measured in the context of AIDS. The Uganda DHS 2000 asked women and men whether women "have the ability to negotiate safer sex." The numerator was defined as "The number of respondents who believe that, if her husband has an STI [sexually transmitted infection], the woman could refuse to have sex with him or propose condom use." The denominator is total number of respondents. Uganda has the continent's highest percentage of women able to negotiate safer sex, by this definition: 91 percent. This compares with 73 percent in Malawi, 87 percent in Rwanda, 55 percent in Tanzania, and 71 percent in Zimbabwe.[35]

Since far more U.S. funds have become available for combating global AIDS, adding emphasis to A and B interventions and involving FBOs (along with schools and other institutions) should not threaten existing programs. A, B, and C programs are all needed. If more funds are available, and if promotion of A and B interventions pays off in abstinence, delay of sexual debut, and partner reduction, then we are talking about adding an important and inexplicably overlooked intervention, not subtracting anything.

At the recent Global AIDS conference in Barcelona, talk was about drugs and especially about how to get antiretroviral drugs to the poor. Of course this is a desirable goal. But there was relatively little discussion about AIDS prevention. It seemed as if the donor community and AIDS experts had given up on prevention. After all, uncountable millions of dollars have gone into condom marketing programs as well as the treatment of standard sexually transmitted diseases, with few apparent results *in Africa*. I suggest that the experts were not looking at other types of behavior that *have* been changing and that now seem to account for at least a significant part of the success that some countries in Africa have had. We should not give up on prevention before it has really been done in the right way.

Acknowledgment: Some of the research for this chapter was supported by the U.S. Agency for International Development through the Synergy Project. Another version of this chapter appears by the same author as: Faith-Based Organizations: Contributions to HIV Prevention. Washington, D.C.: USAID/Washington and the Synergy Project, TvT Associates, Washington, D.C., September 2003.

Notes

1. N. Kaleeba, J. Namulondo, D. Kalinki, and G. Williams, Open Secret: People Facing Up to HIV and AIDS in Uganda (London: ActionAIDS, 2000), p. 58. "Strategies for Hope" series, No. 15.

2. E. Pisani, Acting Early to Prevent AIDS: The Case of Senegal (Geneva: Joint United Nations Programme for HIV/AIDS, 1999), p. 12. UNAIDS/99.34E, Best Practice Collection.

3. N. Iwere, J. C. Ojidoh, and N. Okide, "Engaging Religious Communities in Breaking the Silence on HIV/AIDS" in Abstract MoPeD2729. XIII International AIDS Conference, held in Durban, South Africa, July 9–14, 2000, p. 1.

4. MAP International (November, 1997). Religious-based Initiatives (Arlington, VA: AIDSCAP/Family Health International), p. 1.

5. Z. Lazzarini, Human Rights and HIV/AIDS (Washington, D.C.: USAID/The Synergy Project, 1998). Discussion Papers on HIV/AIDS Care and Support, No. 2.

6. Ruth Bessinger and Priscilla Akwara, "Sexual Behavior, HIV and Fertility Trends: A Comparative Analysis of Six Countries" (June, 2003). Phase I of the ABC Study by ORC/Macro International, Inc., Calverton, Maryland. USAID, "The ABCs of Prevention." Washington, D.C.: USAID, June, 2003. J. Hogle, E. C. Green, V. Nantulya, R. Stoneburner, and J. Stover, "What Happened in Uganda? Declining HIV Prevalence, Behavior Change and the National Response." USAID/Washington and The Synergy Project, TvT Associates, Washington, D.C., September, 2002. R. L. Stoneburner and D. Low-Beer, "Is Condom Use or Decrease in Sexual Partners Behind HIV Declines in Uganda?" Paper presented at the 13th International AIDS Conference, Durban, South Africa, July, 2000.

7. The examples to follow and the present chapter itself are condensed from my book, Rethinking AIDS Prevention: Learning from Successes in Developing Countries (Westport, CT: Praeger, 2003).

8. Kaleeba, et al, Open Secret.

9. Kampala, November 20, 1991.

10. Y. K. Museveni, What Is Africa's Problem? (Minneapolis: University of Minnesota Press, 2000), p. 252.

11. Edward C. Green, Vinand Nantulya, Yaa Oppong, and Teresa Harrison, "Literature Review and Preliminary Analysis of 'ABC' Factors in Six Developing Countries" (July, 2003). Harvard Center for Population and Development Studies in Cambridge, Massachusetts.

12. Bessinger and Akwara, "Sexual Behavior."

13. Green, et al, "Literature Review" and J. Hogle, et al, "What Happened in Uganda?"

14. R. S. Bernstein, D. C. Sokal, S. T. Seitz, B. Auvert, W. Naamara, and J. Stover, "Simulating the Control of a Heterosexual HIV Epidemic in a Severely Affected East African City" in Interfaces, 28 (1998), 101–126. N. J. Robinson, D. W. Mulder, B. Auvert, and R. J. Hayes, "Modelling the Impact of Alternative HIV Intervention Strategies in Rural Uganda," in AIDS, 11 (November 9, 1995), 1263–70. B. Auvert and B. Ferry, "Modeling the Spread of HIV Infections in Four Cities of Sub-Saharan Africa." Paper presented at the "ABC" Experts Technical Meeting, USAID, Washington, D.C. in September, 2002.

15. M. Lyons, Summative Evaluation: AIDS Prevention and Control Project (Kampala: USAID/Uganda, January 20, 1996).

16. BUCEN (U.S. Bureau of the Census), HIV/AIDS Profile: Senegal (Washington, D.C.: U.S. Bureau of the Census, 2000), p. 1.

17. BUCEN, HIV/AIDS Profile: Senegal.

18. W. Sittirai, HIV Prevention, Needs and Success: A Tale of Three Countries Geneva: UNAIDS, 2001), p. 12.

19. Hygea/FHI, Enquete de Surveillance du Comportement ESC 2001 (2001). Senegal Ministry of Health. Republique du Senegal, Ministere de la Sante et de la Prevention, Comite National de Prevention du SIDA CNPS, FHI/USAID Senegal, Eleves Filles-Dakar, p. 31.

20. Ibid, p. 35.

21. Macro International and Government of Senegal, 1994, 1997.

22. Sittirai, HIV Prevention, p. 12.

23. Sittirai, HIV Prevention.

24. E. D. Diouf, S. Paul, and N. Ibra, Religious Action at the International Level in Africa: The Example of International Religious Alliances against HIV in Africa (ARIVA). Abstract MoPeD2741. XIII International AIDS Conference, held in Durban, South Africa, July 9–14, 2000.

25. UNAIDS, Acting Early to Prevent AIDS: The Case of Senegal (Geneva: UNAIDS, 1999), p. 12.

26. Ibid,

27. UNAIDS, Summary Booklet of Best Practices (Geneva: UNAIDS, 1999), p. 13.

28. M. Ladame, GTZ AIDS Network (2)18 (May,1998).

29. Diouf, et al, Religious Action.

30. A. M. Simmons, "In AIDS-ravaged Africa, Senegal is a beacon of hope" in Los Angeles Times (March 9, 2001), p. A1.

31. Sittirai, HIV Prevention.

32. DHS/Measure website.

33. Green, et al, "Literature Review" and Bessinger and Akwara, "Sexual Behavior."

34. E. C. Green and Aldo Conde, "Sexual Partner Reduction and HIV Infection" in Sexually Transmitted Infections (2000), Vol. 76 (2), 145. S. Amara Singham, E. C. Green, and H. Royes, Evaluation of Jamaica's National AIDS Program. Washington, D.C.: USAID/The Synergy Project, 2000.

35. DHS/Measure website.

AIDS AWARENESS AND THE CHALLENGE IN UGANDA

The communities on the outskirts of Kampala, Uganda, are generally rural, and only a few encroach on the suburbs of the city. The primary means of income generation are agriculture and small trade. The area has been recovering from a period of social instability which ended in 1986 with the present government. Though peace and economic development have prevailed in the country as a whole, the rural population has been unable to make equal strides forward due to, among other things, AIDS. The communities have been destabilized because of the destruction of traditional authority structures, including the family, during 20 years of civil unrest. One result has been a massive spread of AIDS.

There has been one regime since 1986 which has been benevolent and under which peace has prevailed. Economic development has occurred under this government. A constitution that includes elections is being discussed, further providing a sense of hope. Many of the rural population have not been able to make many improvements, however, because much of the manpower is dying of AIDS and because many resources are being used on expensive cultural customs such as weddings and funerals. This, in turn, continues to drain money from other key areas, such as education. Many hope to see their children educated in the university and thus place a high priority on money for school fees. But these fees are more difficult to secure in the present environment, and many of these hopes go unfulfilled.

Communities are experiencing greater peace and less fear in their daily lives as they recover from a long period of insecurity. However, the civil unrest has taken its toll. Many of the adults were killed during that time and the result has been a generation ignorant of traditional values and God's law. They have lived "loose" lives and have thus promoted the spread of AIDS. The loss of the adult members of the community has also reduced the number of wage earners and has decreased agricultural output and associated income. The standard of living has greatly decreased during the last 20 years.

Even in the midst of these problems, communities continue to strongly support one another. This mutual support is strengthened by their poverty. Families assist others with weddings, funeral, and educational expenses as a kind of investment toward the same provision in the future when their time of need arises. Life increasingly revolves around death and death rituals. No family is untouched by AIDS—all are involved with someone who is sick and dying from AIDS or someone for whom they have had to arrange a funeral. But even this sense of family and community is under strain. Extended families find their resources further stretched as they take in the increasing numbers of AIDS orphans.

The two main religious forces in these communities are the Protestant and Catholic churches. There is a high church attendance rate in comparison with Western standards. Most of the participants, however, see church as a way to earn God's pleasure rather than as a means of encouraging a personal faith and walk with God. This is also true of many of those who are baptized as infants but who no longer attend services. Interestingly enough, there is a high diversity of understanding among people as to whether or not they are saved.

Christianity does make a difference, however. In many families where there is no commitment to Christ, frequent divorce or multiple spouses unsettle the children. In some cases children have been turned out and made to feel unloved. Many of these youth turn to their peers or to rich benefactors who give them some sense of being wanted, but it is usually at a high cost of exposure to AIDS.

Description of the Project

Our project addresses the lack of care for AIDS patients and their families, and the sexual promiscuity that promotes the spread of AIDS. The project is built on a number of community strengths. (1) The communities desire to do something to express love to the AIDS patients and their families. (But in the past they have not been sure how to do so, and due to the day-to-day necessities for survival they have been unable to set aside time to make plans.) (2) The Anglican Church of Uganda has much influence in the communities. (3) Existing churches have served as forums through which mobilized people could be trained and organized to act on their training.

Technically, our project is considered a health project with a focus on AIDS prevention and improving the care of AIDS patients, as well as addressing the psychological needs of their families. The project began when an expatriate and a Ugandan pastor asked God what he would have them do about the destruction caused by AIDS. They decided to work through Sunday morning church services and other existing church structures such as choirs, youth groups, and Sunday schools. They would discuss the problem of AIDS through music, drama, overhead projections, and exposition of the Bible.

The program's first service was attended unexpectedly by the wife of the president of Uganda, who added her support by expounding on 2 Chronicles 7:14: "If my people, who are called by my name, will humble themselves and pray and seek my face and turn from their wicked ways, then will I hear from heaven and will forgive their sin and will heal their land." This was followed by a play called *Why Me?*, which depicted the impact of AIDS on family life. Many people were moved to dedicate themselves to change during this service.

Food for the Hungry International (FHI) then entered into a partnership with a Church of Uganda diocese. FHI's program was twofold: (1) approach donors with an AIDS prevention proposal called "Youth Challenge" for the Church of Uganda parish youth groups, and (2) start a ministry to AIDS patients and their families in the parishes. Pastors were organized to produce a discussion manual that focused on the dangers of AIDS and what youth needed to do to avoid these dangers. The slogan, "Leap to a Healthier Lifestyle," was printed on T-shirts. Any young person committing to this new lifestyle was taught how to lead a discussion group by using questions to stimulate thought. In Sunday morning services in each parish, the AIDS team would give an AIDS awareness presentation.

The first step in the development process is to secure the cooperation of the diocesan bishop in introducing the program to one of the archdeaconries under him. With the bishop's support, FHI project staff then introduce the program to the chosen archdeacon. With the archdeacon's support, an "Introductory Day" is held with pastors and other leaders of churches in the archdeaconry, to secure their cooperation and set up an action plan.

Following this initial interaction, these leaders and others they recommend are trained by FHI staff in the presentation of the "Challenge of AIDS" to their own parishes, assisted by FHI staff. FHI staff then work with each parish to prepare music and drama to support the AIDS awareness information and the biblical message presented in the Sunday morning "AIDS Challenge Service." In the service, the youth are asked to get involved in the church youth group and begin using the discussion manual developed by the pastors.

At another service, called the "Good Samaritan Service," members receive a challenge to get involved in serving AIDS patients and their families who are socially ostracized. After this an "Implementation Training Day" is held in a specific parish to train leaders and others interested in how to effectively lead the youth group discussions, and how to stimulate care for the sick among church members. The parishes then carry on these programs with occasional follow-up visits by FHI staff.

Critical assumptions in the project are as follows:

1. A changed lifestyle is fundamental to defeat AIDS.
2. Commitment to Jesus as Lord changes lifestyles, which defeats AIDS and allows people to go beyond meeting basic needs to fulfill their God-given potential.
3. God answers prayer.
4. God has called us to be involved in the work under his will.
5. People attend church for cultural rather than religious reasons.
6. Culturally adapted communications will result in a greater knowledge of God's Word and a better understanding of how to deal with AIDS. Music and drama are effective ways to communicate in this culture.

7. AIDS can be conquered as people respond to God's call to repentance.

8. Existing church institutions and structures are a good foundation on which to build the program, and will lead to a greater possibility of sustainable impact.

The key principles we follow:

1. Conform all teaching and training to the Word of God and never compromise.

2. Pray "without ceasing" for the program and beneficiaries, listening to that "still, small voice," and be convinced that God answers prayer.

3. Implementers should be fully committed to the Lord and the program.

4. Identify the key innovators in a community or church who live a Christ-centered life, and mobilize them to commit to the program.

5. Respond to the church's or community's own identified needs—not to the implementer's ideas.

6. Conduct ongoing review with objectives in mind, and seek to avoid dependency.

The local church was involved in the program from its inception. The program began with a pastor and an FHI staff person who shared a burden to do something about the AIDS epidemic. The program has continued to seek the church leadership's cooperation. A primary goal is to use and build on existing church structures and institutions, primarily through training. The church is the primary implementer (e.g., the music and drama are presented by church members and not by FHI staff), with FHI serving primarily as facilitator and trainer.

FHI staff and the church's pastor issue a challenge to the congregation at the presentation during the Sunday service to come forward and accept Christ as their Savior. The staff and pastor will also help to guide them through the problems AIDS presents. The lives of the youth also act as a witness to their peers as they demonstrate the fruit of the Spirit (primarily self-control) and the joy associated with walking with Christ.

The older members of the congregation show the love of Christ by visiting ostracized members of their community and bringing with them gifts of love, listening to their problems, and praying for them.

Results

One of the most significant results is that AIDS patients experience love and affection, rather than ostracism. In one parish alone, after mobilization the number of patients visited increased from 45 to 170 per month. Family members of AIDS patients, after experiencing a compassionate visit, have become involved in the Good Samaritan committees themselves. Visiting Good Samaritans take small gifts (sugar, tea, salt, soap, and clothing) to patients to make them a little more comfortable.

Good Samaritan committee members were frustrated before FHI's involvement, because they saw a need but did not really know how to help the sick. After learning how to visit, they have eagerly ministered the love of Christ. They share their enthusiasm with others, and the membership of one committee has increased from 10 to 40 members. They report that AIDS patients and their families are much more willing to have them visit, thereby making their work more enjoyable. In one church, monthly cash contributions to the committee's work amounted to about $6. This amount increased to $10, and one income-generating project produced an additional $30. (These amounts do not include donated food and clothing.) Committee members benefit from the mutual support and encouragement of the weekly meetings to identify needs.

The program has brought the following improvements in the lives of the poor:

1. Those who were visited no longer feel ostracized by their community.
2. Committed youth who practice a changed lifestyle are protected from AIDS and other sexually transmitted diseases, as well as from physical abuse. They also have lifestyles that avoid drug addiction.
3. Sick people are getting much-needed items, such as sugar and tea.
4. Churches have developed income-generating projects to help their poor members.

5. Individuals have seen the value of income-generating projects and have embarked on other non-church-related areas such as a farmers' association to help improve the farmers' income.

The following are indicators of spiritual change:

1. During the challenges to accept Christ as Savior given at the AIDS awareness services over the past three years, 891 people have come forward.

2. Visiting Good Samaritans have shared the gospel with patients on their deathbeds. In one parish 30 dying people and seven family members accepted Christ as their Savior.

3. At a "Fun Day" organized to help youth better occupy their spare time, 12 accepted Christ as Savior.

4. At a training program for church leaders, 23 accepted Christ as Savior.

5. Attendance in Sunday morning services has increased (in one case going from 500 to 1,000), as have church membership, the number of children in Sunday school, youth group membership, and attendance at various church groups.

6. The Good Samaritan team has motivated one parish to pray every day at 10 p.m. for the sick, the poor, and others in need.

7. Family members of AIDS patients, after experiencing a compassionate visit, have begun attending church.

8. In one parish two young men in wheelchairs who could not attend church are now being brought to church by caring members.

Evidence of cultural and social change:

1. In Uganda many couples live together without formal marriage. They know a church wedding is a commitment they do not want to make. But this program has resulted in couples deciding to sanctify their marriages in the church and committing to each other.

2. Parents and church leaders exposed to training in this program are now asking for education in topics that were once considered taboo.

3. People dying from AIDS were once ostracized by their communities, but now community members visit them and make them feel the love of Christ in their last hours.

4. Parents are having more of an impact in the education (especially sex education) of their children.

5. Youth are spending less time in discos and other places where they are exposed to situations that promote the spread of AIDS. They are spending more time in healthier activities such as sports, reading, and helping others.

6. More people are taking an active interest in their communities and the needs of their members. For example, one young man has volunteered to teach in school wearing the T-shirt that identifies him as a person committed to a healthier lifestyle.

The Process of People Coming to Know Christ

The method with the most easily visible results is the challenge given during awareness services. Leaders attempt to show the need for Christ in one's life during the service, and then make a call at the service's close. The team and church leaders meet interested people for counseling after the service.

Church music and drama groups are trained to present either a clear need for Christ in one's life or a challenge to the congregation to accept Christ. As mentioned above, church members challenged to visit the sick are trained in visitation, including how to share their faith. A number of people have come to Christ by this method, but we don't know how many.

At special events, such as a "Fun Day," organizers present hearers' need for Christ, and give them a challenge to receive him. During training of parish church leadership, attendees learn the facts and implications of AIDS. They also hear the challenge to accept Christ as one's Savior.

One of the key individuals in the program is the project manager. The project manager coordinates with church leaders and key people to secure cooperation and data. She or he is also responsible to see that the project maintains a biblical focus. Another key individual is the music and drama coordinator, who trains the choir and other church participants for the service and sometimes gives the challenge. Both the youth coordinator and the home care coordinator play key roles in the program by participating in the services and training.

Evaluation

To improve the program, I would do the following:

1. Focus on small work areas and on families.

2. Involve Sunday school and primary school children in the program. The youth are the most vulnerable and are influenced most by what they learn from peers and in school.

3. Keep a low profile in the church and community, and be very sensitive to the impact of external visitors on patients.

4. Maintain prayer without ceasing, and listen to God.

5. Work with the pastors and church leaders who catch the vision; they will in turn influence their churches and communities.

We encountered the following obstacles:

1. The pastors' workloads and social habits increasingly revolve around death and funerals. As deaths increase, they find little time to do anything else. Their focus is on the urgent or immediate need.

2. Rain: many social activities come to a halt during rains and rainy season.

3. Some traditional cultural habits prevent change, although these are decreasing as education expands.

4. The traditional church's hierarchy has been very slow to respond to the challenge of AIDS.

5. Major donor policies focus on condom distribution, which promotes promiscuity and confuses the youth when they hear the message of celibacy.

6. There is an attitude that money solves all problems, and that Uganda deserves outside help to solve its problems.

HOME CARE FOR AIDS PATIENTS IN ZIMBABWE

AIDS in Africa reaches into the physical, social, psychological, and spiritual environments of people. Yet the church's response seemed complacent at first. Many felt AIDS was simply a societal problem that did not affect the church. They thought AIDS was God's plan to punish sinners, so the church needed to stay out of it. However, Jesus told the Pharisees: "It is not the healthy who need a doctor, but the sick. . . . For I have not come to call the righteous, but sinners" (Matthew 9:12–13).

Armed with the good news of Christ, the church can help greatly in a situation without good news from a medical or political standpoint. God has called his church to do what Jesus did:

> The Spirit of the Sovereign Lord is on me, because the Lord has anointed me to preach good news to the poor. He has sent me to bind up the brokenhearted, to proclaim freedom for the captives and release from darkness for the prisoners, to proclaim the year of the Lord's favor and the day of vengeance of our God, to comfort all who mourn, and to provide for those who grieve in Zion—to bestow on them a crown of beauty instead of ashes, the oil of gladness instead of mourning, and a garment of praise instead of a spirit of despair. (Isaiah 61:1–3)

A continent with 9 percent of the world's population, Africa is home to 80 percent of the world's HIV-positive citizens. It is estimated that 70 million Africans will be HIV-positive by 2015. In some African countries, one-third of the population is infected. While the cumulative total of reported AIDS cases in Zimbabwe was 41,298 by the end of March 1995, a million Zimbabweans died of AIDS by the year 2000.

Christians and organizations providing care in Africa face a crisis that affects all of us. AIDS is in the world, and AIDS is in the church. Some of the first people to die from AIDS were Christian leaders in our area.

Case Study Context

Zimbabwe is better off economically than most developing countries. People can own land in communal areas, and most grow enough food not only for their families but to sell in good, rainy years. However, two recent droughts in Zimbabwe (1991–1992 and 1994–1995) have created difficult economic times.

Politically, Zimbabwe has been stable since April 1980, when independence and majority rule were established. The country's first black African ruler, Robert Mugabe, was elected prime minister. Mugabe has been reelected three times and continues to rule a socialist government with some leanings toward capitalism.

However, in recent years some religious leaders have accused the regime of using food as a weapon against political opponents. Mugabe has also orchestrated a sometimes-violent campaign of redistributing white-owned farmland to blacks. The results have been chaos, starvation, and continuing economic hardship.

Zimbabwe is nominally Christian. Although most people profess a belief in God, a mixture of both ancestor worship and Christianity is common. Mission hospitals provide more than 60 percent of the rural health care services in Zimbabwe, having established most of the rural health care centers before independence.

Chidamoyo Christian Hospital is in northwest Zimbabwe in Hurungwe District (population 265,000), a communal land where farmers grow maize, cotton, sunflower, and tobacco for cash and for subsistence. Included in this area is the small farming town of Karoi, several commercial farms, as well as large communal farming areas.

The hospital serves approximately 31,000 potential patients in the immediate 30-kilometer radius, and it acts as a referral center for other clinics in the area. It is also the nearest hospital for people in parts of neighboring Kariba and Gokwe districts.

Chidamoyo Christian Hospital began in 1968 as an evangelistic effort of the Churches of Christ in Zimbabwe. Its mission was to holistically treat people with medical and spiritual needs. Many times, however, the overwhelming need for medical care has become more and more time-consuming. Many times the staff has had to reevaluate the ministry focus and get its priorities in order. In 1991, at the beginning of the AIDS crisis, there were more patients than beds. Families were unable to cope with the long hospitalizations; staff members were unable to cope with the ever-increasing numbers of terminally ill patients and their families.

In this region Shona culture predominates. It prizes the family very highly, starting with the local family, then the extended family, and on to people of the same totem (people who believe they have the same original father, and come from the same original area in Zimbabwe). This develops into a sense of community and belonging.

Shona culture sees illness not as an individual problem, but as a community problem. Ill people return to their rural homes to receive care from their extended families. However, Shona people believe that witchcraft causes illness. The logic holds that either someone has bewitched you, or you have not done something to appease your ancestral spirits. Families will go to great lengths and expense to find out the cause of illness by consulting *n'angas* (witch doctors). They believe following the instructions of a *n'anga* will bring healing.

Of course, this belief is widespread throughout Zimbabwe and in many African cultures. Many urban Zimbabweans who believe in scientific causes of diseases nonetheless will turn to *n'angas* when diseases that do not seem to respond to modern medicine afflict them. This often happens when relatives pressure them.

Many Christians hold firmly to their traditional beliefs, blending them into their Christianity. They may go to church on Sunday and go to the *n'anga* on Monday, without seeing any inconsistency. When faced with a life-threatening disease such as AIDS, many Christians will try the *n'angas*, just in case. Again, family members often pressure individuals to find out who is causing the illness.

In response to the AIDS crisis, Chidamoyo Christian Hospital decided to implement a program. It would approach the crisis as a family problem and use the community as the primary caregivers—supported by the medical community—instead of having institutionalized care for terminally ill patients. We were able to draw on the strengths of a strong family and community bond in Shona society in order to deal with the overwhelming disaster that AIDS was bringing in the families and communities in Zimbabwe. From the beginning of the project, we have sought to minister holistically through medical, psychological, social, and spiritual support of people infected with AIDS and their families.

In 1991 the Chidamoyo Christian Hospital medical staff began to shift to a more holistic focus in providing care for both patients and families outside the hospital and into the community. Medical and chaplaincy staff at the hospital formulated a purpose statement and goals for the program (see appendix). The program was to be an integrated part of the hospital AIDS program, offering holistic care to patients and families, and extending care into the community.

The Holistic Ministry Program

The program started in April 1991 with a home care team consisting of one missionary nurse—myself—and one chaplain. This team was to be an integrated part of the hospital care of AIDS patients. From admission through discharge this team would see patients every day. The nurse would plan the in-hospital medical care until discharge, while the chaplain would evaluate spiritual needs and follow-up upon discharge.

HIV infection in Africa is a family disease. Although AIDS enters the family through one person, it affects the physical, social, psychological, economic, and spiritual well being of all family members. The goal of this program was to offer quality terminal care—by family as well as community members—for patients dying from AIDS, and to meet the needs of the family by providing social, psychological, and especially spiritual support throughout.

Patients tested for the HIV infection in the hospital learned of the results from the chaplain and me. The hospital hired the chaplain, who graduated from Zimbabwe Christian College in Harare, specifically to be a chaplain to AIDS patients.

The hospital was committed to integrating medical and spiritual care with AIDS patients and their families. Family members, as well as the patient, were included in counseling sessions. Patients in the terminal stages of the disease could receive home care.

The home care team believed strongly that family members could give quality care to a patient with AIDS as long they received support from the hospital and community. The hospital's responsibility did not end with informing a patient he had AIDS or upon discharge. We needed to follow patients closely to limit the spread of the disease. The home care program would link the hospital to the community.

We realized from the program's inception that the high numbers of patients would preclude the home care team from visiting each more than once a month. With other responsibilities at the hospital, team members were only able to initially invest one afternoon a week to visiting home care patients. Patients sometimes lived far from the hospital, making it impossible to visit more than three or four a week. With so many people to see and so little time, the home care team felt it was impossible to offer psychological and spiritual support immediately after diagnosis.

The time right after an AIDS diagnosis is traumatic for families. Many are in shock. Some patients are major breadwinners who have returned to their rural homes ill and dying.

The team quickly decided to involve local Christians in caring for the AIDS patients and their families. Christians in the community not only care but also, through their churches, have an organized structure for reaching out.

There are thirty-five Churches of Christ congregations within a 60-mile radius of Chidamoyo Christian Hospital. In 1992 hospital staff decided to train two women, two men, and two young people from these congregations as area teams, reaching out to AIDS patients with community and spiritual support. These teams would work with and supplement the hospital's home care team.

We held one-day workshops for the church teams. We taught them how the disease is spread, diagnosed, and treated. We presented videos and role-played situations they could expect during home visits. We stressed that the home visits were only for psychological and spiritual support for the patient and the patient's family. The hospital team would provide the medical support. Churches were to incorporate this ministry into their other outreach activities. They were also to refer people who had come home ill from other areas. The churches would also have to come up with viable projects to care for orphans, support elderly grandparents raising young orphans, provide food, and help in caring for the patient at home, among other issues.

The government paid for these workshops as part of its AIDS prevention and training budget in our area. The hospital cooked the food and provided overnight accommodations.

As the HIV-positive patients are prepared for discharge, we offer them the services of our home care team. We also offer the services of the local church team in their area. If they agree, hospital staff members notify the church leader in that area, and if possible arrange to have church people at the first home care visit with the team.

During the first visit, the home care team explains that the church team will be visiting every week. The family can let the church team know of any change in the patient's medical status, so that it can notify the home care team. Or the family can send word to the hospital. The home care team explains the roles of the hospital and church teams.

The most important part of each visit is allowing patients and their families to talk about themselves, the disease, and how they are coping. Team members spend time reading from the Bible and praying with the patient and family. This kind of spiritual support throughout the illness provides comfort.

The program has greatly strengthened the churches in the Chidamoyo area. Patients and families are coming to know the Lord because of this acute life crisis. Many hear the gospel for the first time when they hear they are infected with AIDS. While responses during these counseling sessions have varied, many have told us they thought about what we said later and drew comfort from our prayers.

Church members are presenting the gospel to people in crisis. Through their compassion and acts of mercy, AIDS patients are joining the community without stigma, and the psychological and spiritual support they receive helps many to end their lives peacefully.

Opportunities arise during many home visits to teach about prevention and necessary behavior changes for those who may not be infected. Children, neighbors, and family members are all included in the visits and discussions. We emphasize preventing the spread of the disease with community members. At times we have talked to groups of fifty or more people. By seeing the disease attack someone they know, members of a community must grapple with the reality of AIDS.

Results

Behavior change in sexual matters is hard to evaluate, but we see change slowly taking place. The home care team encourages open discussion about AIDS and talks frankly concerning the patient's diagnosis. Seeing the reality of the disease in their own families has caused many to reevaluate their lives and behavior. It also opens many to the gospel.

We do not limit visits to church members or to Christians. God's love, compassion, and comfort are for all. AIDS is not a condemnation from God. The church has a biblical mandate to console (2 Corinthians 1:3–5), to reconcile (2 Corinthians 5:19), to love (1 Corinthians 13:1–8), and to minister (Matthew 25:35–36, 40). The home care team works with local churches to help them to minister with unconditional love. Of course, AIDS is in the church. Many church members are already infected and need the hope that Jesus Christ offers.

Home care has prompted some cultural changes. The home care team can talk about issues like *nhaka* (a brother inheriting his brother's widow). This is a dangerous practice if the brother has died of AIDS. Open discussions with the family and emphasis on providing for the widow and her children, without sexual union, take place. We also discuss how to handle the body during illness and in death to minimize possible contamination of caregivers. Many burial practices, such as internal cleansing and washing of the body, are changing through education.

Traditional culture believes someone must have caused this illness, and many times the husband's family blames the wife and takes everything from her, including the children. So the home care team makes sure to talk about care of children and inform women of their legal rights upon the death of their spouses.

In the past, talking about death meant (in traditional Shona culture) wishing for the person to die. In contrast, we seek to encourage the patient and family to talk about the eventuality of death and to make plans for it. We spend a lot of time practicing forgiveness, not placing blame.

People Coming to Know Christ

Through daily devotions and one-to-one sharing between patients and the hospital's chaplains and staff, many come to know the Lord. All three chaplains at the hospital have been trained in AIDS counseling and participate during counseling sessions with patients. As said above, patients hear the gospel when they learn of their HIV infection. They receive follow-up material, and we encourage them to continue talking with the chaplains.

We hold baptisms at the hospital chapel as people commit their lives to the Lord. Other patients at the hospital and local church members attend to offer support and encouragement.

The local congregation near the hospital has a women's group that visits the patients once a week. Members call on any patients from the local area. They sing, read from the Bible, and pray with the patient and family members.

The local church team continues this process when the patient is discharged. During visits they sing, read from the Bible, and pray. They talk about their church and invite family members to attend. Local members provide financial support as needed to families and orphans. They also take charge of many of the funeral services.

A husband and wife who came to know the Lord while they were being treated at Chidamoyo Christian Hospital three years ago have started a church. Ephraim and Juliet were both in their early 30s. Ephraim had been a fisherman in Kariba for several years. After losing his job, he returned home depressed, going to the beer hall with his friends. We discovered that both he and his wife had pulmonary tuberculosis and AIDS. They also had three small children at home.

Ephraim and Juliet received Christ during their counseling session. Upon their discharge, they returned to their home area about 50 kilometers from Chidamoyo, where there was no church. We encouraged them to do their best to find a local church.

Instead, one month later they returned for their checkup and told us they had a group of fifteen meeting at their village every Sunday for church. They wanted teaching materials, songbooks, and Bibles. They were very excited by the change in their lives.

The home care team quickly made an evaluation trip to their area and arranged for a leader from a nearby church to come every Saturday to spend the day teaching and calling on people in the area. He would then spend the night at the village and hold services the next day. Ephraim and Juliet promised to pay his bus fare back and forth and to provide him with food and a place to sleep.

Physically, Juliet and Ephraim improved and were healed of their tuberculosis. They felt well and were able to function normally. Spiritually, a great change took place in their lives, which was apparent to their families and to their community. They were able to talk openly about this.

One year later the home care team was invited to a special "celebration of life" service. There Ephraim and Juliet spoke about the changes in their lives. They had thought they were going to die at the hospital. Ephraim's former drinking friends also testified that they had noticed the change in him, and many came to know the Lord.

Today more than one hundred people regularly attend worship services at the home of Juliet and Ephraim, who are doing well. They have dedicated whatever time they have left to the Lord.

The churches in the Chidamoyo area have been strengthened because of the outreach into the community. They have many new members, and there have been more than 40 baptisms of AIDS patients in the past four years. A portable canvas baptistery has enabled church workers to baptize patients in their own homes. People with AIDS who received counseling through the hospital program are leading two of the new churches. These are fervent young men who have changed their lives and who had not been attending church.

The churches see themselves as coworkers with the hospital who can reach far more people in their community with the gospel. The churches are in constant contact with the hospital concerning the condition of the patients, and if deaths occur they invite the hospital staff to the funerals. Such services are large community gatherings, and the church's presence and message are felt during these times.

Evaluation

Serving approximately forty patients in the program at all times, the staff members involved must also continue their full-time work at the hospital. As of this writing, since 1990 we have had 2,358 new cases of HIV/AIDS. The home care team has been able to make a total of only 408 home visits since April 1991, an average of 3.75 visits per family. Obviously, this leaves out many families who need to be in the program but who cannot be included because of a lack of personnel and time. The current home care team makes visits two afternoons a week.

There were no external obstacles to the program. The government and local churches were very supportive of the hospital's involvement. Zimbabwe's Ministry of Health has recognized the program for leadership and compassionate care offered to AIDS patients.

Given the hospital's uneven track record of holistic ministry, we made integrating spiritual ministry into our program a priority. We refer to the program goals on an ongoing basis. Governmental and nongovernmental observers have seen the need for the spiritual care of AIDS patients. Many of them have introduced Bible reading and praying into their own home care programs, having seen them work in our program.

Through input from our program, the government has included spiritual care at national home care planning workshops. Officials recognize that most Zimbabweans seek spiritual care and comfort when they are ill. Even President Robert Mugabe has called on the church to be at the forefront of the AIDS crisis.

Two government home care programs have asked our advice on appropriate Bible verses and Christian songs to share with patients. Seeing our program in action, one private home care program bought Bibles for home care kits used by its volunteers.

In our program, we have gotten all of the nurses to help with home visits. We have also added two more chaplains, a man and a woman, to meet the needs of our many AIDS patients.

Finances

The government has totally funded our home care program. In 1991 the program operated on just $18,000 (Zimbabwean dollars). It is now $30,000 a year. Most of the money pays for transportation and training.

The government has not attached strings to its financing by limiting the preaching of the gospel. In fact, officials have been very supportive in paying for church leader training as community home care workers. This is because we sold them on the idea that church people have more commitment to patients than do other people in the community. The Christians in the area have demonstrated their love and concern for people. The government has seen that church-related home care programs are the most effective.

We also give food provided by the government from supplementary feeding programs. This is very important in a time of drought, when families do not have enough food and sick patients need proper nutrition to survive.

The main purpose of our program remains to lead people to a personal knowledge of Jesus Christ. Whether people have AIDS or not, we want to prevent them from dying without knowing the Lord. We feel privileged to have this opportunity.

Appendix

Vision for Home Care Program, Chidamoyo Christian Hospital, Adopted April 1991

Believing in Jesus as Lord, we affirm the message that God offers forgiveness to all through his Son, Jesus Christ. God wishes no one to perish but all to be saved. This is our goal throughout this program, as stated in Romans 8:1: "Therefore, there is now no condemnation for those who are in Christ Jesus." We desire to undertake this program with the express purpose of bringing those patients with AIDS and their families to a personal knowledge of Jesus Christ.

We undertake this vision as follows:

1. Patients will be referred to the program by the medical staff working at Chidamoyo Christian Hospital and/or community or church members. First priority will be given to those patients in the terminal stage of AIDS.

2. Patients will be introduced to the Home Care staff while they are inpatients so that a personal relationship can be formed between Home Care staff and the patient and family.

3. Counseling sessions will also emphasize the hope that Jesus Christ is in our lives. Forgiveness is an essential part of this counseling, and the gospel will be presented at each session with the patient and family.

4. Home visits will include medical care, psychological support for the patient and family dealing with AIDS, and spiritual support through prayer and Bible reading, presentation of the gospel to unbelievers, and encouragement of believers.

5. Supplementary food to help the patient nutritionally will be offered as available to those who are in need.

6. Liaison with the local church in the area will be arranged for those patients that do not have a local church. The local church will maintain weekly visits with the patient and family as part of their calling and outreach into the community.

7. We believe strongly in meeting the physical, psychological and spiritual needs of people with AIDS and their families within their communities and home. Community support for these patients will be

encouraged at all times by education, prevention, and openly talking about the disease.

8. We believe strongly that sexual behavior change is desirable and obtainable to stop the disease of AIDS. God has called us to sexual purity outside and inside marriage, and it is important to present God's plan, without condemnation, to bring about change and hope to believers and nonbelievers alike.

9. The Home Care team will work closely together with the hospital staff for encouragement and help in meeting the needs of the patients and their families in the hospital and at home after discharge. The Home Care team will also offer encouragement to the staff on their care and handling of the patients while in the hospital. The responsibility for providing compassionate, nonjudgmental care is upon all staff at Chidamoyo Christian Hospital and the Home Care Team.

10. The goal of our program at all times is to fulfill the biblical mandates:

    i.   To console: "Blessed be the God and Father of our Lord Jesus
         Christ, the Father of mercies and God of all comfort, who
         comforts us in all our tribulation, that we may be able to comfort
         those who are in any trouble, with the comfort with which we
         ourselves are comforted by God. For as the sufferings of Christ
         abound in us, so our consolation also abounds through Christ"
         (2 Corinthians 1:3–5 NKJV).

    ii. To reconcile: "That is, that God was in Christ reconciling the
         world to Himself, not imputing their trespasses to them, and has
         committed to us the word of reconciliation"(2 Corinthians 5:19
         NKJV).

    iii. To love: "And though I bestow all my goods to feed the poor,
         and though I give my body to be burned, but have not love, it
         profits me nothing. Love suffers long and is kind; love does
         not envy; love does not parade itself, is not puffed up; does not
         behave rudely, does not seek its own, is not provoked, thinks no
         evil; does not rejoice in iniquity, but rejoices in the truth; bears

all things, believes in all things, hopes all things, endures all things. Love never fails" (1 Corinthians 13:3–8 NKJV).

iv. To minister: "For I was hungry and you gave Me food; I was thirsty and you gave Me drink; I was a stranger and you took Me in; I was naked and you clothed Me; I was sick and you visited Me; I was in prison and you came to Me. . . . And the King will answer and say to them 'Assuredly, I say to you, inasmuch as you did it to one of the least of these My brethren, you did it to Me'" (Matthew 25:35–36, 40 NKJV).

CHAPTER 9

FLORENCE MUINDI AND LEIGH ANNE DAGEFORDE

███████

HOW CHURCHES IN ETHIOPIA ARE RESPONDING TO THE HIV/AIDS CRISIS

With 67 million people, Ethiopia is one of the world's poorest nations[1] and "has the third largest number of people living with HIV/AIDS of any country."[2] According to the United States Central Intelligence Agency's National Intelligence Council, Ethiopia is one of five nations that will be decimated by HIV/AIDS by the year 2010 due to an exponential growth in the number of cases. The adult prevalence rate of HIV Ethiopia in 2002 ranged from 10 to 18 percent and could reach 19 to 27 percent by 2010.[3]

The AIDS problem in Ethiopia is overwhelming. Many factors have precipitated the crisis, including displaced populations and migration due to war, famine, and widespread poverty. With poverty and family destabilization rampant, rape and oppressive sexual practices increase. Women feel they must provide for pressing basic needs through prostitution because of a lack of other job opportunities. In Addis Ababa, the capital of Ethiopia, the number of sex workers has reached over 150,000. Some 70 to 80 percent of the women involved are HIV-positive. The average age for commercial sex workers in Addis Ababa is fifteen or sixteen.

Alcoholism and drug abuse also lead to irresponsible sexual behavior. Many of the cities along major trucking routes and near military camps have a higher incidence of HIV/AIDS because of the promiscuity of travelers.[4]

Further, the traditional healer also spreads AIDS. In some regions with little to no health care access, traditional healers not only treat illnesses, they also perform both male and female circumcisions. However, they perform these operations without sterile instruments, inadvertently but frequently spreading the HIV virus. Finally, the cultural stigma associated with HIV/AIDS encourages its spread while hindering prevention and treatment.[5]

The HIV/AIDS crisis in many ways is just another problem for a government already overwhelmed with crises. Many people suffer from famine or the economic consequences of a recent border war with Eritrea. Refugees have flooded the country from Sudan on the west and Somalia on the east. Although raising awareness regarding HIV, its modes of transmission, and its severity, the government has done little to modify behavior.

According to 2002 Ethiopian government estimates, the national infection rate will level off at the current 6.6 percent. The government collected its data at thirty-four "sentinel surveillance sites" throughout the country, where health professionals tested pregnant mothers aged 15 to 49. By comparing the number of HIV-positive mothers with the number of HIV-negative mothers, the government could only give a rough estimate of the percentage of HIV-positive people nationwide.

Unfortunately, it is probably an underestimate. HIV reduces fertility by 30 percent, and many mothers cannot afford prenatal care. Additionally, only 12,689 women were involved in the study, representing less than 0.02 percent of the population. Churches and individual caregivers in a variety of communities estimate infection rates of 12 to 40 percent, not 6.6 percent. Accurate statistics are difficult to get, for several reasons: lack of access to services by marginalized populations, the high cost of HIV/AIDS testing, an unwillingness of people to be tested, and political sensitivity to the issue.[6]

Fortunately, the church has heard its call to action and involvement. For several years church leaders believed HIV/AIDS was only a crisis outside the church, but as more church members and leaders died from the virus, that position became impossible to maintain. Now engaged in the problem, churches are concentrating on awareness, prevention, care, and support. (Only the church, not the government, has the resources and people to offer support programs to people who are already dying from the illness.) Church interventions include counseling centers, home-based care programs, anti-AIDS clubs, printed awareness materials, and orphan care.

Just as Christ served the poor, sick, and suffering, churches in Ethiopia are responding to the epidemic through acts of service. Five churches and organizations offer HIV/AIDS interventions. Some developed their approaches recently; others have been in place for fifteen years.

A Case Study in Addis Ababa

HIV/AIDS is not an impersonal statistical phenomenon. It devastates millions of individuals, their families, friends, and churches. In Addis Ababa there is a narrow, rocky path between poorly constructed houses. This poor urban slum, called Mekanisa, is home to 50 thousand people. Children dash around our small group, and a few donkeys squeeze their way past us carrying straw to mix with mud for the walls of nearby houses. We stop at a one-room apartment, only 10-by-10. Our guide, the leader of the Mekanisa New Covenant Baptist Church HIV/AIDS ministry, leads us into the cool, dark room. We sink onto two mattresses close to the ground, the only seats in the house. Despite the grim setting, we exchange greetings and receive a warm welcome.

Almaz, twenty-five years old, sits on a mattress in the corner. She shares this space with her mother and two brothers, whom she supports. Almaz has a small video rental business that pays for their food, rent, and school fees. In her free time, she tells others about AIDS in the Mekanisa community. Through her church, Almaz also visits the homes of women suffering from the disease throughout the community. Almaz praises God for his goodness and that her mother became a Christian in church last week. Smiling in the dim light, she says everyone in her family is now a believer. Almaz has HIV/AIDS.

Greatly saddened at the suffering of our newfound sister in Christ, and amazed at her joy and exuberance, we hear her story. Like 60 percent of HIV-positive married women in Ethiopia, Almaz's husband infected her ten years ago when they were married.[7] Almaz, then sixteen years old, gave birth to her only son. Two years later, her husband left them.

To get money to buy food, Almaz went into prostitution. Six years ago, while in the hospital to receive treatment for hemorrhoids, Almaz learned of her HIV-positive status. Her son also got tested, and he also was HIV-positive. (Thus, Almaz guessed that her husband had infected her, and she in turn passed the disease to her child.) In all those years of prostitution, Almaz must have infected untold numbers of men, who in turn infected others.

Living north of Addis Ababa at the time, Almaz and her son were ostracized by her family—because of their disease, not because of her profession. No longer welcome in the town, they moved to Addis Ababa. Because she was single and completely alone, Almaz left her son at an orphanage upon her arrival in the capital. If still alive, he would be 9 years old. Almaz has not heard from him since she left him there.

Almaz knew she needed to find other work, so she bought a collection of videos and rented them from a landlord's premises. The video business did well. Almaz's mother, who had once kicked Almaz out of the family home, and two brothers came to her for support. But one day the landlord evicted Almaz because she was using the store as a platform to teach people about the danger of AIDS. To continue to pay the rent for her one-room home, Almaz sold half of her video collection. Almaz is currently suffering from pneumocystis pneumonia, which marks the beginning of the end for those living with HIV/AIDS. She has been taking less than half of the medicine she needs, but as we pray with her family, Almaz is filled with joy. She rejoices that God has brought us to visit her, and we are thankful that we will meet again in heaven.[8]

Almaz receives support from Mekanisa New Covenant Baptist Church, which has about 250 adult members and almost 300 children in weekly attendance. Church members are mostly the poor of Addis Ababa, displaced peoples from Eritrea, and leprosy patients from the nearby leprosy hospital. While the average income for a family of seven in the Mekanisa community is about US$2.50 per month, this church has started a holistic HIV/AIDS clinic and counseling center. Like Almaz, women living with HIV/AIDS require not only psychological and spiritual counseling, but also physical care. Thus far, the church can only afford to enroll thirty-two people in the program. Over two hundred are on a waiting list for counseling and home-based care. Eleven trained church volunteers provide care and support.

Facing more needs than resources, the church pastor recognizes the magnitude of the crisis, and the crippling effect of HIV/AIDS on church and community members. Seeking to follow Christ's command and example, the pastor called together his leadership for a day of fasting and prayer. They decided to put their building project on the back burner. Repairs on the rented church building and a church-owned tent can wait, but those who are suffering need immediate help.

Mekanisa Church leaders are also digging deep into their already shallow pockets to find the funds to provide HIV/AIDS victims with food, clothing, housing, rent, school fees, and medicine. Like Mekanisa New Covenant Baptist Church, churches throughout Ethiopia are serving people like Almaz and her family.[9]

Ethiopian Evangelical Church Mekane Yesus

The Ethiopian Evangelical Church Mekane Yesus established an HIV/AIDS prevention and control program more than fifteen years ago. The earliest denomination to found an HIV/AIDS prevention office, it strives to integrate HIV/AIDS awareness into every aspect of the Mekane Yesus church nationwide. Major AIDS programs are in place within its 20 synods. The church recently published the second edition of its *Training Manual on HIV/AIDS/STIs Prevention and Control*. The manuals are part of the church's Training of Trainers meetings at the synods throughout Ethiopia for local church leaders. At these meetings they become educated and mobilized to lead the fight against HIV/AIDS. These leaders learn how to teach about prevention through abstinence and fidelity in marriage. They also form care and support groups for people living with HIV/AIDS. Once trained, they return to their home churches to share their knowledge with fellow community members.

In addition to these twenty major synod HIV prevention programs and six counseling centers, the Mekane Yesus Church is aiming to increase HIV/AIDS intervention activities in all 5,158 of its churches. The church desires to train not only church leaders and evangelists, but also to involve congregational volunteers in counseling, anti-AIDS clubs, and home-based care-giving activities. By training laity, it hopes to reach those churches in even the remotest parts of the country. The denomination's main office in Addis Ababa has many printed supplies, audiotapes, and posters to raise awareness and enhance prevention.

The office also coordinates care and support of AIDS orphans, churches, and community members suffering from HIV/AIDS. The church provides volunteer counseling, testing, and medical care, along with financial and material support, including school fees for some of the children. Finally, the Mekane Yesus Church has established a rehabilitation program for high-risk people in the community, especially female prostitutes. By training these women in sewing, knitting, cooking, and other income-generating skills, they can escape an environment where they are at risk for contracting and spreading HIV/AIDS.

Lutheran churches in other nations, particularly from Finland, have provided most of the money for the Mekane Yesus Church AIDS programs. The Mekane Yesus Church's long-established HIV/AIDS program has been a model for many denominations and organizations.[10]

Ethiopian Kale Heywot Church

Working with the Serving in Mission (SIM) agency, the Ethiopian Kale Heywot Church has created comprehensive HIV/AIDS prevention and control strategies. SIM and the Kale Heywot Church have established strong and active anti-AIDS clubs in churches, schools, and communities. Through dramas, role-playing, interclub competitions, peer educator training programs, and resource centers, information about AIDS goes clearly to youth, the largest population currently at risk for contracting HIV/AIDS. There are three pilot programs run by volunteer staff in cities along major trucking routes. The church chose to work in these cities because of the increased risk of HIV/AIDS infection due to the promiscuity of truckers. Posters and brochures provide information to local and transient populations.

The church's anti-AIDS clubs have instilled a passion in high school students for raising awareness about HIV/AIDS and for providing care to local orphans. In the pilot project, young people from a local high school saw the large numbers of needy AIDS orphans in the area. Many of the children were unable to afford school registration fees, and some children were living on the street or in the local dump. The club hired a teacher to start a school for them. Today more than eighty AIDS orphans attend the small school, which now needs more teachers. The high schoolers, meanwhile, are exploring income-generating activities to sustain the program.

The Kale Heywot Church also works in rural areas. Additionally, it runs a housing complex on the west side of Addis Ababa that focuses on keeping together families of HIV/AIDS victims.

Like the other church denominations, the Kale Heywot Church is searching for more funding for its HIV/AIDS programs. Dr. Alemayehu, the leader of the church's AIDS Prevention Program, says the high number of orphans and patients who need care overwhelms the church. Its funds are too limited to provide medical care, food, and other necessities. Volunteers make sacrificial commitments of time and money to the program, but they must also continue to support their own families. Although the church has been successful in motivating volunteers, more funding is necessary.[11]

Catholic Church

Four Catholic sisters run the Mother Teresa Home for AIDS Orphans. The 250 children they help are HIV-positive and have no parents or relatives to care for them. Moving from a cramped, rented building in Addis Ababa, the new suburban facility has two dormitories and a schoolhouse. Although the life expectancy of the children at the home is about fifteen years, the sisters provide them with the best life possible. The Vatican funded the new campus, and the sisters serve with exceptional commitment, making only one trip home every ten years. In the home, the quality of care far exceeds that provided to many of the 1 million AIDS orphans in Ethiopia. The orphans live in well-kept boarding facilities, receive a balanced diet, and enjoy both basic and creative educational and recreational activities. Most importantly, they receive emotional support.

The Ethiopian government does not fund or operate any orphanages, and few homes focus on HIV-positive children instead of adoptable HIV-negative babies. In the Mother Teresa Home, children of all ages become friends and family. As they learn about their illness—the older ones angry and ashamed, the younger ones afraid—all help one another through life and death. The mother superior told of a boy who recently died. He wanted desperately to move into the new dorms, but he was too weak to live until their completion. One day the sister allowed the young boy to go down the hill for a visit, so his friends carried him to the new but unfinished dorm and laid him on the floor. Surrounded by his friends, he took his last breath there. Although the suffering of innocent young children shrouded our visit, the strength of the Catholic sisters and the hope of a better future for the orphans were great encouragements.

About six hundred children from many different backgrounds live at another Catholic center in Addis Ababa. Some of them are AIDS orphans. The Catholic Church also cares for terminally ill women, although this ministry is accepting no more women until a new facility is completed. Throughout Ethiopia, about half of the Catholic parishes have HIV/AIDS prevention activities focused primarily on young people.[12]

Meserete Kristos Church

The Meserete Kristos (Christ Foundation) Church started an AIDS prevention office in Addis Ababa five years ago. The director of the program, Dr. Samson Estifanos, says that leaders in the denomination, like those in many evangelical churches nationwide, viewed AIDS as a societal, not a church, problem. However, when some elders and pastors started to die of HIV/AIDS, the church finally recognized the magnitude of the crisis. Now its AIDS prevention office is one of the church's five major programs focusing on holistic care.

Prayer is a priority for the church. Leaders believe God can reverse the epidemic; consequently, they send prayer requests each quarter to their 275 congregations. The 200 thousand members of the Meserete Kristos Church pray with the expectation that God will intervene as they fight the HIV/AIDS crisis. The prayer lists include confession of dishonoring marriages and discrimination against infected groups, requests for proper use of HIV/AIDS funds in Ethiopia, and mercy for the nation as a whole. The denomination recognizes that the magnitude of the crisis is far beyond its own power, so members are earnestly turning to the Lord.

Training seminars are an important element of prevention and awareness. Like the Mekane Yesus Church, the Meserete Kristos Church trains church leaders and volunteers. The AIDS prevention office has also printed materials for the congregations. The church is focusing on abstinence and fidelity. In each of the 275 congregations, two trained volunteers do pre-test counseling in the community. This way, not only can people come to the church for help, the church can reach out through the counselors into the homes of people who need care.

Care and support for people living with HIV/AIDS is the third major part of the Meserete Kristos Church's response. Home-based care for both confirmed and unconfirmed cases of HIV occurs in rural areas, because many patients do not live near testing sites, nor do they have the money to afford testing. While the church wants to provide medical kits for the volunteer caregivers, a lack of funding has hindered their distribution. Church volunteers work as home-based caregivers. The church also offers a monthly fellowship meeting for people living with HIV/AIDS at each of its 16 regional offices.

The church also participates in a network with other churches and nongovernmental organizations fighting HIV/AIDS on behalf of not only church members but also surrounding communities. Anti-AIDS task forces meet in local churches to counsel young people and to care for infected individuals. Like many ministries, the Meserete Kristos Church AIDS prevention office needs more financial support. The church's anti-AIDS programs have just twenty full-time employees but 1,100 volunteers, who are giving both their time and money.

The church encourages HIV testing before marriage, but this is an expensive proposition in Ethiopia. The volunteers and the church continue to need money. In fact, the office of AIDS prevention almost closed its doors in 2003 due to lack of funds, but church elders have kept it going on an extremely tight budget.[13]

Ethiopian Orthodox Church

The Ethiopian Orthodox Church, the largest church in the country, has worked with several nongovernmental organizations in fighting HIV/AIDS, including one with the African Medical and Research Foundation (AMREF) called FATE (Fighting AIDS Together in Ethiopia). Like many of its evangelical church counterparts, the Orthodox Church has focused on prevention and care.

In Gonder, in northwestern Ethiopia, a medical doctor has converted a former orphanage into a center focusing on HIV/AIDS care and support. Most people in Gonder earn a subsistence living through farming, and many of them belong to the Ethiopian Orthodox Church. The church has trained 20 peer educators who are involved in behavioral change communications with young people. Just as the evangelical churches train volunteers to teach others about the dangers of HIV/AIDS, the Orthodox Church has initiated a similar program with brochures, posters, manuals, and meetings.

In Gonder, 50 patients and 100 AIDS orphans are being cared for. The Orthodox Church, in conjunction with Life in Abundance and FATE, has begun income-generating activities and home-based care. For patients unable to work, the program provides 50 birr (approximately US$6) for food, medicine, and rent. The program attempts to place orphans with extended family members, relieving the burden by providing money for school expenses and clothing. The project in Gonder is just one example of the Ethiopian Orthodox Church's nationwide ministry.

The patriarch of the church is also very active. He has appeared on television frequently, advocating care and support for patients infected with HIV. The Orthodox Church has established an anti-AIDS office within its development department. This office has maintained a good relationship with the Ministry of Health and is consequently eligible for governmental funds. The church also receives support from Greek and Russian Orthodox churches abroad.

Although the highest Orthodox Church leaders preach abstinence as the main way to control the spread of the disease, as in any church, there are some differences at the grass roots. Many in the church strongly believe that holy water has been "given to Ethiopia to heal HIV/AIDS." They also believe holy water, which they say is available in the country's south, can cure other diseases.

The Orthodox Church provides care and support in several cities with no previous HIV/AIDS programs. We hope that Ethiopia's Orthodox, Catholic, and evangelical churches will better work together in the future to more effectively fight HIV/AIDS.[14] There are encouraging signs that this is indeed happening.

Evangelical Churches Fellowship Of Ethiopia

As the nation faces an alarming increase in HIV/AIDS infections by 2010, Ethiopian churches have responded. The programs and materials established by the many evangelical denominations, the Catholic and Orthodox churches, and several nongovernmental organizations are similar in many ways. To unite the individual churches in their mitigation efforts, and to help the smaller churches that lack the resources for an AIDS prevention office, evangelical leaders have started an Evangelical Churches Fellowship of Ethiopia.[15]

Conclusions

The World Bank has budgeted $59.7 million to fight HIV/AIDS in Ethiopia. Through its Multisectoral HIV/AIDS Project, the bank has designated this money to "finance the Government's 2000–2004 HIV/AIDS strategic plan, that include[s] support for capacity building within, both private and government agencies" in areas of "prevention, care and treatment."[16] While each of the church organizations in this chapter has applied more than once to access some of this money, 75 percent of it has gone unused.

According to coordinators from church and parachurch programs, bureaucratic roadblocks hinder them from accessing the money. Even though the government does not have the capacity to fight AIDS alone, existing policies prohibit churches registered under the Ministry of Justice to receive certain kinds of funds. The government requires specific approaches that may compromise the church's message of salvation. Meanwhile, the people of the nation suffer.

While church members want to respond even more vigorously to the crisis, their capacity is limited. Meeting in simple facilities, Christians say the needs of prevention and support overwhelm their meager resources. Additionally, church members and counselors need more training.

Thankfully, solutions exist. For example, a few holistic training curriculums are in circulation. Further, a recent World Bank conference in Addis Ababa outlined ways to channel program money to faith-based groups through newly created parachurch partners.

Even with all this work going on nationwide, HIV/AIDS is still ravaging the people of Ethiopia. According to the U.S. Agency for International Development, the 11 percent infection level will likely increase rapidly in the next five years.[17] The government doesn't have the resources to fight this crisis, and the nation's poor economy only makes the epidemic worse. Like the government, the church is also short on funds, and the shimmer of hope is starting to tarnish. The Ethiopian church has charged into action and run as far as its resources will reach. Yet despite years of HIV/AIDS ministry, the epidemic is running rampant.

Still, hope for an AIDS-free future in Ethiopia has not died, as we have seen from examples such as Almaz's bedside and a makeshift rented tent called Mekanisa Church. The Ethiopian church has battled strongly with limited resources for years, and it will continue to do so. Looking to the unity of Ugandan churches on the issue, Ethiopian Christians, if they stay unified, have the opportunity to make a similar impact. The Evangelical Churches Fellowship is showing signs of accomplishing this unity, but too many churches still continue to duplicate their excellent efforts. By discarding the denominational differences that are so divisive worldwide, the Ethiopian church will be much more successful.

The church offers the best opportunity to provide compassionate care and emotional healing to those who have AIDS. Therefore, investing resources to empower the church to respond to HIV/AIDS is the most effective way to help people throughout the country. The gospel is a powerful tool not only to change behavior, but also to give the promise of eternal life. Only those individuals who have this hope can live abundant lives.

Over the centuries the Ethiopian church has remained stable even in the face of strong opposition and persecution. The church's structure and leadership, which cut through government, ethnic, and economic status barriers, already touch even the smallest communities.

However, funding for church AIDS programs is limited. Extremely poor church members can hardly sacrifice any more than they already are. All other funding the churches get comes from churches outside the country. Until the church can access money from international agencies, its programs will be necessarily limited. When church leaders beg families of seven living off of $2.50 per month to not only donate volunteer time as caregivers and counselors, but also to give money for HIV/AIDS testing, the need is apparent.

A final lesson can be gained from Almaz and her family. Our brothers and sisters in Christ are suffering from HIV/AIDS. This crisis is not outside the church, and this is of utmost concern to the worldwide community of Christians. Many innocent people are suffering because of HIV/AIDS, and the church has an opportunity to share the love of Christ by caring for all. As the churches in Ethiopia have demonstrated, the HIV/AIDS epidemic must rally Christians to fulfill Christ's commandment to care for the sick, regardless of the stigma.

Notes

1. http://www.undp.org/hdr2003/pdf/hdr03_HDI.pdf. (September 20, 2003).

2. http://www.worldbank.org/afr/et/ctry_brief.htm. (September 20, 2003).

3. National Intelligence Council. "The Next Wave of HIV/AIDS: Nigeria, Ethiopia, Russia, India, and China." September 2002. http://www.odci.gov/nic/pubs/other_products/ICA%20HIV-AIDS%20unclassified%20092302POSTGERBER.htm.

4. Tim Teusink, M.D., Serving in Mission (SIM) HIV/AIDS Prevention Coordinator, and Dr. Alemayehu, Ethiopian Kale Heywot Church comprehensive HIV/AIDS Prevention and Control Strategy Coordinator, personal interview, June 16, 2003.

5. Sr. Etsegenet Hailu, Ethiopian Evangelical Church Mekane Yesus HIV/AIDS Prevention & Control Program Coordinator, personal interview, June 19, 2003.

6. Disease Prevention and Control Department, Ministry of Health, AIDS in Ethiopia, 4th ed. (Ethiopia: October, 2002).

7. UN Office for the Coordination of Humanitarian Affairs, Integrated Regional Information Network. "AFRICA: Religious leaders expose damning attitudes towards HIV/AIDS." September 21, 2003.

8. Almaz, personal interview, June 14, 2003.

9. Tsahaye, Mekanisa New Covenant Baptist Church Counseling Center Volunteer Coordinator, personal interviews, June 14, 2003.

10. Sr. Etsegenet Hailu.

11. Tim Teusink.

12. Sister Superior at Mother Theresa Home for Orphans, personal interview, June 18, 2003.

13. Dr. Samson Estifanos, Meserete Kristos Church AIDS Prevention Office Coordinator, personal interview, June 17, 2003.

14. Dr. Joseph, Life in Abundance, personal interview, June, 20 2003.

15. Evangelical Churches Fellowship of Ethiopia, personal interview, June 19, 2003.

16. http://web.worldbank.org/external/projects/main?pagePK=104231&theSitePK=40941&menuPK=228424&Projectid=P069886 (September 20, 2003).

17. http://www.usaid.gov/pubs/cbj2003/afr/et/ (September 20, 2003).

CHAPTER 10
PAUL KENNEL

███████

GOD'S GENTLE REVOLUTIONARY IN RURAL THAILAND

Radical is not a word that comes to mind when you first meet Pa Malee (Maw-LEE), or Aunt Malee, as people affectionately call her. Now in her early 60s, with short, gray hair, round cheeks, and big glasses, this five-foot-one lady appears quite ordinary. But those who know her quickly dispel that notion.

"She gives me the impression that she could sit with a king and still be herself," says Scott Coats, 40, who has known Malee Charoenboon for several years. Coats grew up in a province about 200 miles from Ban Farm, the child of Christian missionaries. He's now the country manager in Thailand for World Concern, a Christian relief and development organization headquartered in the United States.

Coats describes Malee as "a very caring woman—especially toward people who are suffering. She's quiet and unassuming." When she speaks to groups about AIDS (and she speaks powerfully, according to Coats), she does nothing to hide her northern dialect. The risk of sounding "out of fashion" to most Westernized Thais doesn't seem to bother Malee one bit. She is who she is. And she does what she believes God calls her to do for people living with HIV/AIDS.

HIV in Northern Thailand

Thailand reported its first two cases of AIDS in 1984.[1] Most who were initially infected were heroin addicts sharing needles. But by the end of the 1980s, the virus was spreading rapidly because of an openly flourishing sex trade. The area hardest hit was in the north, around cities like Chiang Rai and Chiang Kham, where Malee's family was living at the time.

Northern Thailand was a convergence zone. Impoverished, minimally educated young women flocked to town to earn money as paid sex workers. The pervasive acceptance of prostitution as part of a boy's passage into manhood and steady patronage from a nearby Thai military base kept the sex business booming.

By 1989, reported AIDS cases in Thailand had grown to seventy-one.[2] The following year the reported number more than doubled,[3] but certainly the actual number of cases was even higher. People were dying. People were becoming afraid.

Fear began to create a strong cultural prejudice in Thailand against anyone with HIV or AIDS. But rather than become immobilized, Malee took action. As other Chiang Kham residents teetered on the edge of panic with misinformation and misplaced anger toward those with the virus, Malee sought the facts.

She began volunteering at a local community center that offered HIV/ AIDS education and counseling. She trained groups on prevention. She distributed literature about the disease. She visited patients in their homes. And over time, she witnessed hopeless, painful deaths. Many victims were young adults about the ages of her four children. Watching them slip away so needlessly, some rejected by their parents, broke Malee's heart.

"She really had a vision, a burden, for caring for other people who had a family member with AIDS," says Coats, who at the time was using his new agriculture degree from Penn State to help farmers in Chiang Rai and Laos. It would be a few years before he and Malee met.

All the while, the Thai government was in denial. Afraid of jeopardizing its lucrative international tourist trade, it tried to keep the rising infection rate a secret and so made matters much worse. Tourist or Thai, child or adult, everyone was at greater risk because the problem was being ignored. The silence meant limited treatment options were available, and it discouraged individuals from seeking treatment. This added to the isolation and shame. Not until 1991 did the Ministry of Public Health finally launch an anti-AIDS campaign, making Thailand the first Asian country to break its silence about the disease.

Christians were at the forefront in the battle against AIDS from the beginning in Thailand. In the early 1990s, as an overwhelmed national medical system turned to the private sector, it found few Buddhist or local groups willing to assist. Despite a subtle anti-Christian bias in this strongly Buddhist country, Christians and nongovernmental organizations took the risk.

The Charoenboons

Malee was one of a very few citizens who stepped forward to help during these early years of the epidemic. It wasn't her job or her training, but she believed it was her calling as a Christian. After all, Jesus cared for those cast to the side by society. And in the process, Malee learned how hard it was in her culture to inspire compassion and understanding for those with the disease.

In a country where being Buddhist is almost synonymous with being Thai, Malee and her family also worshiped as a minority. Only about 0.5 percent of the population of Thailand is Christian.[3]

But Malee's home was clearly Christian. Her husband Yanyong was well known in the community as a Christian leader, and was referred to as *acharn* (teacher or respected one). After attending seminary in northern Thailand, he had evangelized in the area for many years. Yanyong also had worked for World Vision, helping with various Christian-based humanitarian programs. Eventually, Malee's eldest son would go into the ministry, returning to Chiang Kham to pastor a Presbyterian church.

In 1991 600 cases of AIDS were reported in Thailand,[4] and officials predicted that 4 million Thais would become infected by 2001.[5,6] The government finally declared AIDS an "official" epidemic and made condom use mandatory in sex establishments. In other words: no condom, no sexual services. That became the law. Enforcement, however, was another matter.

One of Yanyong and Malee's children, Wayo (WIE-oh) Charoenboon—like seventeen-year-olds everywhere—thought he was invincible. That year he and a group of friends began visiting Chiang Kham's brothels.

Coats was not surprised by the choices Wayo made and the ambivalence the teen probably felt. "Thailand has a culture of contradictions," Coats says. "In this tolerant Buddhist country, men are taught five precepts: no drinking, no smoking, no stealing, no lying, no womanizing." However, no one is actually expected to follow them all. Those who do would have their manhood doubted.

"As I became an adult in Thailand, three questions would generally surface in conversations with men who didn't know me that well. Did I want a cigarette, a drink, and did I like Thai women?" Coats says that any Thai in his late teens who hadn't been to a prostitute was not considered a man. "By the culture's standards, there's obviously something wrong with you. That's just the way it was."

In 1991, a young man visiting a prostitute was common. People saw it as a rite of passage, a business transaction, an acceptable fact of life.

Moving to the Country

1991 was also the year Yanyong decided to move his family to the small village of Ban Farm. He and Malee were thinking ahead to retirement. Peaceful Ban Farm, stretching about one mile alongside the ambling Mae Kok River, was a welcome change, but still close enough to urban Chiang Kham and Chiang Rai for Yanyong to carry on his work a while longer.

Just 50 years earlier, the area had been virgin jungle. There had been no Ban Farm except in the mind of a local Presbyterian missionary who envisioned a Christian community—a working farm where impoverished and homeless families could help themselves and each other.

Eventually, with the local governor's permission, Ban Farm literally took root as a 4,000-acre farm. People from all corners of Thailand— individuals marginalized because of their Christian faith, poverty, and other stigmas—came to plant orchards and vegetable gardens, and to raise fish in small ponds that eventually dotted the flat flood plain. Some of the new arrivals had leprosy, but they were welcomed. At last they had a place where they could live and die with dignity.

When the Charoenboons moved to Ban Farm, most of their neighbors were third- and fourth-generation Christians, the surviving relatives of original founding families. Over 90 percent of the village's 1,600 residents were Christian.

The Farm's compassionate history resonated with Malee. She considered it a blessing that God had brought them to such a place. It felt good to be surrounded by so many who shared her faith—people she could love and count on, no matter what.

Malee wasted no time getting involved in the women's group at church. The Charoenboons joined the larger of the two congregations in the village, Farm Sam Pan Thakit Church, which had been a part of Ban Farm from the beginning.

Meanwhile, Wayo began to settle into Ban Farm in his own way. He applied to a three-year industrial program in nearby Chiang Rai. He filled out the necessary forms, scheduled his classes, and paid his fees. Only one thing remained: Wayo needed to have a blood test.

Wayo had known something was wrong even before the family moved to Ban Farm. He had known, but he didn't want to know. And he certainly didn't want anyone else to know.

Wayo's friends continued to frequent brothels. He went along, fearing that changing his lifestyle would expose his secret. And in his fear, he ignored the obvious: people getting ill, friends dying, and his parents' continued encouragement about making wise choices. He was desperate to pretend that everything was still OK.

It was about this time that the Thai government began to strictly enforce the condom policy and other related laws, even to the point of shutting down a number of sex-service businesses. Public warnings became frequent. But HIV/AIDS continued to be shrouded in misinformation and gossip.

As Wayo became more desperate to hide his confusion and worry, he began to drink heavily. He slept only in spurts, smoked too much, and ate poorly.

A Family's Love, a Village's Fear

The test came back HIV-positive. Without Wayo's permission, officials notified Yanyong of Wayo's blood-test result. It was a shock for them both. But the truth also brought a sense of release that Wayo hadn't expected. He now had someone to share his burden. Right or wrong, father and son decided to keep the secret from Malee for the time being.

Wayo began classes, working toward his welding certificate. Yanyong learned what he could about HIV/AIDS. It was clear that Wayo would need a lot of love, support, and encouragement as the illness progressed.

Of course, Malee—who was still unaware of her son's illness—knew all about the needs of patients and their families from her work with HIV/AIDS cases in Chiang Kham. She was shocked when her efforts to share that knowledge were met with fear and rejection by her Ban Farm neighbors. After all, this was the community built on hope and inspiration, created to accept outcasts, and welcoming even to people with leprosy.

Her church women's group hesitated when Malee urged them to visit and pray with local families living with AIDS, even though a number of victims were members of their congregation.

Many were completely ignorant about the virus, thinking it was spread by casual contact, such as drinking from the same cup, or hugging. Some people completely cut their ties with "infected" families, going as far as to cross the street to avoid them. And there was misdirected judgment and anger toward those who were labeled as having brought the disease into Ban Farm. Some saw HIV/AIDS as just punishment from God for immoral actions.

Malee recalls with sadness those early days when families sometimes had to bury their loved one without even a pastor present to conduct the funeral.

Crisis Changes Lives Forever

By 1994 Wayo's situation had deteriorated. He had become withdrawn and fatigued. He had lost his appetite, and suffered constant headaches and bouts of diarrhea. Malee asked Wayo on several occasions if he was OK and always got the same answer: "I'm fine." Desperately wanting to hear this, she did not push for the truth. But it became obvious that something was terribly wrong. At the urging of Wayo's older sister, a nurse, Yanyong finally told his wife.

"I really think Yanyong was concerned she wouldn't bear up under the news," Coats says. "Like many Thai families, they favored their younger sons." When Malee heard the news that her son was dying, she cried out, "My boy! My dear, dear boy!"

The prognosis was worse than expected. Due to the lack of early medical treatment and the way Wayo had run down his body, the virus was taking over rapidly. A doctor estimated Wayo had only a month or so to live. The doctor advised Malee and Yanyong to give their son whatever he wanted to eat, whenever he wanted it. One day when the Mae Kok River flooded, Yanyong walked all the way to Chiang Rai just to buy a certain food for Wayo.

"Yanyong was unique because he was so actively involved in Wayo's care," says Coats, who by this time had moved to neighboring Laos with his new wife to do community development work. "I'm sure he helped with giving baths and those things that only a patient housewife does."

The Charoenboons knew Wayo had to stay active. He needed to know he still had value, even on days when Malee and her daughter had to help him dress and feed himself. When he became so ill he had to drop out of school just weeks short of graduation, the family gave Wayo the responsibility to tend the family's banana trees and papaya crop. With his family's support, Wayo learned that he was more than just his disease, and that he could still contribute. Malee, Yanyong, and the rest of the family continued to love Wayo and tell him how lovable he was in God's sight. Even as his body got weaker, his faith and trust in his heavenly Father grew stronger.

Confronting Ignorance

However, Malee began to experience firsthand how people respond in cruel and heartless ways—ways that just added to her fear and frustration. Some in the village stopped speaking to her. Close neighbors, who once stopped in to borrow spices, no longer came over. Even the few friends who had the courage and love to rally around the Charoenboons were reserved and uneasy.

Responding to the community's fear and ignorance, Malee tried to educate her visitors, as few as they were. They would sit together on the front porch, looking down on the chickens scratching and pecking the dirt, while Malee patiently explained about HIV/AIDS and answered every question. It helped a little.

Malee prayed regularly. She asked God why he had let this happen to her family. She relied on God, but there were many times when she doubted herself: Had she done all she could to protect her children? Would she be trusted to teach and minister again? Could she give Wayo the care he needed?

Malee knew she could not control the situation—Wayo was going to die soon. But she prayed over and over for God to spare her son the severe physical pain and anguish she had witnessed in other cases.

Meanwhile, the call inside Malee to reach out to other AIDS families was stronger than ever. Now it was more than compassion that drew her. The connection went much deeper to mutual loss, grief, anger, and tears. For the first time, she understood fully what families of AIDS victims go through.

Sadly, HIV/AIDS cases in her village were multiplying, even among Christian families. Again, Malee encouraged her women's group to provide more practical support for those in need. Two women, out of a congregation of nearly 1,100 members, stepped forward to work with Malee in a focused outreach. These three women became the link between several families—going into their homes, praying, offering encouragement and practical information about AIDS.

Malee and Yanyong were among the active members and founders of a group that started calling itself "With Love and Concern." They got together for worship, and sometimes for special events or speakers. But mostly, they were just there for each other, breaking barriers of isolation with love and concern, as the name said.

Soon more and more visitors from other communities started showing up on the Charoenboon porch, seeking Malee's guidance and wisdom.

They wanted to begin their own HIV/AIDS support groups. Ban Farm began coming to terms with the epidemic. Yesterday it had been Wayo. Then it was someone else's son or daughter. Tomorrow it could be an elder in the church. People were finally getting the picture: AIDS does not discriminate.

God Answers Malee's Prayers

By 1995 the government's anti-AIDS campaign was at its peak, with hourly public-service announcements on radio and TV. Sex establishments reported 95 percent condom use (it had been 14 percent only a few years earlier).[7] As a result, Thailand achieved a significant drop in sexually transmitted infections. It was the first bit of relief for the country since the nightmare began.

Wayo had received such good care at home that he only had to go to the hospital once for major treatment. But still the end was inevitable. Finally Wayo died at home, surrounded by family and upheld in prayer, after living a year longer than the doctor originally predicted. Remarkably, there were no bedsores or lesions on his body, and he was not in pain. Malee thanked God; not once did she have to turn her eyes away from her son's suffering, as she always feared she might.

The loss of Wayo was a huge blow to Malee. But her desire to work closely with AIDS patients and their families grew stronger with every funeral she attended.

"She's made a solid commitment to help these families," Coats says. "I think the fact that her son contracted and died of AIDS just strengthened Malee's conviction that this was where God wanted her, and it's what God wants her to do."

During the next year, the With Love and Concern group grew to 26 families. Malee received a grant from UNICEF to provide stipends for the two women working with her. Malee refused to take any pay, believing her work was not a job, but a calling from God.

With Love and Concern continued to coordinate home visits and special get-togethers for families to share stories and comfort. They also began a scholarship program for children, offered supplemental income opportunities for surviving members of AIDS families, provided training for caregivers, and hosted community education events.

As 1995 drew to a close, approximately 40 HIV/AIDS support groups had cropped up throughout northern Thailand, many modeling themselves on Malee's efforts. Today, that number continues to grow at rate of 10 to 20 new groups annually.[6]

"As a result of Thai Christians getting involved in AIDS issues, it's become our trademark: Christians care for people with AIDS," Coats says. "Christians are now known for responding to people who are suffering."

Financial Challenges

The United Nations estimated that the direct cost of HIV/AIDS in Thailand would reach between $7 billion and $9 billion by the new millennium.[7] Clearly, the epidemic threatened to derail the nation's economic productivity as swiftly as it wiped out the savings and livelihoods of individual families. Breadwinners either died or became too ill to work, and recurring medical expenses sometimes equaled half a villager's monthly wages.

No one understood this vicious financial cycle better than the families in Malee's support group, so the group decided it had to do something to help with this part of the AIDS tragedy. Malee's group made and sold crafts, and raised cash crops such as peppers and corn to help with financial needs in affected families. In 1997, two years after joining World Concern and moving to Chiang Rai, Coats found himself climbing the steps to Malee's front porch for a "visit."

Malee proposed obtaining one large loan that she would manage for the group. Individual families could borrow against this pot of money for various income-generating purposes. Borrowers would pay interest to the support group. The interest from these loans would be invested in savings and grow. Eventually, the support group would have enough principal to become self-sufficient.

"So Malee asked us to function like a bank, providing a block loan," Coats says. But unlike local banks that rarely agree to loan to high-risk AIDS families, the support group wouldn't require a person's land title as collateral. "There is a mutual guarantee. Members within the [support] group must partner with each other, agreeing to help if repayment becomes a problem."

Coats and Malee began a 12-month trial run. By the end of that year, Malee's group had paid back all of the 20,000 Baht (US$500) they had borrowed.

After successfully managing a couple more loans through World Concern's fund (now called the Thai Concern Foundation), Malee's group was ready to strike out on its own. By adding a compulsory savings program to their strategy, member families have accumulated approximately 100,000 Baht (US$2,500) of capital in their group fund—five times the amount they initially borrowed from World Concern.

And in the process they had drawn a fractured community together in very real and practical ways.

Hope for the Next Generation

Last year Yanyong died of a kidney infection unrelated to HIV/AIDS. Even though Malee has seen a lot of dying in 12 years, she keeps turning toward life, working to make things better for the next generation.

Malee's two small grandchildren play at her feet, and she wonders, "Am I doing enough to help keep them safe?" Part of Malee's continuing concern stems from reports of rising HIV/AIDS infections among youths and injecting drug users in Thailand. Having made some progress against the disease, the country is experiencing an undercurrent of complacency. She even hears that some teens believe, tragically, that AIDS is curable.

Feeling a sense of urgency for the young people in her village, Malee is organizing a new group: Youth Against Drugs and AIDS. The focus is on prevention and education. Without such programs for young people, the UN has predicted that Asia's number of AIDS victims will balloon—possibly becoming even higher than Africa's.[8]

"AIDS is a tragedy that has affected our country and caused an enormous amount of grief and suffering," Coats says. "Through it all, Christians like Malee, with her commitment and witness, have become recognized as people who care."

So much has changed for the better in Ban Farm. Bewilderment and anger still surround HIV/AIDS, but the community has regained its compassion. In doing so, it has found dignity. Malee and her family teach us that we can choose life in the midst of death, love in the midst of fear.

Notes

1. Family Health International and UNAIDS reports.
2. UNAIDS and World Health Organization 2002 Update.
3. CIA World Factbook 2002.
4. UN General Assembly on HIV/AIDS, June 25, 2001.
5. BBC News Web Site, December 1, 2000.
6. Oxfam Horizons (online), April 1996.
7. Agence France-Presse (online), November 12, 1999.
8. Bangkok Post (online, SEA-AIDS), November 27, 2002.

CHAPTER 11
VINOD SHAH AND MATHEW SANTOSH THOMAS

FIGHTING HIV/AIDS IN INDIA

The Indian Scenario

The context of AIDS: Indian health and development

India has 16 percent of the world's population. Despite major changes in the economy, the health status of the majority of the population, which is primarily rural, continues to be matter of concern.

Indicators	Estimate	Year	Source
Population (millions)	1,027	2001	Census of India, 2001
Decadal growth rate (percent)	21.34	2001	Census of India, 2001
Sex Ratio (females per 1,000 males)	933	2001	Census of India, 2001
Crude Birth Rate (per 1,000 population)	25	1999	UNPOP
Crude Death Rate (per 1,000 population)	9	1999	UNPOP
Total Fertility Rate	3.3	1995-2000	Human Development Report, 2002
Infant Mortality (per 1,000)	69	2000	Human Development Report, 2002
Maternal Mortality Rate (per 100,000 births)	540	1999	Human Development Report, 2002
Human Development Index Ranking	124	2002	Human Development Report, 2002
Literacy (Total in percent)	65.38	2001	Census of India, 2001
Male	75.85	2001	Census of India, 2001
Female	54.16	2001	Census of India, 2001
People below poverty line (%)	35	2000	Human Development Report, 2002
Life expectancy in years	63.3	2000	Human Development Report, 2002
Per capita GNP (US $)	440	1999	UNPOP
Physicians (per 100,000 population)	48	1990-1999	Human Development Report, 2002

(http://www.youandaids.org/AsiaPacific/India.asp)

Socioeconomic scenario

India is a country of striking contrasts. It has a population over a billion, one of the fastest economic growth rates in the world since the 1980s, and a robust Information Technology industry that is projected to earn about $50 billion by 2008. India also has the highest concentration of poverty anywhere in the world.

According to 1999 figures, about 350 million people in India are living below the poverty line. The country accounts for 40 percent of the world's poor. Its social indicators are still poor by most measures of human development. At 9.6 percent of its Gross Domestic Product, its fiscal deficit is one of the highest in the world.

Malnutrition poses a continuing constraint to India's development. Despite improvements in health and in the economy, malnutrition remains a silent emergency in India. The World Bank estimates that malnutrition costs India at least $10 billion annually in terms of lost productivity, illness, and death.

The rise in literacy rates over the last decade indicates India's progress in education. From 1991–2001, the overall literacy rate increased from 52 percent to 65 percent. Yet, just under half of Indian women are still illiterate. About 40 million primary school age children are not in school. Most of these are girls from the poorest, socially excluded households. Only about one-third of girls aged 5–14 years complete the constitutionally mandated eight years of education.

Evolution of the AIDS epidemic

In 2003, 17 years after the first case of HIV/AIDS was detected in India, more than 4 million people were infected with HIV in the country.

Official statistics do not really capture the grim reality.

The World Health Organization has officially acknowledged a massive underreporting of AIDS cases within India. Researchers estimate that fewer than 25 percent of the total AIDS cases in India are actually reported. They say social stigma, lack of awareness, and poor infrastructure are the main reasons for this underreporting. In addition, India may have many carriers who are not aware they are HIV-positive. Very underdeveloped

Figure 1: Evolution of the Epidemic

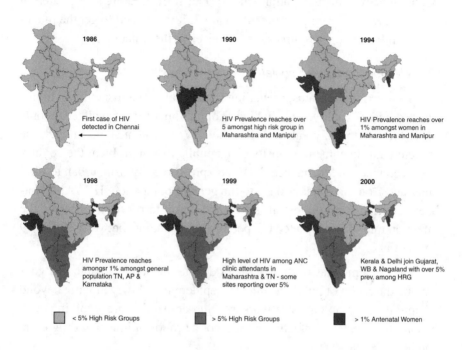

Source: NACO Surveillance, 2000

Key statistics

Estimated number of people living with HIV/AIDS (in millions):

Year	1998	1999	2000	2001
No. of cases	3.5	3.7	3.86	3.97

Estimated number of new infections (in millions):

Year	1999	2000	2001
No. of cases	0.2	0.16	0.16

Source: National AIDS Control Organization

surveillance systems, pervasive migration, and extreme discrimination are also contributing factors. Approximately 75 percent of the country's population lives in rural India. Due to poor infrastructure and clustering of resources and services in the urban areas, it is difficult to get the much-needed information, resources, and services to these people.

Overall impact on Indian society

Socioeconomic status, prevailing traditional social ills, cultural myths on sex and sexuality, and a huge population of marginalized people make India extremely vulnerable to the HIV/AIDS epidemic. In fact, the epidemic has become the most serious public health problem the country has faced since independence. HIV has spread rapidly from urban to rural areas and from high-risk groups to the general population. HIV/AIDS has been reported from almost all states and union territories. Currently the infection rate is an estimated 0.7 percent among adults between 15 and 49 years of age.

The epidemic has become a major developmental challenge that goes beyond the realm of public health. The epidemic is slowly moving beyond its initial focus among sex workers. Sub-epidemics are evolving with potentially explosive infection rates among groups of injecting drug users and homosexuals.

The epidemic continues to shift toward women and young people. About 25 to 45 percent of all HIV infections occur in women. This in turn increases mother to child transmission rates and the prevalence of HIV among children. In India, adverse gender bias adds to the biological vulnerability of women. They are not generally able to insist that their sexual partners use condoms, which provide some protection against infection.

Some 37 percent of the people with AIDS are in the most economically productive age group of 15 to 29 years. In industrialized cities such as Mumbai and Chennai, the high death toll in this age group could severely hurt the economy. The AIDS burden is beginning to be felt in states affected early in the epidemic. Certain referral hospitals in Mumbai and in the states of Maharashtra, Tamil Nadu, and Manipur have recorded 20 to 40 percent bed occupancy rates among HIV-positive patients.

The overburdened, underdeveloped, and underfunded public health care system cannot meet the growing demand for treatment of HIV-related infections. Lack of skilled staff and infrastructure, and easy access to addictive drugs have led to a majority of the population having poorer and poorer access to quality health care.

The Impact of Indian Value Systems on Responsiveness to HIV/AIDS

India is the birthplace of most of the major Eastern religions. Despite the varied belief systems, these Eastern religions have similarities in worldviews and values.

Handed down through generations, these value systems and worldviews continue to permeate every area of life, including attitudes concerning health and medical care, community life and caring, and socioeconomic systems.

In addition, India's centuries-old caste system has hurt development. Unfortunately, it continues to influence health and development even today. Other factors include the continuing low status of women in the community, changing cultural and social norms and values, and the more recent rise of religious fanaticism.

Cultural influences and sexuality

Traditional Indian culture places great importance on the family, which provides strong support to individuals. Most Indian religious systems frown upon any attempt to talk about sex or sexuality.

However, commercialization, Westernization, and globalization are creating chinks in these age-old sociocultural traditional systems. This is particularly true in the changing value systems of the younger generation.

In the midst of traditionally accepted norms—such as high caste men exploiting low caste women, polygamy and polyandry, promiscuous tribal systems, and temple prostitution—a milieu where unsafe sexual behaviors flourish and develop has been created. We can see this in India's high incidence of both HIV and other sexually transmitted diseases in rural and urban communities.

Unfortunately, the Indian response to the AIDS epidemic has focused on condom usage and on so-called safe sex, rather than on behavior change or any revisions of the value system.

Culture and care

Eastern religious worldviews consider the body merely as unclean physical matter. People in these systems see a dichotomy in which the body is a "dirty" prison enclosing a "clean" soul. There is therefore no role for compassion that ministers to the whole person.

This lack of understanding of the connectedness of body and soul has led to the competition-driven commercialization and professionalization of medicine. To exclude lower-paid and lower-skilled community workers, the medical profession has mystified medicine.

In a belief system where suffering is seen as karmic repayment of debt for past sins, caring for the HIV-affected and -infected is not a priority. People fear that alleviating someone's suffering can hinder debt repayment in the karmic system. Those who provide medical care do so largely to earn good karma for their own lives, not because they particularly care for the sick.

HIV/AIDS care is not a financially viable area of health care. In the context of other pressing health care needs, many Indians see palliative and terminal care as wastes of resources. Therefore, it is no surprise that integrating HIV/AIDS care into existing health care systems has yet to take place.

This discrimination by health care systems, the existing misconceptions regarding HIV/AIDS, and the country's cultural taboos have combined to worsen the stigma associated with HIV/AIDS in India.

Worldview and its effect on social support systems

In a male-dominated society where women are seen as second-class citizens, HIV can have a devastating impact. Widows, especially those who are HIV-infected, receive little support. Orphans, prostitutes, and drug users usually become destitute.

Because belief in karma and rebirth are the guiding principles of life, the poor and marginalized do not find any system of care or support. This is especially true if they are HIV-infected or -affected.

Commercialization and HIV/AIDS

A lot of money has flowed into the country to tackle this epidemic in recent years. However, this has led to a commercialization of the response to AIDS. Most efforts address the technically simpler and easier issues: information, education, and communication, such as condom promotion.

This mushrooming of responses to HIV/AIDS has also highlighted the lack of holistic model programs that address root causes beyond providing compassion and continuum of care.

Principles Guiding EHA's Response

The Emmanuel Hospital Association (EHA) is a Christian charitable organization with facilities and a long-term presence in the northern and northeastern parts of India. As the epidemic started becoming visible in these areas, EHA sought to more effectively address the sociocultural issues outlined above.

The principles that guided EHA's response to HIV/AIDS include:

a. Relationship-based behavioral modification: Any attempt at prevention will focus on behavioral modification rather than so-called "safe sex." The focus is on relationships in the context of the family.

b. Care in the context of the family which is holistic: Any intervention for care will focus on caring for the body, mind, and soul and on a continuum of care where the family plays an important role.

c. Abundant life and hope as the goals: We want to bring HIV-infected and -affected families and communities closer to the hope and abundant life available in Christ.

EHA Experience with Behavioral Change

Behavioral change should have the following characteristics:

a. It needs to be integrated with the existing health care and community interventions.

b. It should focus on values, and the target should be young people.

c. Values education will highlight biblically derived principles of sexuality, marriage, and family.

d. Rather than being a one-time interaction, behavioral change occurs over time through repeated encounters.

e. Behavioral change should also include the caregivers—teaching them compassionate, caring, and nonjudgmental attitudes.

Putting these principles into action, EHA created a behavioral change education module with 14 lessons. EHA community health workers and peer group educators are using it to teach adolescents in eight North Indian rural communities.

This module includes topics such as self-image, goal-setting, reproductive health, HIV/AIDS, marriage and family, and so on. Adolescents meet with a group leader once a week for 12 to 14 sessions, using interactive group learning techniques. The hope is that as a new generation imbibes these values, the communities and the families they live in will be changed, thus reducing the spread of HIV/AIDS.

Changing the Culture and Understanding of Care

As EHA's hospitals and units began caring for those affected by HIV/AIDS, we realized that our organization needed to change paradigms in many areas to make an impact in the lives of these people and their families.

The following paradigm shifts were required:

a. From cure to care.

b. From an "in hospital" to a "beyond the hospital" approach.

c. From a "body alone" to a multi-sector approach.

d. From embarrassment and judgmentalism to a respectful focus on the marginalized and "special people."

e. From uncoordinated work to networking for greater impact.

f. From callousness to ushering in a true caring culture of unconditional acceptance.

a. Cure to care

In a culture that has no concept of care, even Christian institutions can lose the needed emphasis on care. Medical education in India prepares doctors and nurses with a narrow "cure only" orientation. Christian institutions are not exempt, and EHA is no exception. Redeeming the caring culture was the first step EHA had to take to integrate AIDS care. This involved redefining the concept of care as being for the whole person: body, soul, and mind.

We had to train the staff in whole person care, and we created teams to carry out this emphasis in these hospitals.

The objective was to make sure that hospitals had staff teams catering to the emotional and spiritual needs of the patients, in addition to their health care needs. Once these systems are in place, AIDS care integration becomes possible, even easy. This approach has worked so well that a few hospitals involved in the holistic care of people living with HIV/AIDS have extended this kind of care to other patients.

Story 1

P.S., now 30, was born and brought up in a small village in Bihar as the eldest son. P.S. started working as a farmer as well as learning carpentry at the age of 14 in his village. At 16, he got married to a girl, 15, from the same village. After two years of marriage, their first daughter was born. They now have three daughters and two sons. The eldest daughter has also married.

At times, it was difficult for P.S. to earn enough money in the village to feed his family. He went to Kathmandu, the capital of Nepal, to seek a better income. There some of his friends suggested that he go to Mumbai where he would be able to easily get a job and earn good money. During his first year in Mumbai, he went home every four months. After that, he did not go home for five or six years and never sent money to his family. In Mumbai, he visited brothels twice. He was also sexually involved with a married woman. P.S. also used prostitutes.

After several years, he became sick and went to the hospital. His blood was tested for HIV, but the doctor did not tell him his test result. Frequently sick, eventually P.S. came back to his family. His health still poor, he went to Patna, the capital of Bihar, and had another HIV test. There the doctor told him he was HIV-positive. His wife was not informed. One day he was very sick and had no money to go to Patna. Some village citizens suggested he go to Duncan Hospital, a unit of Emmanuel Hospital Association, in Raxaul. There he received a blood transfusion, as he was very anemic. The doctor then referred him to the ACT Project. ACT teams are taking care of his physical and spiritual needs. The team has provided blood tests and counseling for the whole family. Unfortunately, his wife and youngest son are also infected. The ACT team is now caring for them. The ACT Project has taken two of the children to a mission school. They may become orphans within a few years.

b. Looking beyond the hospital

Care for people living with HIV/AIDS cannot be confined to the hospitals alone. As a patient passes through the various stages of the illness, he needs care and support at home, in a hospice, and in a community.

At home, he will need emotional and social support. He will also need treatment for minor illnesses. Patients who are admitted and discharged from the hospitals or AIDS hospices run by EHA are followed up in their homes by trained health care workers or volunteers from community-based organizations. These people teach, counsel, and support family members to provide care at home.

EHA had to set up administrative systems to follow up and care for patients at home. This is called home-based care.

EHA hospices provide care for people with acute short-term illnesses. Some terminally ill patients also receive care for pain management. Finally, we seek to set up a community care system for HIV/AIDS affected and infected people. This means community leaders and members will need training and awareness.

EHA had to look beyond the paradigm of mission hospitals to set up "out of hospital" models of care to provide comprehensive care.

c. Multi-sector approach

Involving people who are not health care workers is key. Health care workers have to motivate, mobilize, and train community-based volunteers.

EHA AIDS care programs train volunteers in the community in providing and supervising home care. The involvement of community-based organizations and churches makes care and support more comprehensive, holistic, and sustainable.

d. Focusing on marginalized and special people

Rural mission hospitals cater to low-income communities that do not have access to health care. But even these hospitals do not generally cater to "special people" at high risk for HIV/AIDS: intravenous drug abusers, prostitutes, hermaphrodites, transvestites (known as Hijras in India), migrant workers, and truck drivers.

Regular clinical services generally do not provide opportunities for these groups to receive care. Mission hospitals have stepped in to reduce the transmission of HIV and to provide care and support to those people already infected.

Focused training programs for these groups can go a long way in transforming many of these people. Similarly focused training programs can also change the culture of care in hospitals.

EHA hospitals and projects have implemented a variety of programs, including needle exchanges and detoxification.

Story 2

D.P., now 32, was born in Kathmandu into a middle class family. He had four sisters and four brothers. When he was a boy, pressured by his school friends, he started taking drugs. In college, he began injecting drugs. After years had passed this way, he had to drop out. The family stopped supporting him financially. D.P. married a girl, and they had two children. But the marriage did not change his behavior, and family fights continued. His father gave D.P. his inheritance, which he sold for drugs.

D.P. ran away to the streets, injecting drugs and sharing needles and syringes with his friends. He came to Raxaul because drugs were more available. He had injection abscesses on his legs and hands when the ACT team met him. Found to be HIV-positive, D.P. became a regular client who exchanged needles and syringes. One day he showed up with his whole body swollen and unable to get up by himself. Near death, he received treatment. Slowly he began to feel better. His family members began to visit him and became involved in his care.

e. Networking and partnerships

Mission hospitals cannot function in isolation. Hospitals need to become nerve centers for community networking and partnership. Networking includes opening hospitals to private practitioners, local leaders, and community-based organizations. Working together, they can create a milieu to discourage high-risk behaviors while providing unconditional care.

Many of the projects and hospitals work hand in hand with local leaders and organizations to build the capacity of one another in AIDS care and prevention. Networking in some projects has led to churches or community-based organizations coming forward to support medical care and sponsor anti-retroviral therapy of people with AIDS.

f. Unconditional acceptance

Stigma and discrimination are integral parts of the AIDS phenomenon. To make a difference in this environment, EHA provides unconditional acceptance for people with high-risk behaviors as an entry point for caring, as well as for needed behavioral modification. Safe needle exchange and condom distribution programs, as uncomfortable as they may make us as Christians, are part of this approach. We also seek to reduce the stigma and discrimination these people experience.

Hospital and community-based safe needle exchange programs and condom promotion programs become a bridge of communication with these communities. Once we build rapport with them, caregivers can influence them to seek professional and spiritual counselling along with drug detoxification. EHA has seen radical transformation in the lives of many through this approach. It also plays an important role in reducing the stigma and discrimination these communities experience.

This can happen only in the context of what we call an AIDS-friendly health care system. AIDS-friendly hospitals have staff who are properly trained and motivated to care for and support people with HIV/AIDS. Such hospitals also must provide infection control and waste management systems.

As AIDS care gets integrated into these hospitals, the stigma related to the infection wanes in the community.

Networking and partnering with community-based organizations in reaching out to high-risk communities and people living with HIV/AIDS helps reduce the stigma associated with the epidemic. This paves the way for unconditional acceptance.

Story 3

L.N.T. was an unwilling divorcee who had to leave behind a husband and three children. Feeling a void in her life, she started drinking. Soon, she was an alcoholic.

With no reliable family support, she left home. Soon she did not even have enough money for a drink, so she decided to sell her body. Involved in unprotected sex, she soon contracted HIV.

We met her during our outreach and asked her to come to our hospice.

Fed up with her life, she joined a spiritual camp organized by SHALOM, one of our ministries. There, she was deeply convicted of her sin and accepted God's unconditional divine love.

Today she attends church services and has a burden for her family members.

Developing Replicable Models

Creating replicable models and increasing impact through multiplying responses is important in a vast country like India. EHA programs focus on developing model responses that will fulfill needs in individual communities. These programs in turn train and build the capacity of other organizations.

Other EHA units and other nongovernmental and governmental organizations have taken up some of these programs, including the Manipur continuum model and the needle exchange program.

Lessons Learned

- Addressing an issue like AIDS involves a multipronged approach and paradigm changes in various care-related issues.

- AIDS-friendly health care systems happen only when organizations intentionally address them.

- Setting up AIDS care systems helps health care organizations to re-gain a culture of care, which many have lost or create a culture of care, which many have never had, such as in the case of India.

- Hospitals can play a major role in changing the culture of care in a community and reducing the stigma and discrimination associated with the infection.

- Unconditional acceptance of the infected is absolutely essential for any program or project.

- Care has to go beyond the hospital to the homes, hospices, and community.

CHAPTER 12

PETER MEADOWS

A LETTER TO THE U.K. CHURCH

Dear Church in the United Kingdom,

Greetings from just one of your number who stands amazed at your visionary and sacrificial response to the HIV/AIDS crises. I am truly humbled to be counted as part of you.

So easily could your knees have jerked in the direction of judgmental condemnation. Churches through the centuries have managed that with great skill. But not you. Instead, you gave birth to pioneers who have shown courage and compassion. Better still, you have not stopped there. To their vision you have added your own commitment and sacrifice, making an impact on your own nation and even the global community.

Not that this is a time to bask in the past. The incoming tide of need seems relentless, and of those to whom much has been given, much will be expected. Before this letter is through, I will spell out a little of what that could mean. But first, let's honor your heroes. Those among you who have never stopped to reflect on their accomplishments probably think you have better things to do, more urgent tasks to perform, more important needs to meet.

So please step back and glimpse what these warriors of yours have already done. You'll be impressed.

The signs of this strange new disease first hit the U.K. headlines in the early 1980s, to be greeted with ignorance and fear. Thankfully, only a fringe minority among you were heard screaming "gay plague" and "divine judgment." Meanwhile, from your midst arose those with a more biblically thoughtful and Jesus-inspired response. Among them was Patrick Dixon.

"How Could I Possibly Turn Away?"

Dixon, a hospice doctor and an active lay Christian, first encountered the virus while watching a man in a hospital side room, suffocating to death.

"I was completely traumatized," Dixon says. "The man was on his own; with no family around. No one held his hand. He wasn't even getting the right treatment. Until then, I'd been rather unsympathetic towards people with AIDS. Now I realized here was a human being, made in the image of God—and how could I possibly turn away?"

Dixon was appalled by the cruel combination of discrimination and medical ignorance being dealt to AIDS sufferers then. Even some of his colleagues were unwilling to look after them. Worse, the patients he came across were "dying badly"—as he puts it. So, seeking to obey Jesus Christ, Dixon helped set up a new team within Britain's National Health Service to focus on their care. That's right, U.K. Church, one of your own got the ball rolling. Before long, others were helping, too, as Dixon talked to local congregations about what he saw.

After fighting through the mist of doubt, fear, and confusion, Dixon caught the attention of a Christian publisher. The result was a groundbreaking book, *The Truth About AIDS*, published in 1987. It exposed the myths and cover-ups, urging the church to join the fight. And you did.

One result was the pioneering Christian organization ACET—AIDS Care Education and Training—that Dixon founded. Now it is an international network. To date, more than 1.3 million pupils have received ACET booklets about HIV and sexual health. More than 1,500 with AIDS have received practical help at home.

Today, the vision of Patrick Dixon's book is still being worked out. And the author has found large numbers of fellow activists. Many went to work with ACET before starting their own initiatives. As Dixon himself comments: "There are many who have selflessly sacrificed and given of themselves to show God's unconditional love, to save lives through effective prevention, respecting historic Christian values. In the 1980s, everywhere I went, if I was talking about the Christian response to AIDS,

I would find people coming up, saying, 'The same Holy Spirit has spoken to me; I need to act.'"

"This Is Where God Wanted Me to Be"

Such a response created another of your great pioneers. The famous Mildmay mission hospital was founded in 1866 as a Christian response to a cholera epidemic among London's poor. Today it is at the forefront of compassionate action in the U.K. and around the world. And, in 1988 it provided Europe's first AIDS palliative care unit, staffed by Christians from the very top down to the volunteers who cleaned the soiled sheets.

At the heart of Mildmay's story is Dr. Veronica Moss. In 1986, she was established as a family doctor in a country town. Yet she agreed to go for an interview at the old mission hospital and was unanimously appointed by the board.

"What I came to was a derelict old building, with one refurbished ward and kitchens, but little else," she remembers. Asked to research Mildmay's possible responses to the AIDS epidemic, she was both excited and challenged. Mildmay entered the AIDS arena by developing an AIDS terminal care facility.

The first AIDS unit opened in February 1988. Initial referrals were for terminal care—young men and women who thought they had only a week or two to live. But in the care of Mildmay's intensively trained staff, many improved. The good news spread, although some people opposed the hospital's Christian ethos. But as Dr. Moss explains, "We were simply responding, as a Christian organization, to a need in the same way that we saw Jesus behave towards marginalized people in the Gospels."

Mildmay—*your* Mildmay—swiftly became the national model for a Christian response, setting your light on a hill, displaying the good works Jesus prepared for his church. New research and academic initiatives have followed, with Mildmay now leading the field in specialist HIV/AIDS care. Each year, the hospital admits hundreds of men, women, and children.

Veronica Moss became a success story in her own right, awarded the prestigious Fellowship of the Royal College of Physicians in 1998, and three years later a Hero in Medicine award for her outstanding contribution to HIV/AIDS care. And she has done it all simply because Jesus called her, and God gave her the strength to respond. As she puts it, "Through it all I have had the conviction this is where God wanted me to be."

The impact has reached to the heart of the U.K. Health Service and touched individual lives from the late Diana, Princess of Wales, who made several visits to the hospital, to anonymous patients who have died with no other friend to hold their hand.

Making all this possible is a whole army of Christians who give financially and encourage others to do the same. Without church support—*your* support—Mildmay would never receive the £1 million a year needed to keep its doors open.

Foundation Stones

As the saga of Mildmay shows—with its history of helping the infirm—the foundation stones had long been laid for your remarkable response to AIDS. In your own "golden age" of the early church in Britain and Ireland—during the fifth and sixth centuries—Christian monks dedicated themselves to prayer and gave hospitality to the poor and sick. The monastery at Kildare founded by Brigid was renowned for its generous hospitality, becoming known as "the City of the Poor." When King Oswin gave a horse to Aidan of Lindisfarne, Aidan promptly passed the gift on to the first poor person he met.

Such acts of selflessness have shaped your spiritual DNA down through the ages. Centuries later, that joint mantle of social concern and spiritual transformation fell on an Anglican evangelist named John Wesley. He preached a gospel that inspired people to take up social causes—such as the emancipation of slaves—in the name of Christ. Just before his death in 1791, Wesley urged William Wilberforce to continue the good work. Wilberforce and the so-called "Clapham Sect" pioneered Christian activism in the dark days of eighteenth and nineteenth century England.

Sadly, for much of the twentieth century, the shining sword of social activism and spiritual renewal became a rusty relic. Those of us committed to the historic faith used more of our energy fighting Liberal theology than combating social injustice and helping the poor. We were more fearful of embracing a social gospel than of not embracing those desperately in need of God's love in action.

All of which makes it surprising that you were able to grasp the HIV/AIDS crisis so firmly. But the reason why also comes from our own ranks. Take a bow, such influential thinkers as Anglican theologian John Stott, who mightily contributed to the first Lausanne Congress. Here, commitment to the good news being both word and deed—with the two being totally inseparable—set the tone for what was to come.

It did not take long for such radical rethinking to become deeply ingrained in the Christian community. Senior evangelicals took up the Lausanne challenge—putting justice and compassion high on the agenda of thinking Christians in the U.K. The launch and activities of TEAR (The Evangelical Alliance Relief) Fund fanned these flames. It became both a means to express a growing Christian social conscience and a major influence toward individuals having one. And who can dare underestimate the impact of the annual Easter-time event Spring Harvest, which continues to draw some 70,000 Christians of all ages? Here the good news in word and deed is not only taught but demonstrated through championing initiatives against poverty and injustice.

In that social climate John Stott even included a section specifically about AIDS in his groundbreaking book, *Issues Facing Christians Today* (IVP). After some declared HIV/AIDS to be God's judgment on homosexuals, Stott wanted you to face the facts. He proposed a threefold Christian response with three clear characteristics:

1. *Theological*: Jesus warned us not to interpret calamities as God's specific judgments (Luke 13:1–5), yet Scripture's timely warning is that a person will reap exactly what he sows (Galatians 6:7). AIDS is part of the cost we all pay for society's permissive "experiment."

2. *Pastoral:* As one AIDS patient said, "Don't judge me. I'm living under my own judgement. What I need is for you to walk with me." Sufferers need most of all the care and fellowship of the Body of Christ.

3. *Educational*: Churches should play a major role in challenging society to sexual self-control and faithfulness, and pointing to Jesus as the source of forgiveness and power.

Rather than merely making occasional evangelistic raids into enemy territory, Stott called you to "go out into the lost and lonely world, in order to live and love, to witness and serve," giving you compelling biblical reasons to do so.

Stott urged you to be a "healing community": "We do not deny that many people have contracted AIDS as a result of their own sexual promiscuity. But this provides us with no possible justification for shunning or neglecting them, any more than we would those who damage themselves through drunken driving or other forms of recklessness."

Of course, you could have chosen to be rabid and condemning—simply wagging fingers from afar. But instead you gave birth to Britain's hospice movement. Once again, you stepped in to bridge the gap and offer love to the unloved.

"The Kingdom is the Answer"

Just one of your number who has responded to the challenge is Amanda Willimans, a volunteer with ACET before moving out on her own. This former "prodigal"—a wandering daughter of the church—rediscovered her faith while helping on an AIDS ward. She made quite a leap from being an oil company executive to pushing a tea trolley down hospital corridors. But it turned her life around. "My heart started to break for what I saw happening in the young men's lives," she explains, "and I became passionate about the Jesus I'd learned about in Sunday school."

In 1989 Amanda visited a small residential unit for HIV-positive children in Washington D.C., called Grandma's House. Two children tumbled into the room and sat on her lap. The experience caused her to think about such youngsters in England. ACET helped to link her with a family whose 2-year-old son was HIV-positive. Amanda cared for him until his death. "It was the closest to heaven I have ever walked," she recalls. "I felt God say he wanted to call his people to minister very practically in the way that I had done. Out of that, Grandma's was born."

The aim of Grandma's is to demonstrate God's love to children and families affected by HIV/AIDS regardless of race, religion, sexuality, lifestyle, or any other factor. The name aims to convey a sense of extended family. Grandparents can have a special relationship with a child. Often in the case of HIV, it may actually be a grandparent who becomes the caregiver.

From those humble beginnings, Grandma's has touched 500 families in London, usually helping them in their own homes. The organization is currently working with 200, with 50 on a waiting list. So the challenge is considerable. "We give child-focused, practical support," says Amanda, "and reflect the Father's heart to them. They all know we are Christians. If people want to know about our faith, then we share that with them."

Grandma's has an unpaid full-time team of 14 and 120 part-timers. It has also launched initiatives in Ireland and India. "I'm passionate about the fact that the kingdom is the answer to this issue," Amanda explains, "and if God has the answer, it gets worked out through us, his people."

No Time to Fade

But, Church, as wonderful as all this is, is it enough? Dare we sit back to count our heroes and assume our role is done? For God's sake, no. You know all too well the size of the global challenge. The statistics are numbing. The human stories behind each number are heartbreaking. So, having started so well, don't fade now. This is not the moment to dust your trophies but to raise the level of your game.

As you do so, please be spurred on by five vital principles:

1. *HIV/AIDS is vastly more than an issue of human sexuality.* It is all too easy to assume the ravaging impact of HIV/AIDS is partly, if not mainly, "their fault"—that it's the result of widespread promiscuity, that if only they had "morals like ours" they wouldn't be in the mess they are in.

Suppose, in the U.K., we had written off the first deaths as being the result of witchcraft, not disease, because those deaths came mainly to businessmen in cities and were assumed to be the result of the powerful magic of their business rivals, rather than something directly related to sexual behavior. And suppose, as a result, the virus had become deeply ingrained in the "system" before our government knew enough to respond. That's exactly what has happened in Africa.

Suppose we had lacked both the money and the know-how to get the message out to the population—which was true of Africa. And when it came to doing so, the population we had to reach was exactly like theirs— including many which were scattered, rural, and not able to read. Suppose we had to face the prohibitive costs of screening blood supplies, a health system vastly more antiquated than our own, vast numbers of migrant workers separated from their families for long periods, the prevalence of rape by warring factions, and the impact of poverty in leaving women with the "choice" of either selling their bodies or seeing themselves and their children starve.

Suppose the basic cultural climate of the U.K. was that sex was not something you talked about. And suppose our government steadfastly refused to accept a link between HIV and death. Then what?

There are many similarities and parallels. Should you try to write off the global crisis as simply due to a lack of sexual morality you will be wide of the mark. Just imagine how the West would fare given our own prevailing morality. What would our own death toll and head count of AIDS-generated orphans be? We have been rich not only in material wealth but also in the knowledge and resources to help us minimize and respond to the threat of HIV/AIDS.

2. *Have a clear understanding of need.* You must see beyond simply those whose lives are at risk of ebbing away. Caring for those who are sick and dying is vital. But what of the wider fallout—the tens of thousands of children who now must care for younger siblings, cousins, and even ailing grandparents? Let's consider those communities where the economy, now and for the future, has been decimated. Think of the able-bodied people now missing and no longer able to contribute their knowledge, experience, and participation. Consider that those still left are sick, weak, and having to care for those around them. How can such communities compete in a global economy? How can they survive?

3. *Look beyond the statistics and begin to feel the pain.* If it is true that when one part of the body hurts, it all hurts, then how are you, the Church, hurting now? Where is the evidence of the pain that should be ours? As those behind the numbing statistics bury their dead and fight to survive, how does it impact our 68-TV-channel homes and three-calorie-rich-meals-a-day lifestyle? Where is the world AIDS crisis on the agenda of our wider network of churches, our denomination, our congregation, and our home group? How is it reflected in the way we as churches think, behave, plan, spend, and set our priorities? Would they be any different if HIV/AIDS didn't exist? One of the big frustrations for Amanda Williams, project director of Grandma's, is trying to crack a church culture that's busying itself so much with prayer meetings and home groups, that every diary is bulging with commitments.

In the face of a global mess, how about a church response of equal proportions? How about saying "no" to spending any more on ourselves for 10 years than the church in, say, Ephesus or Galatia would have spent on themselves during their first 10 years? Such a comparatively minor sacrifice would release vital resources to fund what must happen if those with no hope of a future are to receive one.

How about making sure that those who share our common humanity, including so many who also share our devotion to Jesus Christ, are never forgotten? Could you put a big red ribbon somewhere visible when you meet for worship and always include prayers for some aspect of the issue as part of your service? Could you pause for a minute of silence every time you meet to hold before God those in anguish? Could you use "Ideas For AIDS-Themed Worship," published by Mildmay, and available at www.mildmay.org.uk?

4. *Think internationally.* This will mean helping the churches in the developing world face up to the issue. Sadly, in many parts of the world, the impact of HIV/AIDS may be public though the issue is very private. The culture shies away from any mention of sex and its impact. The government follows in that wake—and so does the church.

Think about the contacts you have with national churches, either directly or through the agencies you support. How can you help them move from silence and secrecy to openness and honesty? What can you ask them? What example can you set?

5. *Help people become more holistic in their understanding of the gospel.* Don't assume they grasp the inseparableness of "word and deed." Some of our fellow believers in the most needy parts of the world are the least well taught on issues like this. Don't blame them; they have mainly been planted and nurtured by our own missionaries, and left without the scriptural insights of people such as Stott who have enriched and informed our own thinking. We need to help them be good news in deed as well as in word.

Dear sisters and brothers, you have started so well. Some of your people are already working in the fields under the heat of the day and the terrors of the night. Let us recognize anew God's overwhelming goodness to us and the responsibilities and opportunities this brings. Let us bring good news in word and deed to all impacted by HIV/AIDS—bravely, sacrificially, joyfully, and humbly.

As Jesus touched lepers with his hands and his life, may we do the same for those affected by HIV/AIDS in the twenty-first century. May the grace of our Lord Jesus Christ be with us all as we do.

Amen.

Sources: Interviews with Dr. Patrick Dixon, Amanda Williams, and Claire Wheatcroft; Highlights, Mildmay Mission Hospital's newsletter; Issues Facing Christians Today, by John Stott (IVP); ACET International's website (www.acet-international.com).

CHAPTER 13

E. ANNE PETERSON

FROM MISSIONARY DOCTOR TO POLICY-MAKER: HOW ONE CHRISTIAN CONFRONTS AIDS

My life has been full of extraordinary and unexpected opportunities. I have seen first-hand the devastation of AIDS on individuals, families, and communities. While the HIV/AIDS crisis seems hopeless, today there are signs that we can win the war against this deadly disease. This is the story of my personal journey as a doctor dealing with AIDS. It will not only chronicle some of the history of the epidemic but also show the opportunities for individual Christians and the church to bring hope and leadership to the war on AIDS.

Going to Ground Zero: Zaire

I began my career in medicine at the same time that the world began to recognize and grapple with the AIDS pandemic. In 1982, while young American men were dying of a mysterious disease in New York and San Francisco, I was in Central Africa, treating patients in a mission hospital in Zaire. I was a fourth-year medical student, not yet a doctor, and among the many new diseases I saw were patients with an unknown disease that was not yet called AIDS.

My husband Dan and I were in Zaire to work at the Nyankunde, a 200-bed, interfaith hospital near the Ruwenzori Mountains, "the Mountains of the Moon," and about as far away from our home in Minnesota as it was possible to get. Our two-and-a-half month mission was funded through Medical Assistance Program (MAP) with a scholarship from Reader's Digest. We were new Christians trying to determine if our career calling included missionary work in Africa. Little did we know that it was a call that we would hear again and again.

It was our first trip to Africa. To get to Nyankunde, we flew to Nairobi, Kenya, where the airport abuts a game park. As we landed, an impala seemed to race along beside our plane along the runway. We then switched to a tiny Mission Aviation Fellowship plane headed west to the northeast corner of the Zaire near the Uganda border. Touching down in Entebbe just months after the Israeli raid to save the hostages held by Idi Amin, we saw this eerily empty airport, the only other plane a burned out hulk and the beautiful, practically new terminal building with bullet holes in the walls. It was an early reminder that African governments rise and fall but the people, the church, and the need for ministry go on.

Once in Zaire, our nascent medical training was immediately put to the test. On the men's medical ward, there were three patients with strange, hard purple skin lesions, known as Kaposi's sarcoma. We were only able to offer the most superficial care, and all the patients went home eventually to die. Kaposi's sarcoma is a rare cancer. The Mayo Clinic, where Dan and I went to medical school, is a world-renowned referral center where physicians see the rarest disorders and diseases, what we called the "zebras" of medicine. Even at Mayo, we hadn't seen Kaposi's sarcoma. Kaposi's should have been rare at Nyankunde, but it had become as common as horses.

We didn't put it all together until we came home in the summer of 1982. Dan's roommate, Paul Axelson, told us of similar cases he had seen during his rotation in San Francisco. Later that summer, doctors at the Centers for Disease Control gave the disease a name: Acquired Immune Deficiency Syndrome, or AIDS.

In many ways, our patients were the fortunate ones. They had made it to Nyankunde, a real hospital with only one patient in each metal bed, cement floors, and local and missionary doctors on staff. The vast majority of those who died of AIDS in Africa never made it to a hospital or clinic, never saw a doctor or nurse. We also visited a 120-bed hospital hidden just inside the Congo rainforest at a village called Oicha that hadn't had any doctors in four years, but all the patient care and surgery were done by very capable nurses. For most Africans, there is limited access to modern health care even as we now can offer extended and better quality of life for AIDS patients.

While African nations have health care systems that provide at least some care to their citizens, today, millions of Africans are still kept healthy and alive by missionary hospitals and other faith-based organizations. Church-based health care providers were among the first to recognize AIDS, the first to care for its victims and are still in Africa, preventing new infections, caring for the sick and providing treatment—where possible— to extend the lives of those living with AIDS. While in Washington we debate, give speeches, and hold conferences, the real work has been going on since the early 1980s in Africa, for the most part by people of faith who have given their lives over to God to serve others far less fortunate.

After our rotations were over, Dan and I returned to America, but we left our hearts in Africa. Almost immediately, during my internship at a hospital on Long Island, I was treating my next AIDS patient, an ex-heroin addict. Twenty years later it's hard to remember individual patients well but Mary remains one I will never forget. She was filled with sadness, loneliness, and bitterness. Her children hadn't visited her in over a year. We didn't know how her disease was transmitted, but already the stigma of AIDS and fears about its contagiousness were isolating and hindering the delivery of care to this young woman dying alone and in pain.

While it was clear that needle and blood safety were important precautions, I needed to give her some human contact and show her that I wasn't afraid of her. Young and perhaps a little too idealistic, I had more exposure than one would allow now and while I was tapping her intravenous blood line for lab samples, her blood got on my skin. I was pregnant and had the opportunity at this time and in a later episode to think deeply about what risks one accepts in answering the call to work with AIDS patients. God doesn't promise perfect safety, but both my new son, Chris, and I stayed healthy.

Back to Africa

In 1985, after further medical training and now with two toddlers, we went back to Africa with a small missionary agency from Minnesota called Mission: Moving Mountains. We had planned to go to Uganda, but the government of Milton Obote, who was nearly as bad as his predecessor,

Idi Amin, was in the process of being overthrown by Yoweri Museveni's rebel movement. We ended up next door, in Eldoret, Kenya.

Eldoret is a stop on the trans-Africa highway, which goes from ocean to ocean across the African continent. The road, which disintegrates to large potholes through the middle Congo River basin, is the same road in Zaire we took from the village clinic at Oicha to the hospital in Nyankunde. It is also the major transport route that truckers take from the coasts into the interior of Africa and back again. By the mid-1980s, we knew that AIDS was spread by blood and sexual contact. Most epidemiologists believe that these truckers, who are on the road for months at a time and who are frequent clients of prostitutes, did much to spread HIV through Central Africa in the 1970s and 1980s. Eldoret had less than a 1 percent HIV prevalence rate at that time. AIDS was hitting Uganda hard, and it seemed like whole villages were dying. Eldoret was just over the border from this catastrophe. It was clear that AIDS would roll down the trans-Africa highway and repeat the Uganda story in Eldoret and the rest of Kenya if not dealt with promptly.

In Kenya, our boss was a young, dynamic Anglican bishop, Alexander Muge, who cared about development as part of his political and spiritual leadership calling. The day we met him, he had been praying for someone to lead his newly funded community health initiative. When the bishop heard that our Uganda plans had been thwarted and we were now looking to work in Kenya, he told us, "You are angels in answer to my prayer."

Our program in Kenya was called Tulinde Afya Kijijini (TAKI), Kiswahili for "protecting the health of the village." It covered many seemingly mundane interventions: dish racks, safe fireplaces, water protection, and nutritional improvements. As missionaries, we used these household-level programs to reinforce spiritual growth and discipleship. We also trained community health workers known as barefoot doctors. In the villages, I was called Mama Taki. From a public health perspective, it was difficult to measure our successes—there were simply too few people in the individual villages to measure change in health indicators such as infant mortality rates. But we knew each small change could and did make a difference for that individual: extending a life, saving a baby, or building a stronger marriage. The hardest place to intervene was with AIDS.

While the government was not yet acknowledging or acting to prevent the spread of AIDS, the women were well aware and despairing of risks out of their control. Faithful wives, who remained on the home farm, or shamba, would come asking for medical advice. A story we heard too often from women in the villages would be something like, "My husband is coming back from Nairobi. I know he has been sleeping with the prostitutes there. He is sick with that disease. What can I do? I can't refuse him, but I want to stay alive so someone can care for the children."

In public health, we call these couples "sero-discordant," meaning one spouse is HIV-positive and the other is HIV-negative. This term doesn't begin to describe the fear we saw in the village women's eyes. In almost all of these cases, the only option is the use of condoms to protect the HIV-negative spouse. This time the lesson of stigma was wrapped up in gender vulnerabilities that I would have the opportunity to address a decade later in Zimbabwe.

The government and the medical community shared in the silence and stigma. At the Kenyan Medical Association, doctors told us that they would rather commit suicide than know their HIV status. Our boss, the young Anglican bishop, understood all this and encouraged us to make AIDS education part of our community initiatives. It helped for the few people with whom we had contact, but for much of Kenya, there existed a terrible combination of silence, ignorance, and irresponsible decision making. The seeds of a devastating epidemic had been planted.

Today, adult prevalence of HIV/AIDS in Eldoret is almost 20 times higher than when I was there and twice as high as in its neighbor, Uganda. This discrepancy is largely explained by Kenya's failure to deal with the AIDS crisis and Uganda's aggressive efforts to prevent the spread of the disease. President Museveni and his wife, Janet, deserve enormous credit for going to villages, towns, and cities with a basic message: Change your behavior or die.

It was the beginning of the ABC approach to AIDS prevention: abstain, be faithful and, if necessary, use a condom. In Uganda, the epidemic turned around, and HIV prevalence went from over 20 percent to only 5 percent. In Kenya, it has steadily increased and only now the first glimmers of a turnaround are in sight. Today, the Kenyan government has declared HIV/AIDS to be a national emergency and is finally taking action.

But AIDS and medical care in Kenya weren't just professional concerns. A personal experience gave me real empathy and understanding for those whose lives are affected by HIV/AIDS. I was pregnant with our third child and was likely to need a caesarian delivery. Given serious complications in my previous two deliveries, we needed to be sure of good medical care. The nearest trustworthy care was the mission hospital in Kijabe, a three-hour drive.

Even there, I had to plan in advance to have a matching blood supply in the event that I would need a transfusion during or after giving birth. Because AIDS was beginning to spread in Kenya, the local blood supply was not an option, and I had expatriate friends with my blood type on call in case they were needed. In the end, they were not needed, but I thanked God that I had that safe option.

Next Stop: Zimbabwe

We spent three years in Kenya, then brought our young family back to America. Our African adventures were not over, however, and we returned to Africa in the mid-1990s, this time to Zimbabwe. I wanted to work with young people on AIDS prevention with a faith-based approach. I got to do all of that and more. I worked with street kids, taught in the public schools with a local faith-based organization, designed and taught curricula at the local university, and tried to mobilize the churches in Harare to respond to AIDS. This ministry was so exciting that I didn't want to leave.

The AIDS epidemic in southern Africa began almost a decade later than the East African epidemic, but it surged much more quickly. By 1994 when we arrived in Harare, the epidemic was already maturing. One of the saddest consequences of this was the growing orphan problem. The streets of Harare had hundreds of street children, some of whom had family to go home to at night, but many others who had no place to go. I began to take bread when I went downtown so that I would have some appropriate way to respond to the begging. But I realized it wasn't enough.

Nancy Warlick, an energetic Presbyterian activist who had lived for years in Kinshasa, Zaire, helped me learn and serve in an additional way. Her friend, Joan, known as the Bread Lady, would bring bread every day to about 50 street children. Nancy and Joan gathered a group to have a weekly Wednesday night outreach to the street children at City Presbyterian Church. Nearly one hundred children, ages 6–19, would come. (They were almost all boys, because it was dangerous for girls to be on the streets.) Many had either biblical or character-based names such as Ezekiel or Innocent.

The central activity was dinner, preceded by game time and followed by a lesson. Occasionally I would bring my own children, now in grade school, to play soccer in the church gym with the street children. During the lesson time, the littlest ones would sit on our laps, happy to have someone, even a stranger, hold and care for them even for a few minutes.

Initially, I provided medical care to those who needed it, usually between 5 and 10 patients a week. My hope was to build a relationship with the kids so that eventually I could talk to them about their risk for AIDS. The major medical problems that I saw, diarrhea and pneumonia, were hygiene-related. A month or so into our weekly visits, I prepared to lead a discussion on "How to stay healthy while living on the streets." (We had already instituted hand-washing prior to eating as part of the dinner routine. I was content that there were some small things that we and they could do to respond to the challenges of daily life on the street.)

I hoped that in a few weeks, we could talk about AIDS. So I was astounded when they told me right off the bat that their biggest problems were hunger, diarrhea, sexually transmitted diseases (STDs), AIDS, and having to sell themselves to get food. These were brave boys, admitting to homosexual prostitution in Africa, where this is a hidden and forbidden topic. In that very first lesson, they were ready to learn about AIDS and discuss ways to change their lives and, if possible, to reduce their exposure to AIDS.

A college student who was doing a summer internship asked them about their lives before they lived in the streets, what it was like now, and what their hopes and dreams were. They said they wanted to have families, go back to school, and be warm and safe. With all they endured, they yearned for normal lives. Over the year, the informal ministry for street children morphed into a board of a new organization that founded a home for some of the children, tried to reconnect them with families and school, and trained them how to stay alive.

When I taught in the public schools, I asked the students, "What is your greatest fear about AIDS?" Consistently, the biggest fear, from the best of schools to the worst, was not that they would get AIDS. It was the fear that their parents would get AIDS. Most children knew someone who had died of AIDS. Often the first sign of AIDS in a child's home was his or her increasingly sporadic school attendance, as the family could no longer pay school fees or needed children, particularly girls, to stay home and care for the family.

Seventh-grade classes in Zimbabwe were typically 45 students per class. For our AIDS sessions, two classes jammed into a single classroom the size Americans would use for 20 to 30 students. We discussed the very difficult realities of AIDS with stories, games, drama, and posters. The program, designed by Scripture Union, was welcomed into nearly all of the public schools with the open invitation to pray with the kids, quote Scripture, and see their lives changed. The curriculum very forthrightly explained anatomy, sexual maturation, AIDS, and STDs within what public health professionals would refer to as an "AB" (abstinence, be faithful) message.

My favorite teaching tool was a poster that I still put up on the wall of my office wherever I work. A friend of mine in the public health department at the University of Zimbabwe developed it. It shows a man lounging against a car gazing at a girl in a school uniform. She is looking back over her shoulder at him. Every student in Africa immediately recognizes the situation. The rich, older man (or "sugar daddy") is an authority figure in a patriarchal, authoritarian society. He expects the schoolgirl to have sex with him in exchange for money, gifts, or possibly good grades. My students' initial response was that the girl had no choice. But as the students and I worked through what the girl could do, the students learned that they could say no to this arrangement. I learned that an abstinence message alone has no power unless the girls know how to say no.

The girls faced these situations regularly but it had less personal reality for the boys. I would ask the boys, How would they feel if this were their sister or girlfriend? What could they do to protect the girls? Would they be a sugar daddy when they grew up? A light went on in the eyes of a few of these boys, telling me they had begun to understand their responsibility not only for their own behavior, but also to protect the women in their families and communities.

Back to America

After two years in Zimbabwe, we returned to the United States. I extended my professional skills by becoming board certified in public health and preventive medicine (a specialty like pediatrics or surgery). I worked with Georgia's state department of health and later consulted for the Centers for Disease Control and the World Health Organization (WHO). I expanded my public health expertise doing disease outbreak investigations, social marketing, food safety, surveillance of sexually transmitted diseases, diarrheal disease control and formative research, and patient education material design for the management of elephantiasis. The work with elephantiasis seems unrelated to AIDS work, but I saw stark parallels of stigma, discrimination, and hopelessness.

God has a great sense of humor. Everything I categorically said I would never do has now become part of my life. When I was 16, I was determined to help people so long as I didn't have to go to Africa. In Kenya, Dan and I started to realize the political implications of many of our programs. Our concerns led him to become interested in American policymaking. My less than supportive spousal response was, "Oh no! Don't make me a politician's wife." Well, he didn't, but I made him a politician's husband.

Back in the United States, a confluence of connections led me to be the commissioner of health in Virginia. It was an unexpected offer that allowed me to build on my international youth work but in my own country. In Virginia, we instituted new youth programs such as Right Choices for Youth, which President Bush had started while governor in Texas. Overall, I had 35 health districts and 120 health offices, 4,200 employees and a $420 million budget when we weren't struggling with shortfalls.

It was a terrific opportunity to learn politics and management at the same time. I learned to deal with legislation, managed health programs from birth to death, and learned more than a thing or two about the managed care industry and sewage regulations. Our department responded to floods, the 9/11 terrorist attack on the Pentagon, and the anthrax attacks. It was enormously challenging, but I missed the work oversees. I couldn't have known it, but God was faithfully preparing me for a bigger role in international health as a policymaker and administrator.

In the midst of the anthrax crisis, I was named by President Bush to be the head of global health at the U.S. Agency for International Development (USAID). From the genteel southern politics of Virginia, I moved my office across the Potomac River to Washington. I was now the head of a bureau charged with providing technical assistance and policy guidance to health programs in more than 90 countries with a staff of 200 and a budget of $1.6 billion. The AIDS portfolio, about a fourth of the bureau's work, was soon to soar.

I was honored that the president had chosen me, but I was also overwhelmed by the challenge. I learned that the scariest verse in the Bible is: "To whom much is given, much is required." I faced the question that had challenged us to go to Africa for the first time: "Lord, you have unexpectedly put me in this place at this time. What do you have for me to do?" All the preceding years, wonderful opportunities in themselves, now fit together clearly as necessary preparation for the new plans that I never planned or expected.

Working with the Church

To win the war against AIDS, the U.S. government and its resources must work closely with faith-based organizations (FBOs). The biggest limiting factor for progress in international health today is not uncertainty about what needs to be done, or not knowing what to do, or even a lack of money. We know AIDS can be prevented, and treatment costs are declining, bringing them in reach for more of the world. We have seen success, particularly in Uganda, and we know what works. We have the resources to beat back this pandemic. With President Bush's commitment to spend $15 billion over five years for the international battle against AIDS, money is no longer an issue.

What we need are the people who are going to do the work. AIDS is increasing the burden on health staff while simultaneously decimating the ranks of those same health care workers. We need people to run programs, teach children, and care for the sick and dying.

The church has vast barely tapped networks of people. In many countries, FBOs are the major—and often some of the best—providers of health care. Caring for the poor, sick, needy, and hungry, for the widows and orphans, is part of God's call to the church. AIDS is creating millions of these people who desperately need love, compassion, and spiritual support. The potential to reach millions is only possible through the millions of people of faith. A recent UNICEF study looked at the role of church networks in orphan care in six countries. It found that if every congregation cared for just 20 orphans, then all the orphans who need assistance would get it.

The American government has money, technical expertise, and the best practices to share. But, for many faith-based organizations, tapping into government resources has been difficult because of bureaucratic barriers. Early on I put together a faith-based task force to identify and help new FBOs overcome these hurdles.

Last summer I was with President Bush and First Lady Laura Bush when they launched a new program to stop the transmission of HIV from mother to child in Nigeria. I stood in the courtyard of a hospital watching President Bush warmly greet HIV-positive women who had received Nevarapine as part of the U.S. government program, thus cutting in half the chances that they would pass the virus on to their babies. President Bush has made the ABC approach a cornerstone of his bold war on HIV/AIDS.

A New, Balanced ABC Approach

The ABC approach teaches AIDS prevention this way: A—abstain from sexual activity; B—be faithful to your spouse; and C—when necessary, correctly and consistently use condoms. This book, very appropriately, contains a chapter devoted to the ABC model.

In America, there is a bias in the public health community against teaching abstinence, but in Africa, the ABC message is clear and compelling. As my kids would say, this was a "no brainer" for me. I had seen it work both in Virginia and in Africa. The B message of being faithful (or "zero grazing," as it is known in some parts of Africa) particularly resonated within African culture.

I knew, however, that I needed an approach firmly based on scientific data for any policy change to last beyond the current administration. God is a God of truth, and I expect objective research to be consistent with his plan. I was very comfortable in requiring data as the basis for policy change. The result was a series of publications from my bureau: *What Happened in Uganda, The "ABCs" of HIV Prevention: Report of a USAID Technical Meeting On Behavior Change Approaches to Primary Prevention of HIV/AIDS*, and *Phase I Report of the ABC Study: Summary of HIV Prevalence and Sexual Behavior Findings*.

New evidence documents the success of the B interventions of "Be faithful" and partner reduction. There is much more we can learn about the relative contributions of A, B, and C and, in particular, how Uganda has moved so many people to make such significant changes in behavior. We are continuing to fund ABC research, but clearly we have sufficient evidence to demonstrate the effectiveness of the ABC model.

Changed Policy Emphasis

With these new studies, we established a more balanced ABC policy. USAID had been using the ABC model for a long time. In fact, the agency was a major contributor to Uganda's success in the 1980s. But in the 1990s the program heavily favored the C intervention: condoms. Very few of our programs took advantage of A and B.

The new policy, promoting a balance between all three interventions, was included in the training required of all agency personnel in the field every two years. The policy was also the subject of congressional briefings and cables sent to our missions around the world. It allowed for variations based on the local population. In generalized epidemics, however, such as those in most African nations, we needed to have a balance between the three interventions.

Broadening the Provider Base

In the past, USAID had in practice required providers to be willing to disseminate all three components. Many FBOs were not comfortable with the controversial condom message. Religious leaders, however, are uniquely positioned to speak effectively about the A and B messages, and I wanted to fully use their leadership potential.

Seeing that Muslim and Christian leaders in Uganda had done this effectively, we instituted another policy change: while the U.S. government would pursue a balance among the three interventions, we did not require each of our partner organizations to provide all three. We only required that our partners not disparage the interventions they chose not to offer.

At the end of 2003, I was with Secretary of Health and Human Services, Tommy Thompson, and the State Department's AIDS Coordinator, Ambassador Randall Tobias in Kampala, Uganda, where the ABC message began. We were able to thank the Ugandans for showing us the way to go.

Child Health

Our response to the AIDS pandemic necessitates other policy changes that need the attention of the church. Primarily, we must redouble our efforts against other childhood killers. Children affected by AIDS are dying primarily of familiar diseases—measles, pneumonia, diarrhea, malnutrition, and so on. AIDS is devastating the health care infrastructure and sapping resources in many African nations. The poor, neglected, and orphaned are highly vulnerable to these changes. Alarmingly, improvements in infant and child mortality rates that were a long time in coming are being reversed in some southern African countries.

We have a moral mandate to provide treatment for people living with AIDS, but we cannot let that mandate divert resources and attention away from our programs that save the lives of children who die every year from diseases we can prevent with cheap, effective, known prevention tools. If Africa is to survive this devastating pandemic, it needs a healthy generation of children. In a few years, today's children will be leaders, parents, farmers, and teachers. The economic backbone of African countries depends on keeping these youth healthy, educated, and free from HIV/AIDS. So as we address AIDS, we must be sure to simultaneously address the needs of AIDS orphans and all other children by promoting better access to quality child survival interventions.

Life Extending Treatment (LET)

When we think of treatment, most of us think of the anti-retroviral (ARV) drugs. They have proven people can live for many years with AIDS. For some time, I have been pondering the evidence and implications of whether there is such a thing as non-ARV life extending treatment and what it would mean to international efforts in fighting the AIDS pandemic.

We know that some people with AIDS live longer than others. Prior to ARVs, drugs to treat and prevent opportunistic infections (OI), such as Kaposi's sarcoma and tuberculosis, helped bring comfort and extend life. These treatments have been far less available in the developing world. Thus, we should expect that life expectancy there is less than it could be. Mounting evidence from the CDC and the National Institute of Health show disease-specific interventions that significantly decrease mortality in HIV-positive individuals and those living with AIDS. Thus, there may be a combination of interventions—providing food, nutrition, safe drinking water, and medicine for tuberculosis, malaria, and OI—that could be provided to these nations in order to extend lives.

This is an urgent policy item because people are dying now. Children are being orphaned, and it could be years before ARV drugs are available for them. These life extending interventions could go to people cheaply and quickly. Life Extending Treatment could help overcome the stigma of HIV testing—remember the Kenyan doctors who would rather commit suicide than know their status?—and enhance voluntary counseling and testing. The treatment package could keep hundreds of thousands, perhaps millions of people, alive just a few more years—perhaps long enough for ARVs to be more widely available in Africa.

Treatment is the current call to action. The moral mandate is to provide for the developing world what the developed world has access to. If this package of interventions can make a real difference, we will need political will, resources, and determination to launch it. Without immediate interventions, many, many will die before ARVs can reach them; many children will be orphaned; and the devastating impact on economics, education, and societies will continue.

Conclusion

There is hope for the world and for turning around the AIDS epidemic. We have more interest and resources ever. President Bush has led the way with the founding contributions to the Global Fund for AIDS, TB, and Malaria; the Prevention of Mother to Child Transmission Program; and the $15 billion President's Emergency Initiative. But all this will still not be enough if the church does not provide manpower, leadership, and hope.

My journey in responding to AIDS has spanned 20 years and several continents; covered the range of prevention, care, and treatment; and moved me from missionary to federal policymaker. I've been honored to work with people from across the spectrum of human experience: from nomadic tribesmen to street children, to African heads of state, and now to President Bush. When I stepped on that plane to Zaire 20 years ago, I could never have imagined the calling and career God had in store for me. If God can use me, then he can use you.

CHAPTER 14
DICK DAY

PREVENTING HIV/AIDS VIA BIBLICALLY BASED CONCEPTS OF SEXUALITY, LOVE, AND MARRIAGE

Africa has undergone dramatic political, economic, and social changes. Changes that occurred in Europe and North America over centuries have been compounded into several generations. The cornerstones of traditional African culture, which are the family and community, have been profoundly affected.

When the "wind of change" began to sweep across Africa, John Mbiti said, "The change means individuals are severed, cut off, pulled out and separated from corporate morality, customs and traditional solidarity. They have no firm roots any more. They are simply uprooted but not necessarily transplanted."[1] There is little doubt that this profound upheaval has contributed to the rapid and extensive spread of HIV/AIDS.

William Rushing, former chair of the Section on Medical Sociology of the American Sociological Association, put it well when he said, "In the final analysis, whether the HIV/AIDS epidemic in Africa slows down will depend on millions of people changing their behavior. And since behavior is anchored in cultural norms, social institutions and the structure of social rewards, change will be hard for health care professionals to bring about. . . . African programs must be adapted to the traditional social practices and culture of Africa."[2]

We are dealing with a pandemic that is essentially a behaviorally transmitted disease. Yet the world is looking to the West for a scientific answer. Many people are relying on condoms which do not address the main causal factors. Condoms provide a technical solution to a problem that can be addressed only through fundamental changes in social attitudes, values, and behavior. To combat AIDS, there needs to be a transformation of one's mind—a change in worldview.

Worldview Failure

What is a worldview? On the personal level, it is one's perception of reality. It may be true, partially true or entirely false; it may be held consciously or subconsciously; it may be consistent or inconsistent. One's worldview determines one's beliefs, values, and behavior. It involves the mind, the emotions, and the will. As Proverbs 23:7 states, "For as he thinks within himself, so he is" (NASB). Without the transformation of one's worldview, there is no transformation of behavior.

Cultures also have concepts of what is real. Cultural values are not selected arbitrarily, but they invariably reflect an underlying system of beliefs. At the heart of any culture is its worldview. This cultural worldview helps shape the individual's worldview and consequently his or her behavior.

In Africa, perhaps as nowhere else, people's approach to life is holistic. According to William Dyrness, holism means that the "material and spiritual worlds are ultimately part of a single reality, and the line between the one and the other is difficult to draw. But to all Africans, the belief in a single, all-powerful God is unquestioned."[3]

Promisingly, Africa's holistic worldview makes the biblical worldview culturally appropriate in addressing behavioral change. Yet over the years, Christianity has failed in any significant way to build upon this foundational African worldview—to build a biblical worldview either in the individual or in the culture.

Tokunboh Adeyemo, former general secretary of the Association of Evangelicals of Africa and Madagascar, agrees. "For decades in Africa, evangelism and missionary activities have been directed at getting people saved (that is, spiritually), but losing their minds," Adeyemo says. "Consequently, we have a continent south of the Sahara that boasts of over 50 percent Christian population on the average, but having little or no impact on society. In actual fact, it sounds like an irony that within our own rank and file, such practices as witchcraft, traditional religions, orgies, tribalism and the like are regarded as normal."[4]

At the dedication of the Billy Graham Center at Wheaton College, September 13, 1980, Charles Malik, former president of the United Nations' General Assembly and the Security Council, warned, "The problem is not only to win souls but to save minds. If you win the whole world and lose the mind of the world you will soon discover you have not won the world. Indeed, it may turn out that you have actually lost the world."[5] Unfortunately, this appears, by and large, to be what happened in Africa. In essence, Africa has been evangelized, but the African mind has not been captured for Christ. Yet as tragic as the HIV/AIDS pandemic is, it has opened doors to build a holistic, biblical worldview into the next generation. One attempt to respond to this opportunity is the "WHY WAIT?" Family Enrichment Educational Program.

Key Concepts Addressed by the "WHY WAIT?" Program

Much of human sexuality depends more on what individuals think than on biology. Thus, it is essential to develop a biblical worldview that rightly relates the individuals to God, themselves, and others in true love. To do this, the "WHY WAIT?" curriculum focuses on the following key concepts.[6]

The Foundation: God's Creative Plan

Young people are special and have been created in God's image, both male and female. God loves them and wants them to have a meaningful relationship with him, others, and themselves (Matthew 22:36–40).

Human Needs

The program is built on meeting two basic felt needs: the need for security (a sense of belonging) and the need for significance (a sense of being able to contribute).

The Basis for Meeting Needs: Love

The basis for meeting these needs is love—being loved and being able to love. Love is both a basic human need as well as a learned behavior

(1 John 4:19). Loving others is the ultimate witness of the Christian faith to the world (John 13:35).

Affirming Human Dignity

We are living in a day and age of racism, sexism, tribalism, poor self-concept, and drug and sex abuse, all of which deny the very essence of God's creative plan. This adversely impacts not only the society at large, but the individual. God's creation declares the worth and dignity of each human being, the equality of male and female, and the responsibility of each individual. Therefore, we must first affirm God's creative plan, which has been proven by his redemptive plan and secured through identification with Christ in spiritual birth.

Human Dignity in Relationships

We have been created in God's image so that we might have a living relationship with him and honor and glorify him. The Christian life is built upon relationships and developing godly character through these relationships (Luke 6:40).

Family Reflects the Image of God

The family is vital in God's plan. God created people in his image, both male and female (Genesis 1:27). He created the family so that the image of God is reflected to the children through the father and the mother and passed from generation to generation. When a family is disorganized (i.e., through divorce, separation, death) or dysfunctional (i.e., lacking character, values, etc.), the growing child lacks the proper role models to develop a Christian worldview (Romans 12:2).

Love Provides and Protects

Establishing individual human dignity is the basis for accepting all humanity, including one's enemies. But we need to go deeper and understand that true love is critical. This kind of love both provides and protects. We see it in action through the Bible, Jesus Christ and his example, and the Christ-like character demonstrated by those created in his image.

Cultural Boundaries—Cultural Expressions

In our book *WHY WAIT? What You Need To Know About The Teen Sexuality Crisis*, Josh McDowell and I list 37 reasons why young people do not wait to engage in sex, and 27 reasons why they should.[7] These reasons encompass the physical, emotional, psychological, relational, moral, and spiritual realms. Although research for the book was based on American youth, the principles apply in virtually every culture. In working with students at the University of Malawi, I found that at least 30 of the 37 reasons for not waiting are relevant to Malawian youth.

Human needs know no historical timelines, and no geographical or cultural boundaries; however, they have different cultural expressions. Therefore, biblical principles are extremely relevant for addressing these human needs. As we apply these universal principles, we need to understand the culture. In teaching the principles, we must make the activities relevant to the culture. We need to advocate values that will become internalized and result in healthy (i.e., biblical) behavior patterns or behavioral change.

The Mind Matters

Associated with affirming the dignity of humanity, both male and female, we need to emphasize the mind, so that it knows the truth and chooses to act upon that knowledge. Youth need to know that they can make right choices and change their behavior with the power of the Holy Spirit—something that much of contemporary philosophy rejects. They also need to understand that the mind is the greatest sex organ and, as such, needs to be protected.

Human Sexuality is Learned

Compared with other species, human sexuality is: (1) involved with human psychology as well as physiology; (2) under conscious control rather than instinctual biological control; (3) affected by learning and social factors, and thus more variable within the species; (4) largely directed by an individual's beliefs and attitudes (i.e., worldview); (5) less directly attached to reproduction; (6) able to serve other purposes in addition to reproduction, such as pair bonding and communication; and

(7) a source of pleasure.[8] Without built-in guidelines, human sexuality is dependent on learning. Different societies and groups teach different things about sexuality. Therefore, people need a biblical worldview to properly express God's creation of human sexuality.

Love is a Choice

Young people need to understand that true love is first and foremost an act of the will. Christ said, "A new command I give you: that you love one another."[9] A commandment is an appeal to the will. The great love passage of 1 Corinthians 13 describes acts of the will, not expressions of the emotions.

A Clean Heart for a New Start

With right thinking and right behavior, there can be new beginnings through the grace of God and his forgiveness. We can maintain these new beginnings by abiding in God's principles, through the power of the Holy Spirit.

Vision and Virtue

There is a connection between vision and virtue. One has to see correctly before one can act correctly. It is for this reason that the person of Jesus Christ becomes the ultimate model of character and moral development.

"WHY WAIT?" in Africa

Background

"WHY WAIT?" Africa was initially presented in 1992 at the first annual weeklong Uganda Youth Conference, hosted by First Lady Janet Museveni. In 1993, the Malawi Ministry of Education requested Sub-Saharan Africa Family Enrichment (SAFE) to develop an African-oriented curriculum addressing sexual abstinence, life skills, and character development that could be used in schools to help address HIV/AIDS.

University of Malawi Professor Moira Chimombo put together the first draft of the "WHY WAIT?" Family Enrichment curriculum. In 1994,

SAFE conducted the first teacher training and training of trainers (TOTs) workshops. The program was launched nationally at convocation of 3,000 students and 500 teachers hosted by State President Bakili Muluzi at Sanjika Palace in 1995.

Curricula Development

A four-year curriculum has been developed, field tested, revised, and printed for secondary school students. Also, a four-year primary school curriculum for grades 5 through 8 has been developed. Malawians have been trained and mobilized, and more than 2,000 teachers have been trained in four- to five-day workshops. In addition, both a semester course and a "WHY WAIT?" training workshop are available for education majors at the University of Malawi. While the program's integrated, value-based approach is built on biblical principles, it also reflects a holistic African worldview and traditional morals.

Expansion to Other Countries

Malawian TOTs have trained Kenyan TOTs, who have conducted 12 training workshops in Kenya. These workshops have trained over 1,500 teachers and Ministry of Education officials, as well as educators from Tanzania, Uganda, and Congo. In 2003, Nigerian TOTs, trained by senior Malawian TOTs, initiated the program in Nigeria.

What Happened in Uganda?

Information in itself is not enough to change sexual behavior. According to a 1988 survey, 95 percent of all Ugandans were aware of AIDS and how it is transmitted.[10] In a speech which was broadcasted live on April 7, 1990, the minister of health, Zaker Kaheru said, "The only way people will survive this epidemic is by adopting disciplined social behaviour."[11] Yet even with this awareness, the killer disease continued to spread until peaking in 1991.

Before one can change behavior, beliefs and values must change. This is what happened in Uganda, particularly among the youth, beginning in 1992. Much to the surprise of most international agencies and authorities, the turnaround was not primarily due to condoms and the large amount of money invested in their distribution. Rather, the shift was primarily due to changes in behavior, particularly among the youth.

Addressing the House Committee on International Relations, Subcommittee on Africa, Hearing on HIV/AIDS Steps to Prevention, September 27, 2000, Vivian L Derryck, Bureau for Africa, U.S. Agency for International Development (USAID), stated: "Religious leaders [in Uganda] were instrumental in inculcating ideas about sex within marriage and delays in the age of sexual debuts."[12] At a USAID sponsored consultation (February, 2002), four individuals with long-term experience in HIV prevention substantially agreed with Derryck.

Following are excerpts from a summary document of the USAID meeting:

> "Now considered to be one of the world's earliest and best success stories in overcoming HIV, Uganda has experienced substantial declines in prevalence, and evidently incidence, during at least the past decade, especially among younger age cohorts . . . Estimates by the U.S. Census Bureau/UNAIDS are that national HIV prevalence peaked at around 15 percent in 1991, and had fallen to five percent as of 2001."[13]

> "Uganda's President set the example for the nation with his matter-of-fact approach in dealing with the HIV threat, and inspired thousands of community, religious, and government leaders to talk candidly to people about delaying sexual activity, abstaining, being faithful, 'zero grazing.' and using condoms (roughly in that order)."[14]

> "Mainstream faith-based organizations wield enormous influence in Africa. Early and significant mobilization of Ugandan religious leaders and organizations resulted in their active participation in AIDS education and prevention activities."[15]

Uganda's "ABC" strategy—Abstinence, Be faithful, use Condoms, in that order—has received much of the credit for the turnaround in that country. Anne Peterson (see chapter 13), M.D., who heads the USAID global health bureau, says the emphasis has been on the first two components. "The historical approach to HIV has been little 'a,' little 'b,' and big 'C,' but Africans were far ahead of the worldwide public health community on this," Peterson says. "The core of Uganda's success story is big 'A,' big 'B,' and little 'c.'"[16]

From the beginning, President Museveni has strongly advocated big "A," big "B," and small "c," as indicated by his address on June 20, 1991, to the Seventh International Conference on AIDS. "I don't support the idea of condoms myself," he stated, suggesting instead that "abstinence and self-control must be taught to our young people."[17]

The following November, addressing the first AIDS Congress in East and Central Africa, held in Kampala, Museveni again emphasized the need for big "A" and big "B": "I have been emphasizing a return to our time-tested cultural practices which emphasized fidelity and condemned premarital and extramarital sex. . . . I feel that condoms have a role to play as a means of protection, especially in couples who are HIV-positive, but they cannot become the main means of stemming the tide of AIDS."[18]

In May 1992, the First National Youth Forum was initiated. The theme was "WHY WAIT?—Because you are special and worth waiting for!" The program affirms the God-given dignity and equality of every human being. The forum, which is now an annual event, is a seven-day conference attended by thousands of Ugandan youth, including the President's children. The First Lady, Mrs. Janet Museveni, as the patron and honorary chairperson, continues to serve the youth in that capacity. As the principal speaker at the first two forums (1992, 1993), I addressed the youth on the topic "WHY WAIT?" I participated again in 2000.

On February 20, 2002, at the Prescription For Hope HIV/AIDS Conference held in Washington, D.C., Janet Museveni attributed the country's HIV/AIDS turnaround to the annual Uganda Youth Forum, accompanied by the involvement of the faith community. The faith community has a key role in fighting the HIV/AIDS pandemic because it has the biblical principles to implement both the "A" and the "B." This worked in Uganda. It is now working in Malawi and in other countries.

Justin Malewezi, vice president of Malawi and chairman of the Cabinet Committee on HIV/AIDS, stated, "The many faith communities' programs in the area of behavior change and life skills training have proved very effective in reducing HIV transmission among our youth. These programs should be implemented on a national scale."[19]

"WHY WAIT?" Makes a Difference

In 1999, the "WHY WAIT?" program was introduced into Ndirande Full Primary School, in a squatter village in Blantyre, the main commercial center of Malawi. It has an enrollment of over 8,000 children in grades 1 through 8. Twenty-eight percent of the children are orphans, mostly due to AIDS. Ninety percent of the children live in poverty.

Because there are 121 classes and only 20 classrooms, the vast majority of the classes must be held outdoors. Even in the school, there are no desks or chairs for the children. The primary instructional equipment is a chalkboard, either hanging on a wall or under a tree.

The year before the program was introduced in Ndirande Primary School, 121 girls dropped out of school due to pregnancies. Two years after the program was implemented, the pregnancy dropout rate fell to zero. Even with the lack of physical facilities, the children have excelled in character and academic development. The headmaster says the teachers have modeled the program well, and the message has connected with students, who have been actively involved in the learning process.

The Need Worldwide

What is needed in Africa, is needed worldwide. Urie Bronfenbrenner, professor of human development and family studies, Cornell University, stated, "We have learned that stresses being experienced in both worlds (developed and developing) have common roots and call for common strategies grounded in the basic requirements for survival and growth of all human beings in all human ecologies."[20]

Billy Graham made a similar observation in his book, *World Aflame* (1967). "Man is the same all over the world. His hopes, dreams, problems, difficulties and longings are essentially the same whether he is in the heart of Africa or in the heart of America. As Goethe said, 'Mankind is always advancing. Man remains ever the same.'"[21]

God has created every human being with certain basic needs of the soul that he desires to meet through the Spirit. However, if people do not understand how God wants to meet the needs or rejects God's way, the tendency is to meet the needs of the soul through the physical senses. This leads to indulgences such as sex, alcohol, drug abuse, materialism. All of these can contribute to the spread of HIV/AIDS.

A Closing Thought

Stephen Covey describes how caring people have an Area of Concern and an Area of Influence.[22] *Proactive* people focus on their Area of Influence. They work in areas where they can effect change; and as the nature of their energy is positive, enlarging, and magnifying, their Area of Influence increases. On the other hand, if the focus is on the Area of Concern, they tend to become *reactive* rather than proactive. They tend to blame and accuse others. They feel like victims of circumstances. The negative energy generated by this focus causes their Area of Influence to shrink.

As caring people, we will have concern, but our focus must be on our Area of Influence—ourselves, our family, our neighbors, our students, our community, and, for a few, even national policy.

If caring people band together in a caring network, we can greatly increase our Area of Influence and begin to bring about change in our Area of Concern. We need caring communities of parents, teachers, neighbors, and church members. Anthropologist Margaret Mead was known to believe that a small group of thoughtful, committed citizens could change the world. Indeed, it's the only thing that ever has.

Professor Robert Webber of Wheaton College describes how the leaders of the "Great Awakening" of the eighteenth-century America held a holistic view of salvation: "They did not separate the body from the soul. Rather, their approach to revival stimulated the improvement of social conditions and the bettering of human life."[23] The results were changed lives and a changed society.

Acts 17:6 describes the disciples as "these that have turned the world upside down." Let's do it again. Help turn the world upside down. It appears that the only hope for the HIV/AIDS pandemic in Africa is a biblical worldview attained through the discipling of nations.

Notes

1. John S. Mbiti, African Religions and Philosophy (London: Heineman, 1967), p. 219.

2. William A. Rushing, The AIDS Epidemic (Boulder, CO: Westview Press, 1995), p. 235.

3. William A. Dryness, Learning About Theology From the Third World (Grand Rapids, MI: Academic Books, 1990), p. 44.

4. Tokunboh Adeyemo, The Christian Mind in a Changing Africa (Nairobi: The Association of Evangelicals of Africa and Madagascar, 1993), p. vi.

5. Charles Malik, The Two Tasks (Westchester, IL: Cornerstone Books, 1980). pp. 31–32, 34.

6. Moira Chimombo and Dick Day, Why Wait? Family Enrichment Curriculum, Unit 1, Secondary Level (Zomba, Malawi: Sub-Saharan Africa Family Enrichment, 1996).

7. Josh McDowell and Dick Day, Why Wait? What You Need To Know About the Teen Sexuality Crisis (San Bernardino, CA: Here's Life Publishers, 1987).

8. Frank D. Cox, Human Intimacy: Marriage, Family and Its Meaning (St. Paul, MN: West Publishing, 1987).

9. John 13:34 NASB.

10. Monte Leach, "Hope among the Ruins." A paper made available by Share International, 1970.

11. David Musoke, "Ugandan Life Not Affected by AIDS Scare" in New African (August, 1990), 41.

12. Vivian Derryck, An independent news briefing about the United Nations. UN wire. n.d.

13. Jan Hogle, What Happened in Uganda? Declining HIV Prevalence, Behavior Change, and the National Response (Washington, D.C.: USAID, 2002), p. 2.

14. Ibid, p. 10.

15. Ibid, p. 5.

16. Anne Peterson, An independent news briefing about the United Nations. UN wire. n.d.

17. Tony Barnett and Piers Blaikie, AIDS in Africa (London: Behaven Press, 1992), p. 61.

18. Yoweri K. Museveni, What Is Africa's Problem? (Kampala, Uganda: NRM Publications, 1992), p. 273.

19. Justin Malewazi, "The Government: Faith Community Consultation to Strengthen Collaboration in HIV Prevention and Care" (2001), p. 2. A paper on the keynote address, made available by the Office of Vice President, Lilongwe, Malawi.

20. Urie Bronfenbrenner, Who Cares for Children? (Paris: UNESCO, 1998), p. 2.

21. Billy Graham, World Aflame (Westwood, NJ: Fleming H. Revell, 1967), pp. 51–52.

22 Stephen R. Covey, The 7 Habits of Highly Effective People (New York: Simon & Schuster, 1987).

23 Robert E. Webber, The Church in the World (Grand Rapids, MI: Zondervan Publishing, 1986), p. 58.

CAN CHRISTIAN AID ORGANIZATIONS IGNORE THE CRISIS?

One day an expert in religious law stood up to test Jesus by asking him this question: "Teacher, what must I do to receive eternal life?" Jesus replied, "What does the law of Moses say? How do you read it?" The man answered, "'You must love the Lord your God with all your heart, all your soul, all your strength, and all your mind.' And, 'Love your neighbor as yourself.'" "Right!" Jesus told him. "Do this and you will live!"

The man wanted to justify his actions, so he asked Jesus, "And who is my neighbor?"

Jesus replied with an illustration: "A Jewish man was traveling on a trip from Jerusalem to Jericho, and he was attacked by bandits. They stripped him of his clothes and money, beat him up, and left him half dead beside the road.

"By chance a Jewish priest came along; but when he saw the man lying there, he crossed to the other side of the road and passed him by. A temple assistant walked over and looked at him lying there, but he also passed by on the other side. Then a despised Samaritan came along, and when he saw the man, he felt deep pity. Kneeling beside him, the Samaritan soothed his wounds with medicine and bandaged them. Then he put the man on his own donkey and took him to an inn, where he took care of him.

"The next day he handed the innkeeper two pieces of silver and told him to take care of the man. 'If his bill runs higher than that,' he said, 'I'll pay the difference the next time I am here.'

"Now which of these three would you say was a neighbor to the man who was attacked by bandits?" Jesus asked. The man replied, "The one who showed him mercy." Then Jesus said, "Yes, now go and do the same." (Luke 10:25–37 NLT)

Christ has called us to be modern-day Samaritans walking an age-old road of suffering. Forty-five million people lie along this road. And there will be even more tomorrow. A ruthless bandit has attacked them and left them for dead. Many people have crossed to the other side to pass them by. This bandit's name is HIV/AIDS, and some of those passing by are Christians.

Every nongovernmental organization has a specialty. Christian nongovernmental organizations do, too, but Christian groups have an extra responsibility in the kingdom to teach, serve, reach out, and share the eternal hope that comes only from a personal relationship with Jesus Christ. God's word mandates these actions for Christians in every walk of life. Christian nongovernmental organizations thus share a higher calling, a higher accountability, and a higher responsibility in the fight against HIV/AIDS.

The Human Toll

HIV/AIDS used to be a shadowy and fearful subject. Today, however, AIDS has made public discussion of sexually intimate acts necessary. The human toll is staggering. An estimated 28 million people worldwide have already died, including 3 million last year alone.

In sub-Saharan Africa, a region I've traveled to many dozens of times over the last two decades, the situation is catastrophic. More than 29 million people there are infected with HIV/AIDS. Of that number, 3 million are children under the age of 15.

In many ways the children are bearing the greatest burden. Over 14 million youngsters have lost one or both parents to AIDS. Every day another 2,200 children are infected.

Numbers alone do not tell the story, however. HIV/AIDS is devastating the very fabric of the societies where its victims live. Families, food supplies, social structures, and economies—both large and small—

are under relentless attack. For every person who dies, there are usually six to ten family members directly affected by the loss of income and leadership, drained resources, and less available labor. More often than not, family and victim suffer shame and are ostracized by their neighbors and community.

Christian NGOs

Nongovernmental organizations (NGOs) cannot and have not ignored this crisis. But more importantly, Christians cannot ignore this crisis. The stakes are simply too high. Eternity is waiting at the doorstep of the 42 million people around the world who are right now living with this disease. Some of these 42 million know and serve Christ, but many do not. Christians everywhere have a mandate not only to love and care for these people, but also to share with them the hope of Christ.

The path is clear and the role is unique for any Christian organization that brings physical assistance to people in need. We cannot ignore the HIV/AIDS crisis.

Why?

1. *HIV/AIDS is everywhere we work.* We encounter its impact in every sector of relief and development. No program or project can be undertaken today without first taking into consideration either the direct or collateral impact that HIV/AIDS already has on the recipient group or intended outcome.

2. *Our role as Christians in the fight against HIV/AIDS is unique.* Governments and aid agencies are working diligently to fight HIV/AIDS—engaging hundreds of thousands of politicians, educators, health care providers, and ordinary citizens around the world. Many worthy policies and programs have been put into place to educate the world about this disease and to care for those living with it.

I believe Christians bear the greatest responsibility in developing international HIV/AIDS strategies. And with this responsibility comes tremendous opportunity to share the gospel in word and deed. HIV/AIDS allows Christians to demonstrate Christlike love, compassion, and grace to a world that may not otherwise hear or see this message.

Franklin Graham, the president of Samaritan's Purse, recently told delegates to an HIV/AIDS conference we hosted in Uganda that the church has a unique challenge. He said:

> The world's finest doctors, richest donors, and strongest governments cannot match the worldwide Church in terms of earthly care and eternal hope . . . Our response to HIV/AIDS will be a defining moment in the history of the Church.

Can a Christian nongovernmental organization ignore the HIV/AIDS crisis? The answer, of course, is "no." Christ's own example demands a response.

Impact in Developing Countries

To better understand how and why NGOs are tackling the HIV/AIDS crisis, you first have to understand how completely pervasive the impact of this disease has been within every level of society where infection rates are soaring. No level of society or government can afford to consider itself immune. To achieve any degree of success, strategies and systems of emergency relief and long-term development must take this into consideration. HIV/AIDS is no longer only a health issue. Nongovernmental organizations have no choice but to understand it in these terms and consider HIV/AIDS components in all their programming.

Family and Social Structure

While HIV/AIDS severely impacts the economics and politics of many countries, its most devastating and personal effect is at the family and village (local community) level. Each loss magnifies and multiplies itself many times over, weakening and unraveling the threads of societies throughout cultures. Families are disintegrating, and entire nations are paying the cost.

Women and children are the most vulnerable members of any society. The enormous extra burden and pressure that HIV/AIDS forces upon them is impossible to accurately measure or comprehend. As husbands and fathers (the primary breadwinners) succumb, women and children become increasingly susceptible to high-risk behavior—behavior they may feel is their only option. A woman's weak legal, social, and political status only compounds this problem.

In many cultures, men commonly marry the widows of their dead brothers. If a brother has died of AIDS, then it is likely that the wife is HIV-positive. If she is, then he will be infected.

The tragedy of AIDS orphans is one of the most visible impacts. Already more than 14 million children have lost parents to AIDS. Many have no other relatives to care for them. They often must care for themselves and younger siblings. Without older family members to raise, educate, or even love them, they will be forced to look elsewhere for this support. Again, high-risk behavior usually presents itself as their only survival option. This is one of the largest factors driving the explosive growth in street children globally, a group at extreme risk for HIV/AIDS.

Few things break my heart more than seeing scores of homeless and abandoned children roaming city streets. Some are beggars, some are thieves, and some are prostitutes. The idea of a formal education is beyond their grasp. So is any hope in the future.

Last year in Uganda, I met a young girl named Agnes. She used to live on the streets of Kampala, surviving by begging and scavenging for food in garbage bins. Agnes saw other children on their way back and forth to school. She admitted to me that this made her envious because she couldn't even recognize the first letter of her name. To her, going to school was an impossible dream. I'm glad to report that a street ministry rescued Agnes. She now lives in a Christian children's home, eats regular meals, has a bed to sleep in, and is excelling in school.

Food and Agriculture

HIV/AIDS has had a severe impact on food security. Losing the day-to-day productivity of one, or maybe two, family members, the weaker members must then care for the sick and also do the farming themselves. Those sick with the disease need special nutrition to maintain their health. Families with sick members need extra food to make up for what they cannot produce.

Already fragile food supplies are in jeopardy of becoming either inaccessible or unavailable entirely. Agriculture is the primary means of sustenance in many areas. The implication for farmers and their families, and eventually their countries, is staggering.

AIDS is stealing agricultural expertise and farming techniques from whole populations. Millions of subsistence farmers are dying, leaving behind children who do not have survival skills. This tragic pattern will eventually leave behind populations and countries without enough farmers who know how to seed, cultivate, and harvest a crop. People will have to rely even more heavily on limited supplies of donated food from governments and aid agencies or on expensive food imports they cannot possibly afford.

Education

The tragic pattern unfolding in the agricultural sector is being mirrored in the classroom. Countries where HIV infection rates are the highest are also recording significant declines in school enrollment. Children who do not have HIV are often forced to stay home to care for sick family members. Too often they become the primary breadwinners themselves.

HIV/AIDS is robbing schools of both students and teachers. The situation is especially bad in rural areas, where teachers are already scarce. Many communities cannot find replacement teachers. In the cities, replacements often cannot be trained fast enough to match the AIDS death rate.

Impact on Traditional Development Strategy and Practices

HIV/AIDS is destroying years of economic and social advancement while reversing decades of development. Conventional development and assistance strategies must change both in their design and implementation.

The epidemic only adds to the heavy burden on countries, societies, families, and individuals already at tremendous development risk. For example, people with limited access to food are the most likely to be vulnerable in other areas. They will get sick sooner, stay sick longer, and be less likely to stay in school or keep a job. If you multiply this condition often enough, an entire country becomes at risk. Aid agencies must adjust their programming accordingly. We see negative spirals in every sector of a nation—health care, education, industry, development, and any other area that an NGO may work, including programs directly with churches.

Personnel

New outreaches require our staffs to be educated in all aspects of HIV facts and risks. The disease has created the highest demand for health professionals ever, putting unprecedented strain on health care systems throughout the developing world. Unfortunately, AIDS is killing qualified medical people, and there are fewer professionals to replace them.

In fact, AIDS is decimating entire workforces in developing countries. The disease hits hardest between the ages of 15 and 49, the time of greatest productivity. Children lose their mothers, offices lose their workers, universities lose their professors, hospitals lose their doctors, armies lose their commanders, and on the list goes.

Nations are calling upon nongovernmental organizations to supply more trained staff to hospitals, clinics, community health programs, schools, universities, and orphan care activities. The need for community health professionals has exploded. Samaritan's Purse is recruiting, training, and placing community health specialists faster than ever before. Like many, we are also developing HIV/AIDS awareness and prevention programs—and we cannot keep up with the demand.

Financial

HIV/AIDS programming costs a lot. Generally, the more that an NGO spends on HIV/AIDS, the less it will have for other worthy programs. Seeking funding from governments is no panacea. Christian groups and national churches sometimes look to governments or the Global Fund to support their activities. When they do, conflicts often arise over the issues of evangelism and proselytizing.

AIDS is a long-term problem and requires a long-term response. Unfortunately, donors often have a shorter-term focus. Regular donors are asked to support a chronic emergency that is going to be with us for many decades. Thus, we need to revise our funding strategies.

Donor Education

Christian NGOs must carefully help donors understand the disease and the unique challenges and strategies required to fight it. This type of donor education often requires a candid, and sometimes explicit, discussion of sexually related matters. Explaining a school construction project or the science behind water purification is much easier. Sex is a sensitive topic for many people. Typically, the more conservative a person or group, the more uncomfortable it can be. But to help people thoroughly understand the causes and impact of HIV/AIDS, we must talk about these things.

A Holistic Approach

HIV/AIDS is causing nongovernmental organizations to take a more holistic approach. In most cases, the impact of the disease is so pervasive within a population group or region that no single organization can cover each sector (food, water, education, shelter, medical care, etc.). Coordination with other agencies is the only way to make a significant impact.

In another sense, battling HIV/AIDS is like peeling an onion. There are many layers, and if you want to see a long-lasting and effective change in people's lives, you have to peel away all the layers.

For example, prostitution in southeast Asia is no simple matter. Women and children—both girls and boys—prostitute themselves in the cities and resorts of Thailand, Cambodia, and Vietnam. They are also contracting HIV at a record pace.

Most of them are not in the sex trade by choice. Most think they have no other option to survive. I have met many young women and children who come from impoverished refugee or rural families. Profiteers offer to find the child a job in the city for a price. The parents pay part of the fee thinking the child will work in a factory or a farm. Instead the child is forced into a brothel and now owes the balance of the debt on behalf of the parents. This debt rarely gets paid, and it puts the child in bondage. In some instances, parents sell their children to these profiteers knowingly. Tragically, some of these children even go willingly, believing this is the only hope for their families.

Many of these women and children will eventually contract HIV/AIDS and need medical assistance. If they are fortunate, perhaps a group that can provide the training and skills to earn a safer living will rescue them. Or maybe a female prostitute will get pregnant, have a baby, and then abandon it to an orphanage run by a nongovernmental organization. Perhaps that child will be HIV-positive.

And while all these varieties of help are important and valuable, in the end there are still thousands of women, men, and children dying of AIDS in Bangkok and Phnom Penh.

After you peel away all the complex reasons why a person has AIDS, you finally arrive at the cause: somewhere, in a mountain village in northern Thailand or in a refugee camp along the Mekong River, you will find family members in such critical need that they agreed to trade their daughter or son for a couple bags of rice or a new roof.

I believe it is in that village where the need is the greatest and we can do the most to help. Unfortunately, the more immediate impacts of HIV/AIDS require that we use our resources, staff, and expertise elsewhere.

The Christian Aid Organization—Responsibility and Role

Christians, and Christian aid organizations—both in the United States and elsewhere, whether in a pulpit or in an AIDS hospice—have a message, a position, a mandate, and an opportunity like none other. We have eternal life through Jesus Christ, and we have a biblical responsibility to share that hope and the love of Christ in our words and deeds.

Christ made himself very clear on this matter. In Matthew 5:14–17 he tells a crowd:

You are the light of the world. A city on a hill cannot be hidden. Neither do people light a lamp and put it under a bowl. Instead they put it on its stand and it gives light to everyone in the house. In the same way, let your light shine before men, that they may see your good deeds and praise your Father in heaven.

We need to shine our light—the light of Christ in us—before men and women. We need to show unconditional love, compassion, and grace to the people around us. This means being true to the gospel and speaking the truth that sex is ordained by God to be between a husband and wife in a monogamous relationship. It means saying that AIDS is spread through human behavior and the only way to defeat AIDS is for people to change the way they behave. Speaking truthfully demands we condemn sin while loving sinners. By doing this, we must hold, and allow others to hold, ourselves to the highest standards.

AIDS has created an evangelism opportunity for the body of Christ unlike any in history. However, regardless of the number of people who do or do not accept Christ as Lord and Savior, Christians are responsible to act. Service, compassion, instruction, love, forgiveness, care, and humility are all vital expressions of Christianity, and they are all required as we respond to HIV/AIDS. Christians should take the lead in this effort as part of our worship to the Lord.

The world is watching our response. While the subject is sensitive, we cannot afford to fail. Even secular experts in the HIV/AIDS field recognize the strategic importance of churches in the fight against this disease and its ravages.

In a 2002 speech to the African Religious Leaders Assembly on Children and HIV/AIDS in Nairobi, Stephen Lewis, special envoy of the United Nations Secretary General for HIV/AIDS in Africa, said:

> As always, children and women carry the burden of abandonment, vulnerability, stigma, poverty, and desperation. They constitute, for you, the cause you must lead. You constitute, for them, the meaning of salvation in terms both spiritual and practical. Who else, beyond yourselves, is so well placed to lead? Who else has such a network of voices at the grass-roots level? Who else has access to all communities once a week? Every week, across the continent? Who else officiates at the millions of funerals of those who die from AIDS-related illnesses, and better understands the consequences for children and families? Who else works on a daily basis with faith-based, community-based organizations? In the midst of this wanton, ravaging pandemic, it is truly like an act of divine intervention you should be physically present everywhere, all the time. I ask again: who else, therefore, is so well placed to lead?

The Stigma of HIV/AIDS

What keeps people from confronting the realities and implications of HIV/AIDS? After awareness happens, there is only one answer: stigma.

Stigma keeps North American churches from being involved with the AIDS crisis. Stigma keeps people in isolation as they suffer. Stigma condemns and labels the sick and dying as sinners. Stigma keeps people from getting tested. Stigma keeps sick people from seeking medical help. Stigma keeps people from getting help from their neighbors. Stigma cuts off relationships and destroys families. Stigma causes people to lose their jobs or keeps them from getting jobs. Stigma causes communities and countries to deny the reality and impact of this disease.

Examples are plentiful. Some people have been secretly diagnosed as HIV-positive but are afraid to tell anyone for fear of being ostracized from their family, church, job, or home. Others have family members dying of AIDS and are embarrassed to tell anyone. Church members are sick or dying and then rejected by their Christian community, who feel this person has received a judgment from God.

No people group, country, or religion has a monopoly on HIV/AIDS stigma. In southeast Asia, teenage daughters who have been sold into prostitution by their families return to their villages as castoffs who have been abused, exploited, and are now HIV-positive. They are shunned and have no hope of marrying. In parts of Africa, sweeping shame under the proverbial rug is not enough for some families. Instead, they lock relatives into back rooms to die, where no one else can see them or has to deal with them.

The original Greek word for stigma refers to the marks created on Christ's body by the wounds of his crucifixion. Our Lord, Jesus Christ, was stigmatized himself. After his resurrection, he confirmed his identity to the disciples by letting them see his scars. During his ministry, Christ touched lepers, not asking how they became afflicted, only showing compassion while meeting their needs.

Since HIV/AIDS was first identified over 20 years ago, tragic misconceptions and misunderstandings have taken root in the church. Many Christians believe that AIDS is a disease primarily of homosexuals, prostitutes, and drug users. Many others believe that AIDS is a judgment from God for sin. It is true that every action has a consequence, and when we choose to act outside of God's mandate for sexual purity, we should also be prepared to deal with those consequences. However, the Bible teaches that "*all* have sinned, and come short of the glory of God" (Romans 3:23 KJV). We are all sinners and deserve eternal death. But through Christ we can be forgiven.

God calls Christians to tell others of the redeeming love of Christ and the eternal life they can have through him. We also must demonstrate that love and grace. God's grace can overcome stigma. One of the most beautiful demonstrations of his grace is found in the story of the Good Samaritan.

The Good Samaritan Model

The name of the organization I work for, Samaritan's Purse, comes from Luke 10. It is a well-known story that perfectly describes a model of unconditional assistance. Any aid organization—Christian or not—would do well to consider the actions of this anonymous Samaritan traveler.

For Christians in particular, this story is of utmost importance. In it, Christ tells us how to treat people in need. By helping the man lying at the side of the road, the Samaritan performed an act of gracious, spontaneous, and unconditional compassion. He didn't ask the man who he was or what circumstances brought him to this road. He didn't question the man's ethnicity or religion. There is no record of the Samaritan suggesting to the man that this assault was something he deserved or brought on himself.

The Samaritan simply took pity on the man, went to where he was, and helped him. By the end of the story, this Samaritan had provided the beaten man with medical care, transport, shelter, clothing, and other basic needs. He did his job thoroughly. Should anyone be surprised that this ancient story so perfectly sets all modern standards of humanitarian assistance?

The Missing Ingredients: Grace and Leadership

Not only is the story of the Good Samaritan a perfect model of humanitarian assistance, there is an even more important message

Christians can glean. It is a message of magnificent grace. It is a message of how we must reach out in unconditional love and compassion to people locked in the shackles of HIV/AIDS.

Christians, more than anyone, have an unprecedented opportunity to show grace. We cannot walk away from Christ's mandate of grace. It is freely given to us and we in turn are compelled to freely give it out.

Christians must come to recognize those with HIV/AIDS not as hopeless sinners reaping the consequences of a wasted life, but as people God loves and values. And as we reach out to them in love and compassion, they will see Christ in us. This is our calling.

Apart from God's grace, we all would be hopelessly lost in our own sin. How can we respond any differently to people who are sick and perhaps living without any hope for eternity? If we can't live grace, then we are living in a deficit. If we can live it, then we have an unprecedented opportunity to share the good news in word and deed.

If grace is scarce in the Christian response to HIV/AIDS, then we also need to add leadership to that list. Any effective, long-lasting response to the HIV/AIDS crisis demands strong moral leadership within every level of the body of Christ and society. This goes from leadership at international levels, to country levels, to community levels, to church levels, to our individual lives. The bar of direct leadership is high for those groups purporting to give aid in the name of Christ.

This leadership must begin at the individual level. We must practice biblically based standards of abstinence and fidelity. This personal leadership takes the form of obedience and daily surrender to God. With this as our foundation, we can show leadership in our families, organizations, jobs, and churches. And we must demand strong moral leadership from our pastors, denominational leaders, and public office holders at every level.

In every country on every continent where HIV/AIDS is cutting its deadly swath, dismal Christian leadership has allowed ignorance and apathy to grow in churches and communities. The lack of leadership, perhaps more than anything else, has allowed HIV infection rates to soar to unimaginable heights.

Certainly there are some exceptions. Uganda stands as a shining example. Many years ago, when the virus first appeared, government leaders decided to act. Strong political and moral leadership from President Yoweri Museveni and First Lady Janet Museveni has paid its dividends. Infection rates have dropped dramatically.

Ugandans, under the leadership of the Musevenis, were among the first to acknowledge the essential role of faith and biblical principles in fighting HIV/AIDS. Uganda has answered the call to moral leadership and proven that it works. Many Ugandans have demonstrated faithfulness and compassion.

Conclusion

In Matthew 24:12–14, Jesus warns of what will happen in the final days before his return:

> Sin will be rampant everywhere, and the love of many will grow cold. But those who endure to the end will be saved. And the Good News about the Kingdom will be preached throughout the whole world, so that all nations will hear it; and then, finally, the end will come. (NLT)

Christ declares that the love of many will grow cold. This truly frightening thought must challenge Christians and everyone who works for a Christian aid organization.

We have the privilege and responsibility to bring spiritual and physical help to poor, sick, and needy people around the world. Christian nongovernmental organizations also have the obligation to share their stories with the world. We must encourage Christians to get involved in the fight against HIV/AIDS. We should applaud examples of hope, compassion, and leadership to spur others to do the same. We can reach people who lead people.

Only Christ knows the name of every person who has ever lived or died with HIV/AIDS. These are not anonymous faces or soulless statistics to our Creator. Though they may suffer and die alone, Christ, who has already done the same, is lovingly watching over them and wants us to love them and tell them about his redeeming love.

We are all walking on the Samaritan road, a road littered by those who have needlessly died from the wounds of a bandit named AIDS. When history's final page is written, I pray that it will not be said that Christians walked by on the other side. Let our legacy be love, compassion, and grace. Let our history be one of action. Let our story say that we did not let our hearts grow cold.

The King will reply, "I tell you the truth, whatever you did for one of the least of these brothers of mine, you did for me" (Matthew 25:40).

CHAPTER 16
DOROTHY BREWSTER-LEE

PROVIDING AIDS TREATMENT AND CARE

The World Health Organization estimates that there are 42 million people infected with HIV, 6 million of whom need antiretroviral therapy (ART). In sub-Saharan Africa, less than 1 percent of those who need treatment are receiving antiretroviral (ARV) therapy. Over the past three years, the prices of ARV drugs have fallen dramatically. Other good news: The World Health Organization has recently committed to ensure that at least 3 million of those who need treatment in resource poor countries get enrolled in ART programs by 2005. The United States AIDS Emergency Plan seeks to get 2 million people in treatment by 2008. Both the World Health Organization and U.S. initiatives aim to increase the access of poor communities to treatment.

Seventy percent of the people living with HIV are in sub-Saharan Africa. Church hospitals and Christian community health programs have been some of the first organizations to care for patients with HIV infections. Their programs include treating opportunistic infections and providing palliative care and home-based care. Many of these hospitals have now added ART programs.[1]

In fact, faith-based organizations provide up to 50 percent of the health care in this region. Given this reality, how should Christian hospitals and other health institutions respond to the challenge of increasing access by the poor? What ethical questions need to be answered before a Christian hospital establishes an ART program? Who should be treated? Should Christian hospitals charge for ARV treatment? What will happen to patients when the crisis ceases to dominate the global center stage and ARV drugs no longer receive huge subsidies? There are many questions and few clear answers.

Ethical Questions

There are many practical and ethical reasons why Christian hospitals might want to avoid initiating ARV therapy. One compelling reason relates to the concern that most mission hospitals will not be able to guarantee long-term, affordable access to these drugs, which need to be taken over the course of the patient's life. This is particularly true for poor patients who are candidates to receive drugs either free or at heavily subsidized prices. Without heavy overseas support, most Christian hospitals cannot maintain the equipment and staff required to provide optimal programs for diagnosing new cases, monitoring drug-related complications and compliance, and conducting community surveillance for drug resistance. Inappropriate use of drugs might quickly lead to resistance and render a generation of drugs useless. This has already occurred with both tuberculosis (TB) and malaria drugs.

Clinicians in Christian hospitals also fear that committing scarce resources to fight one disease may undermine the fragile health infrastructure at a time when many Christian hospitals are struggling to deliver care to millions of patients dying from other killer diseases such as malaria, TB, upper respiratory infections, and diarrhea. Committing church resources to AIDS treatment also runs the risk of undermining efforts to strengthen primary behavior change, which may ultimately be the most important contribution of the church to the AIDS crisis.

Despite the uncertainties, Christian hospitals continue to initiate new ARV treatment programs. While these hospitals are not confident that this is the most effective approach, particularly in the long term, they are certain that using all available and appropriate technologies to prolong life in the most optimal state is central to the mission of every Christian hospital. One Christian hospital coordinator said, "We prayerfully and with trepidation felt drawn to enter the ARV treatment arena as another way to serve others."

How Should Christian Hospitals Become Involved with ARV Therapy?

ARVs will soon be available for the poor in sub-Saharan Africa. But making drugs technically feasible and affordable for poor communities does not ensure that they will actually reach the right communities. Numerous studies document the failure of both governments and nongovernmental organizations to get desperately needed resources to the most vulnerable populations. We need to develop, implement, and carefully monitor solid strategies so that the poor, particularly in rural communities, can get ARV therapies. Christian health institutions, many founded specifically to help poor rural communities, are well placed to see that this happens.

Here are several vital questions such institutions need to answer:

1. How does disease-specific treatment impact Christian efforts to treat the whole person?

From their inception, Christian hospitals have set out to treat the whole person—mind, body, and spirit. This founding principle has remained central. Church health ministries have expanded to include community-based and congregation-based approaches. Some Christian hospitals have expanded to include community development programs that directly impact health, such as water management, food security, and income generation. Integral to all these outreach programs has been the emphasis on community participation, which is the cornerstone for long-term sustainability.

Disease-driven agendas, with predetermined goals and methods for implementation, are frequently thrust upon communities, allowing little room for integration into the overall health strategy. Christian institutions need to insist that they are well integrated into their existing prevention, care, and support activities. They will need to constantly remind their medical colleagues that they are called to minister to people and not simply to dispense pills. Church institutions engaging in ART programs must see that communities, not simply experts, design and implement these programs. Community ownership will be integral to success. Reserving leadership roles for people living with HIV/AIDS is another prerequisite.

2. Is it possible to provide AIDS treatment in a community setting?

Many have suggested that treating patients outside the walls of the Christian hospital might increase access for the poor by bringing services closer to communities. Community-based programs would theoretically also be more affordable. Direct observation therapy (DOT) programs for TB are held up as a model for community-based ARV distribution. At first glance, the approach looks very feasible. On closer review, however, one begins to see difficulties. As the administrator of one DOTS program asked, "Practically speaking, how can we maintain a program for a lifetime, when it's so tough to maintain patients on a six-month course of TB treatment?"

Jodi McGill, R.N., M.P.H., is responsible for primary health care in three Christian hospitals in Malawi. She said, "Community-based treatment seems to work only for those who have been correctly diagnosed, then moved through their initial ARV treatment without major side effects. The patients also need to demonstrate their ability to be consistent about taking their meds before they are released to follow-up in the community setting."[2]

Volunteers are recruited through the various church denominations. Recruitment and retention of volunteers are high because of the social respect that comes with being a volunteer. Volunteers are also motivated by the frequent visits of the program supervisors, who are chosen from among each group of volunteers in an area. Some of these volunteers also are active in the home-based care (HBC) and TB DOTs programs.

The emergence of a resistant virus is always an issue of concern, particularly when drugs are being administered beyond hospital walls. In Malawi, drug resistance resulting from patient noncompliance with drug therapy is generally due to one of three causes: (1) poor comprehension about resistance; (2) difficulty getting to the drug distribution site; and (3) lack of funds to purchase medications.

Drugs cost about US$30 per month in a region where the average income is US$170 a year. Forty percent of the people earn less than US$40 per year. Program organizers hope that providing affordable, fixed-dose combinations (FDCs) in well supervised and supported local community settings will increase patient access and compliance.

3. How would AIDS treatment and care provided by Christian health facilities differ from what a government would provide?

There is little debate about the added value Christian organizations bring in implementing primary behavior change prevention and stigma reduction. Do Christian organizations also make a unique contribution in AIDS treatment and care? Holly Frietas, B.S.N., HIV/AIDS resource facilitator, Medical Ambassadors International, notes, "Christian health facilities are generally better equipped to provide holistic care to individuals and families, focusing on the whole person rather than merely curative care pharmaceutical distribution. They often have outside resources for funding, personnel, medical supplies, and training. Most significantly, Christian care providers have a unique internal motivation to provide ongoing and loving care to those affected by HIV/AIDS and Christ as their model of compassion and care."

4. Is there a role for short-term players?

At the 2003 Global Missions Health Conference, Louisville, Kentucky, Jodi McGill, mission coworker with the Presbyterian Church (USA), said that national staff and long-term expatriate staff in many of these institutions desperately need relief, additional helping hands, and updated information. Short-term volunteers are needed for relieving the long-term permanent staff, providing technical training updates for staff, assisting at community-based childcare centers, and providing nutrition education to patients.

Examples of Christian Involvement

Local health institutions working with community leaders must be empowered to build ART programs, which address the needs of the local stakeholders and draw on the community's strength and resources. Below are three examples of Christian health responses.

Ekwendeni Mission Hospital, Church of Central Africa, Malawi

The AIDS epidemic has hit Malawi very hard. Malawi has one of the highest infection levels in the world, with 16.4 percent of those aged 15 to 49 and 8.9 percent of the total population infected. AIDS is the *leading cause of death* for people 15 to 49 years old. The disease has orphaned more than 300,000 children, deepened the country's already widespread poverty, and continues to burden countless families with loss of health, income, and life.

Malawi's initial public health response to the epidemic was robust. It consisted of education, prevention, and palliation for those in the later stages of the disease, social support programs such as orphan care, and prayer by those with faith. This disease itself, however, was not treated because the obstacles were too great. Treatment was too expensive and demanding (numerous pills to be taken at specific times throughout the day and evening), the health care resources and infrastructure were too limited, and the risk of resistant HIV strains emerging was too large.

Ekwendeni Mission Hospital is situated on the main road to Karonga, about 13 miles from Mzuzu City. The hospital, with 200 beds and a nursing school, serves an area of approximately 360 square miles and 60,000 people. Approximately 45 percent of the people admitted are HIV-positive.

The overall goal of the Ekwendeni program is to reduce the burden of opportunistic infections and number of deaths caused by HIV/AIDS. The program provides voluntary counseling and testing (VCT), prevention of mother to child transmission (PMTCT), home-based care (HBC), palliative care, and treatment of opportunistic infections. In 2003, leaders expanded the HIV/AIDS program to include ART.

A weekly ARV treatment clinic screens and enlists eligible clients into treatment. Eligibility is based on the National AIDS Commission ARV guidelines. Treatment generally consists of a fixed triple drug therapy (one tab taken twice a day). The program expects most patients to contribute to the cost of their ARV treatment. Patients with sufficient income pay the full amount for drugs. The program accepts referrals from VCT clinics in the area as well as from other health institutions.

Quarterly the program manager reports on interventions, the number of people reached, the quality of treatment, and the number of people voluntarily tested and counseled. The Ministry of Health and National AIDS Commission receive copies of the reports. During the project years

2004–2005 the program hopes to place 500 people living with AIDS on ARV treatment. This number is expected to increase along with the capacity of the clinic to process patients. The scaled-up ARV program will require retraining of staff in patient clinical management and tracking. It will also require better laboratory equipment and technician skills.

Not surprisingly, program start-up costs are high. The running costs, which are minimal, can be absorbed into the hospital budget. Drugs represent the largest ongoing project expense, but the program anticipates that patients will be able to pay increasing proportions of the costs as the drug prices fall. The per-patient overhead hospital costs should also fall as patients move to community monitoring sites.

Catholic Relief Services HIV/AIDS Programs

Catholic Relief Services (CRS) has been responding to the HIV/AIDS crisis since 1989. It supports more than 160 HIV/AIDS projects in 30 countries, reaching more than 4 million people. The aim of the CRS HIV/AIDS program is to provide holistic care and support to patients and families while building local capacity that can respond to immediate needs, address the underlying causes of AIDS, and reduce the spread of HIV. An extensive network of partners (which include local churches, community-based organizations, other faith-based organizations, local governments, and government health ministries) implements the program. Program activities include:

- Home-Based Care (HBC) and Support: palliative care, treatment of opportunistic infections, psychosocial services and nutrition;

- Orphans and Vulnerable Children (OVC) care and support: functional school aid (tuition grants, fees, uniforms, books), training in vocational and life skills;

- Information, Education and Communication for awareness and prevention: behavior change, VCT, and PMTCT;

- Peer support groups for People Living with HIV/AIDS: psychosocial support, income generation, agriculture, youth anti-AIDS clubs, and food security.

After months of research, CRS decided to provide technical support to its overseas affiliates wishing to add ART to their extensive care and support services. Affordability, sustainability, and potential emergence of resistant viruses were all considered. Ultimately, CRS created an advisory board to review the program's development, monitor activities, and provide guidance for setting ART policy. In 2003 CRS initiated a partnership with the South Africa Catholic Bishops' Conference (SACBC) AIDS Office to expand their care and support services to include ARV treatment.

South Africa Catholic Bishops' Conference AIDS Office

The South Africa Catholic Bishops' Conference (SACBC) AIDS Office, created in January 2000, coordinates work in South Africa, Swaziland, Botswana, Namibia, and Lesotho. It provides technical assistance and funds to 187 projects run at the diocese and parish level. Among these projects is a network of 44 home-based care programs, which serve approximately 22,000 clients.

Over the past year, SACBC has taken a radical turn on ART access. It now strongly supports the rapid implementation of a comprehensive treatment plan, which includes free universal access to ARV therapy. In 2003, it selected 12 home-based care sites to include an ART component. By the end of 2004, SACBC intends to have 1,000 clients on ART; by 2006 it will have 4,800.

Sister Alison Munro, who coordinates the office, notes that the church has always been involved in various community activities relating to health, education, and relief. She notes, however, that the Catholic Church got off to a slow start in southern Africa, "influenced by sociopolitical realities, by ethical dilemmas, and by an inability on the part of the church and community leadership to recognize the signs of impending calamity."

"Today," she adds, "the Catholic Church is a major provider of care, treatment, and support to affected and infected people."

The new initiative to scale up ART programs has three goals:

1. To provide ART to patients living with AIDS in resource-limited setting through an open access program.

2. To provide comprehensive support services at the 12 sites, including counseling and emotional support, AIDS education, Positive Living Programs, food security and nutrition programs, peer support groups, and clinical services.

3. To provide a protocol and framework to initiate a comprehensive, coordinated, and planned assault on HIV/AIDS.

The ARV treatment will be prescribed and monitored by the program doctor and nurse. The program clinical team will also be able to provide treatment for TB and other opportunistic infections. Referrals to the ART program will continue to come from the home-based care programs, the hospitals, community members, and local doctors.

Once on therapy, patients will return quarterly for clinical assessments to determine the continued efficacy of the treatment regime. Sister Munro notes, "It is important that the clinical and support services are not seen as separate services in the program, but that they work and coordinate as a unit to ensure the long-term sustainability of the project."

A steering committee of community members will provide oversight and guidance. It will define program policies and procedures, review the financial plan, create program objectives, and monitor implementation.

The program addresses concerns about the emergence of antiretroviral drug resistance through its adherence program and support groups. The adherence program is modeled after, and works in close cooperation with, the TB DOTS program. Home caregivers and nurses already collaborate with the Department of Health on monitoring patient compliance to TB treatment. A "buddy system" and Nutrition and Food Security support groups also encourage adherence. Prior to being placed on ARVs, patients must also complete the Patient Compliance Assessment protocol. Patients must live within walking distance of the care site.

The SACBC HBC volunteer network will continue to be integral to the success of the ART program. "What is emerging clearly in many areas throughout the region is that people are taking seriously the call of the gospel to love their neighbor in need," Sister Munro says. Volunteer Home Caregivers receive training in basic nursing skills, counseling for the patient and immediate family, AIDS education, data gathering, and program adherence counseling. AIDS core training topics also include understanding ART; sexually transmitted infections and TB; spiritual, cultural, and religious issues; infection control; and nutrition.

The extensive community reach of the SACBC program into an area of approximately 8.8 million people will complement the government initiative announced on August 8, 2003, to license and manufacture generic ARVs and to implement a national plan for ART services.

Medical Ambassadors International (MAI)

The MAI Mission Statement reads, *"Transforming nations through the seamless combination of disease prevention, evangelism, and community development."* The MAI program is based on the Community Health Evangelism (CHE) method. The primary purpose is to recruit, train, and mentor nationals in the developing world to take responsibility to reach their own people physically and spiritually.

Medical Ambassadors International is currently working in 56 countries and 894 villages. A comprehensive manual addresses the challenges for communities. Program objectives include:

1. Educating and involving communities and community leaders to become active in HIV prevention.

2. Strengthening and mobilizing local churches for HIV/AIDS ministry.

3. Improving the ability of families and neighbors to meet the holistic health needs of their HIV-positive family members.

4. Improving the emotional state and coping skills of PLWHA and their families.

5. Helping communities to develop strategies to care for children and adults.

6. Decreasing the risk of transmission from mother to child.

7. Bringing HIV/AIDS to the forefront in planning and funding.

8. Bringing hope through Christ to individuals and communities.

The Vertical AIDS Transmission Prevention (VATP) program is the only MAI initiative involving the distribution of ARVs. MAI collaborates with local clinics to provide Nevirapine to pregnant women and their newborns. Trained CHEs provide counseling and follow-up.

At present, MAI's AIDS care and support programs do not include ARV treatment. The goal is to produce self-sustaining programs run by community members who take active ownership of the project and do not require oversight or continuing funding by MAI. Providing affordable, accessible, lifelong ART regimes is not impossible but certainly would be a formidable undertaking for many poor communities. While MAI attempts to provide ART in appropriate settings, it emphasizes that the church must treat the whole person, particularly in remote areas where access to ART will always be limited or nonexistent.

Christians have organized many approaches to treatment and care. But medical realities and the high technology required by ART have placed the burden primarily in the hands of medical institutions. Many of the community-based ART programs have been developed by doctors desperate to extend the life saving drugs beyond the narrow limits of their hospital. The SACBC ART program differs because it emerges from the HBC program, a program initiated not by a medical institution but from the church and community leaders.[3]

Each community will need to decide on the right balance of technologically appropriate, medically sound, spiritually based, and compassionate care and treatment.

Christian Contribution to AIDS Treatment and Care

Christian health providers must not simply contribute our extensive capacity for reaching rural communities with high quality services, but we must also bring our perspective on justice, holistic care, long-term engagement, insistence on community participation, and commitment to increased health access for the poor. In the rush to get drugs to the field, we must monitor the long-term implications of the short-term quantitative goals principally set by foreign experts.

Christian health professionals, leaders, and laity need to increase advocacy for affordable drugs and comprehensive programs that do not simply dispense pills but address the need for treatment of opportunistic infections, home-based care, behavior change counseling and peer support, nutritional enhancement, and support for vulnerable children living with sick parents. We need Christian prayers and compassion to bring hope and spiritual healing to those who are sick and dying in spite of ART and the best comprehensive psychosocial support programs. We need Christian leaders to condemn stigma and discrimination as sinful. An environment that encourages massive testing, disclosure of HIV status, and access to ART can only exist when communities have eliminated stigma and discrimination.

Christian health professionals both in sub-Saharan Africa and the United States are well placed to monitor the flow of resources and insist on appropriate levels of funding not only for ART but also for primary behavior change activities. We need to implement more national prevention strategies to reduce the rate of infections and bring the epidemic to a halt.

Conclusion

AIDS is robbing Africa of many of its most productive people. In South Africa alone, there will be an estimated 1.5 million AIDS orphans by 2010. Even if an effective vaccine were developed today, we would still need to help the 28 million people already infected and dying. While ARV drugs are not a cure, they do reduce mortality and morbidity. ARV drugs can thus improve the quality of life of those infected, allowing them to contribute to their communities and their nations.

Notes

1. In the words of Dr. Lungu, medical director at Ekwendeni hospital:

"In spite of the relative success of Malawi's prevention and support programs, their impact on the AIDS epidemic has been limited, because they have not been comprehensive and didn't strike at the disease itself, i.e., there has been no antiretroviral therapy. Two significant developments have occurred in the last few years that have removed the obstacles associated with antiretroviral (ARV) treatment of AIDS patients in Africa. First, ARV treatment regimens have been simplified and their cost has decreased (from more than several thousand dollars for one year of treatment per patient to about $300 per patient/year in Africa). Second, the rest of the world (i.e., developed countries) [has] finally come to appreciate the awful toll that AIDS is taking in developing countries and are now recognizing their responsibility to help. They are now funding African countries such as Malawi (through the United Nation's Global Fund) to develop the healthcare infrastructure necessary to enable ARV treatment of AIDS patients to occur. These recent developments have created an environment in Malawi where it is now possible for the Synod of Livingstonia to add ARVs to its many already existent AIDS programs.

". . . The disease mostly affects the young and productive that may also just have started a family. Recurrent illnesses result in the loss of working days and being unable to support their families. Farmers are unable to produce enough food crops, which threatens the food security of the whole nation. When the people become terminally ill, not only family resources are diverted to caring for them but also [there is a] double loss of labour and thus inevitable low productivity, food shortage and poverty level worsens. And when they die they leave an ever-increasing number of orphans placing a socioeconomic burden on the community.

"Ekwendeni hospital, located in the rural area, will mostly treat farmers and traders. Treating farmers and traders will ensure food security, protect the rural economy and reduce the number of orphans and financial loss incurred in taking care of the orphans. The cost-benefit analysis of this intervention has much greater gains than the loss of capital to be invested in it."

2. McGill describes the process of transitioning patients to community programs:

"In the hospital programs a person who is diagnosed as seropositive for HIV is given the name of volunteers in his/her area. If the person agrees, the volunteer is also given that person's name. If the person agrees to disclosure, the volunteer visits the client shortly after receiving the information and determines what is needed at that time and how often visits will take place. If the client wants to take the responsibility for contacting the volunteer, then the time from 'referral' to volunteer contact is quite variable. Both types of referrals have a little paperwork involved. Volunteers refer or suggest referral for clients as needed."

3. Sister Munro states, "Commitment to the response of the Catholic Church to AIDS comes from all levels. Bishops who take a hands-on approach inspire the laity to take seriously the call to serve God in their brothers and sisters. When clergy, as gatekeepers, open the gates to various initiatives of their parishioners, much good work ensues."

CHAPTER 17
ANDREW TOMKINS

![black bar]

NEEDS, NICHES, AND NEW LEADERSHIP STYLES: EMERGING CHALLENGES AND OPPORTUNITIES FOR CHRISTIANS IN THE HIV/AIDS EPIDEMIC

Many interventions for the prevention and management of the HIV/AIDS epidemic are now understood, but the necessary manpower and finance are way beyond the capacity of most national governments. International agencies are increasing their financial contributions to poor countries afflicted by HIV/AIDS, and national health workers are increasingly skilled, but the sheer scale of work frequently overwhelms them. Christian churches and organizations have a key role but need to move beyond their traditional activities of evangelism and spiritual nurture.

This chapter aims to provide a framework for Christians to become more proactive. It identifies the needs, including behavior change, medical care, personal care, and spiritual care. It discusses the niches for Christian organizations—filling the gaps that national and international programs cannot fill—and outlines the commitment, approaches, and resources that Christian organizations need for their programs to be effective and sustainable.

It reviews leadership models. Hierarchical models that focus on preaching and teaching need to be replaced by those focusing on Christ-inspired servanthood. This requires leaders to lead by example—getting alongside and caring for those who are affected or afflicted, helping with the myriad of physical, emotional, and spiritual care issues that accompany the HIV/AIDS epidemic. Such leaders in HIV/AIDS-afflicted countries need support from Christian leaders and churches in industrialized countries on a much larger scale than at present.

There has never been a greater opportunity for Christians in every country to work together to show the love of Jesus in action.

What are the Needs?

Behavior change. Sexual abstinence, faithful sexual partnerships, and a cure for Intravenous Drug Use (IDU) are all possible. However, many find these things difficult, as evidenced by the impact of HIV among church members in many countries. We need greater appreciation of the relative impact of knowledge-based, as opposed to skill-based, prevention programs. Conventional programs assume that individuals who are informed of the risks will change behavior. But low self worth, lack of skills in negotiating in threatening sexual environments, cultural subservience of girls to older males, and macho sexual cultures often overcome a person's "head knowledge" of what is right.

There are good examples of training programs (such as child-to-child programs) and self-awareness activities in schools and youth groups. Process evaluations show that they are popular with students, particularly when the program has been developed with the full participation of children. But whether they have resulted in behavioral change is usually unknown. The challenge is to assess the impact of behavior change programs more carefully.[1]

Harm reduction. Male condoms are of proven benefit in the prevention of transmission of HIV between adults. Drugs are important in the prevention of Mother to Child Transmission (MTCT) of HIV to an innocent, developing child during pregnancy. Supplying sterile needles to intravenous drug users results in a reduction in hepatitis B and HIV.

Prevention of MTCT. The detection of HIV and other sexually transmitted infections in individuals before they become parents is increasing in industrialized countries. While it is extremely painful for one partner to discover that he or she is HIV-positive while the other is HIV–negative, such knowledge provides couples with information they can use to base their decisions about future life together, sexual activity, and parenthood.

Churches are increasingly offering HIV testing and counseling before marriage. Such activities are not new.[2] Premarital testing for genetic blood disorders such as thalassaemia has been a key strategy in reducing the prevalence of this devastating fatal disease of children. Sterilization is also increasingly requested by women who know they are HIV-positive but who do not wish to risk infecting their infant. If an HIV-positive woman is pregnant, there are interventions (e.g., nevirapine) that reduce the risk of MTCT.

This assumes that women know their HIV status, but for the majority of women in sub-Saharan Africa, HIV testing is unavailable. Even when it is, the testing rates vary considerably. In Lusaka, Zambia, less than 10 percent of women attending routine prenatal clinics agree to be tested. But in clinics with specially trained staff the rate is over 70 percent. Fear of the consequences of disclosure to partners is a major problem. The testing rates in certain Nigerian centers are 100 percent because testing is enforced. Globally, there are unfulfilled needs for compassionate, confidential HIV testing and counseling.

Anti-retroviral drugs and their cost. While there are high-level, international initiatives (e.g., a global fund that focuses on HIV, malaria, and tuberculosis) that promise increasing resources for HIV-affected nations, the costs of anti-retroviral drugs (ARVs) has been too high (a year's supply costs many thousands of dollars) for most poor countries where the average annual expenditure on health/individual is below US$20. Low-cost drug regimes are increasingly available (around US$350 per year), but this does not cover the cost of testing the CD4 white blood cell count and viral load, which are necessary for monitoring treatment.

Considerable efforts are being made to "fast track" low-cost ARV regimes to adults and children with HIV/AIDS. There is a great need for advocacy to make ARVs more widely available.[3] But agencies and governments ask how many extra months of life will these drugs achieve in each situation? Could these extra months be achieved by other use of the money that is being spent on ARV programs? These are painful but necessary questions. At present there are major anomalies in distribution of ARVs.[4]

Improved management of conditions that affect the transmission and severity of HIV/AIDS. This includes malaria, sexually transmitted diseases, intestinal parasites, TB, and nutritional deficiencies.[5] Prevention and rapid treatment of these conditions has been a central part of primary health care. These interventions need greater attention than ever if HIV transmission is to be prevented. Common conditions need basic, affordable treatment for diarrhoea, skin infection, mouth ulcers, and pain. There are now good examples of basic treatment regimes that non-professionals can use.[6]

Personal care. Few governments have enough staff to cope with the massive needs of HIV-infected individuals. They need clean clothes to replace those which are soiled, bathing when they feel too weak to bother, food prepared when they feel too tired to cook, and help with household chores.

Emotional and spiritual care. HIV-infected individuals have special needs for support. Their guilt, anger, despair, isolation, stigmatisation, and other afflictions all drain the capacity to keep going. HIV-infected individuals really appreciate consistent, unjudging, and ungrudging compassion, care, and support. But governments or agencies cannot provide these. Love does not come in bottles; neither can it be injected. Many testify to the effect of believing prayer on the physical and emotional condition of the HIV-positive individual. Over the last decade a variety of care-models have been developed, but few have been evaluated. Whereas the literature is brimming with evaluations of different doses and regimes of ARVs, there has been remarkably little evaluation of emotional/ spiritual care regimes. However, methods are available to monitor health and wholeness.[7]

Finances and food. Individuals and families living with HIV/AIDS are nearly always poor. Their income may have been drastically reduced; they may be less able to farm; they face problems finding money for housing, food, water, and education for their children; and they face considerable costs for health care. Program managers, community leaders, and households have to make painful decisions about what they should focus on. Increasing their income and household food security is crucial if HIV-infected subjects are to feel well enough to work, survive, and nurture their children. Thus income-generating activities, improved water supplies, agricultural extension, and small animal projects are increasingly seen as vital interventions in support of HIV/AIDS. Revolving loans have been used extensively. Nongovernmental organizations have much experience with these.

Orphan care. Previous epidemics and wars have left children without parents. But HIV/AIDS has several characteristics that cause children more stress than in previous crises.[8] Children have often seen their parents take a long time to die. They may well have been lied to, as parents and relatives refused to tell the children why their parents are so ill. The children, especially the girls, may be prevented from going to school because they have to look after sick relatives and do household and farming chores. They may have been excluded from key family events. They may not have been allowed to go to the funeral. Relatives may have stolen the family land. Children may be hungry, confused, anxious, tired, and ill themselves. Lacking parental nurture, they may grow up without the wisdom and support of adults, getting into bad company and desperately trying to get enough to eat and clothe themselves. There are many programs for care and support of Orphans and Vulnerable Children (OVCs) but few evaluations of their effectiveness and sustainability.[9]

The Niches

Behavior change. Working with ordinary, vulnerable people is more effective than simply preaching from the pulpit. Development of strong life skills is more effective than telling people what to do. There are now helpful materials for HIV/AIDS education within schools, youth groups, child-to-child programs, and programs for commercial sex workers and intravenous drug users.[10] It is possible to achieve an increase in abstinence rates.[11]

A review of 20 HIV/AIDS programs run by Christian organizations supported by Tear Fund in East, Central, and South Africa indicates that several key elements are important.[12] These include: (1) basing interventions on what young people say they want in sexual health information; (2) accepting that changing adolescent behavior may require intensive efforts for at least two to three years; (3) using small group instruction and learning; (4) using a variety of interactive teaching encouraging participants to develop and own the messages for themselves; (5) addressing the influence of social pressure on adolescents; (6) ensuring effective training for individuals implementing the program; and (7) encouraging openness in communicating about sex.

Tackling harm reduction with compassion. Programs run by Christian organizations are welcomed if they are effective and consistent. "Fly by night" programs without follow-up and support are not. Christian organizations need to develop a clear, compassionate stance on the promotion of condom use. It is quite possible to be involved in more than one track. Promoting the ABC approach (Abstinence, Being faithful, and use of Condoms by those who do not keep to the first two) is feasible. Preventing fatal infection in adults and children by condoms is a rational parallel message.

Premarital testing. Churches have many opportunities to introduce testing and counseling in a supportive way.

Protecting children. Christians have many approaches to keep the infected from infecting their children.[13]

Advocacy for ARVs. Christians need to take a realistic view in light of local circumstances. This requires Christian organizations to plan carefully for the use of their own resources and to work with others who are advocating for more widespread availability of ARVs.

Primary Health Care (PHC) for the prevention of HIV. Many Christian organzations have been active in PHC for many years. Recent data support their vital role in prevention and management of HIV/AIDS.[14]

Personal Care. Professional qualifications are not necessary to care for sick people, wash their clothes, and prepare and feed them nutritious meals when they lose their appetite. Health workers rarely have time to do these tasks. The love shown by non-professional Christians points the ill toward Jesus' love.

Emotional care. Patients and relatives need a friend to listen, support, serve, and counsel.

Spiritual care. Most people with HIV/AIDS, whether committed Christians or not, have concerns about dying and what happens when they die. Listening, praying, and anointing where appropriate are vital care activities only Christians can provide.

Financial/food security. Most families touched by HIV/AIDS are hungry. Handouts, though welcome, are not sustainable. HIV/AIDS requires Christians to be more innovative in community and social development programs.

Orphan care. Children have low status in many communities.[15] While proud parents often dearly love them, children are often regarded as a resource for the future rather than of value here and now. Christian organizations that encourage discussion of the true causes of parental death should ask children where they would like to live after their parents die, avoid separating them from siblings and friends, prevent their exploitation as cheap labor in new adoptive families, and protect them from sexual and physical abuse.

Those organizations that recognize children's special needs have much to offer in "child unfriendly" cultures.[16] Such programs can support adults as they face up to telling the truth about their impending death, as they draw up a proper will that protects children from loss of ancestral land by relatives, as they develop photo memory books, and as they discuss who will look after the children when they die. There is strong scriptural basis for letting children know that heaven is a good place,[17] but we cannot end the discussion there. Children need support as they grieve over parental death.[18]

Support for education. School attendance is dropping in many countries. OVCs are often withdrawn from school to work at home or in the fields or business.[19] A child needs at least four years of education to gain skills and experience in getting a job and climbing out of poverty. Many traditional schools are just not coping with the numbers of children because so many teachers are dying. The church needs to develop novel approaches. In Bangladesh, BRAC (Bangladesh Rural Advancement Committee) runs 30,000 community schools.[20]

New Leadership Styles

Traditionally, "leadership" in Christian circles means leading people in their devotional lives, preaching, teaching, and encouraging prayer, evangelism, and pastoral care. Rather disappointingly, there is little evidence that this has made a lot of difference in limiting the spread of HIV/AIDS. The continent of Africa has many preachers and many really committed Christians. It also has the highest prevalence of HIV per-capita in the world. If Christians and Christian organizations are going to have an impact, radical changes are necessary.

They will need to develop new styles of "leadership," especially in communities where HIV is decimating the entire fabric of society. This will require a radical restructuring of what theological colleges and churches teach. While this chapter does not have space to prescribe what these should be, there are two guiding principles: (1) a renewed commitment to follow the commands and example of Christ as a servant leader; and (2) a need to identify and follow the lifestyles of Christians who are making a difference.

Examples. The Assemblies of God program based in Jinja, Uganda, has more than 140 member teams who visit the seriously ill. They provide home care and support. This enables them to continue to work with children after parents die. The envisioning process has come through strong servant-leadership by church pastors.

A group of Christian women in the Evangelical Fellowship of Zambia started a soup kitchen for the large numbers of orphaned children in Lusaka. They were overwhelmed by the enormous numbers who came and by the sadness of the children as they left the women's compound. The women changed their approach to working in pairs, each pair responsible for visiting around 10 families affected by HIV/AIDS.

In Zimbabwe, the ZOE program involves visiting homes in pairs, encouraging one another, and helping with around 10 families per pair.[21] A series of church-based responses to HIV/AIDS in Namibia, South Africa, and Mozambique have also started.[22] One was stimulated by the loss of parents, leaving a grandmother to set up a program that looks after orphans. In Pretoria, South Africa, a drop-in center uses very basic facilities and some free food provided by local business organizations. Initially the church elders rejected doing this kind of ministry but then relented.

In Umtata, South Africa, a group of women (the Umtata Women's Theology Group) writes Bible study material, visits families affected by HIV/AIDS, sets up information centers, and visits churches to inspire them to take on a range of HIV/AIDS awareness and care programs.

An Anglican church in Cape Town, South Africa, developed a strong tradition of applying the biblical principles of justice and advocacy during the apartheid years. It started a Treatment Action Campaign (TAC) for youth in and out of the churches.[23] Campaign leaders initially experienced opposition from church leaders, who viewed HIV primarily as a judgment for sexual sin. However, campaign leaders believed their response had to emphasize the love and forgiveness of Jesus. A sister in a Catholic church in Durban, South Africa, described how her first response to people with HIV/AIDS was one of fear and incompetence. But as she prayed, she developed a vision of training and care both inside and outside the church.

While there is no template for such ministries, many leaders refer to the work of Nehemiah in rebuilding Jerusalem as a scriptural stimulus to their work. Many openly acknowledge that their personal faith is vital in keeping them going. This strength in diversity seems to be a common element in a number of Christian HIV/AIDS programs.

There are now many opportunities for partnership in mission because of the HIV/AIDs epidemic. Churches in industrialized countries are waking up to the opportunities they have of linking in new ways, including sharing information, financial support, and fellowship. Increasing numbers of Christians are now visiting and supporting leaders in HIV-afflicted communities as they become overwhelmed with the never-ending needs. National and expatriate Christian leaders in poor countries appreciate this kind of help enormously.

Conclusion

There are several ways of looking at the global epidemic of HIV/ AIDS from a Christian perspective. It is possible to become judgmental about human behavior, downcast that a "God of love" could ever allow this to happen, or mesmerized by the scale and the horror of the epidemic. Yet these responses, though they each have an element of truth, will keep us on the sidelines, contributing nothing and having little worthwhile to say. But there is an alternative strategy—accepting that HIV/AIDS is here, for whatever reasons theologically and behaviorally, and deciding to make a difference.

There is no blueprint of response for individual Christians and Christian organizations. Yet governments of poor countries and international agencies (including those in North America and Europe) now readily admit that their resources and programs are insufficient. They are crying out for assistance by Christian organizations. There has never been such an opportunity for Christian organizations to intervene in an effective, credible way showing the love of Jesus in action. For those Christian organizations unwilling to change radically, there will be no impact and no mission. For those who are prepared to change, as some are already doing, the opportunities for Christian action and witness are limitless.

Notes

1. S.H. Miles, and J. Song, "Behavioral assessment for HIV prevention: a model program design," *Int.J.STD AIDS*, 2001, vol. 12, no. 11, pp. 710–716 and J.R. Scotti, et al, "Evaluation of an HIV/AIDS education program for family-based foster care providers," *Ment.Retard.*, 1996, vol. 34, no. 2, pp. 75–82.

2. B. Modell, et al, "Population screening for carrier of recessively inherited disorders," *Lancet*, 1980, vol. 2, no. 8198, p. 806.

3. Graham Gordon. "Understanding Advocacy." (Tear Fund, U.K., 2002) and Graham Gordon and Bryan Evans. "The Mission of the church and the role of advocacy" (U.K.: Tear Fund, July 2002), 1–53.

4. F. Dabis, and E.R. Ekpini, "HIV-1/AIDS and maternal and child health in Africa," *Lancet*, 2002, vol. 359, no. 9323, pp. 2097–2104.

5. A. Tomkins, "Nutrition and maternal morbidity and mortality," *Br.J.Nutr.*, 2001, vol. 85 Suppl 2, pp. S93–S99.

6. E. Van Praag, and J.H. Perriens, J. H. "Caring for patients with HIV and AIDS in middle income countries," *BMJ*, 1996, vol. 313, no. 7055, p. 440.

7. V. Makame, C. Ani, and S. Grantham-McGregor, "Psychological well-being of orphans in Dar El Salaam, Tanzania," *Acta Paediatr.*, 2002, vol. 91, no. 4, pp. 459–465.

8. G. Foster, and J. Williamson, "A review of current literature on the impact of HIV/AIDS on children in sub-Saharan Africa," *AIDS*, 2000, vol. 14 Suppl. 3, pp. S275–S284 and E. O. Nyambedha, S. Wandibba, and J. Aagaard-Hansen, "Policy implications of the inadequate support systems for orphans in western Kenya," *Health Policy*, 2001, vol. 58, no. 1, pp. 83–96.

9. G. Foster, "Supporting community efforts to assist orphans in Africa," *N.Engl.J.Med.*, 2002, vol. 346, no. 24, pp. 1907–1910 and F.L. Cohen, W.M. Nehring, K.C. Malm, and D.M. Harris, "Family experiences when a child is HIV-positive: reports of natural and foster parents," (Pediatr.Nurs., 1995), vol. 21, no. 3, pp. 248–254.

10. Amelemba, W. D. "Growing together—a guide for parents and youth." (MAP International, 2002).

11. K.H. Shears, "Abstinence: an option for adolescents." *Family Health International*, 2002, vol. 22, pp. 4–7.

12. Rachel Savage. "Sex Education in East Africa. Review of Sex Education Programs and their evaluation process in young people in East Africa." (London: Centre for international Child Health, Institute of Child Health, 2002), www.cich.ich.ucl.ac.uk.

13. M.L. Newell, "Prevention of mother-to-child transmission of HIV: challenges for the current decade," *Bull. World Health Organ*, 2001, vol. 79, no. 12, pp. 1138–1144.

14. H. Grosskurth, et al, "Control of sexually transmitted diseases for HIV-1 prevention: understanding the implications of the Mwanza and Rakai trials," *Lancet*, 2000, vol. 355, no. 9219, pp. 1981–1987.

15. HIV/AIDS Viva. "HIV/AIDS in Reaching Children at Risk." (U.K.: VIVA), pp. 1–13.

16. A.M. Tomkins, *Celebrating Children.* "The Basis for the Design of Child Development Programs" (Paternoster Press, 2004).

17. "He will wipe away every tear from their eyes. There will be no more death or mourning or crying or pain" (Revelation 21:4).

18. G. Foster, et al, "Orphan prevalence and extended family care in a peri-urban community in Zimbabwe," *AIDS Care*, 1995, vol. 7, no. 1, pp. 3–17 and Paula Manuel. "How do orphaned children and their caregivers cope with the stresses created by parental death?" (London: Centre for International Child Health, Institute of Child Health, 2002), www.cich.ich.ucl.ac.uk.

19. "Education and HIV/AIDS a window of hope." (World Bank, 2002), pp. 1–79, www.worldbank.org.

20. R.S. Drew, C. Makufa, and G. Foster, "Strategies for providing care and support to children orphaned by AIDS," *AIDS Care*, 1998, vol. 10 Suppl. 1, pp. S9–15.

21. M. Derbyshire, "Friends in Need—a Handbook for Care of Orphans in the Community." (U.K.: VIVA, 2002), 1–83.

22. G.S. Byamugisha, "Journeys of Faith—church based responses to HIV and AIDS in three southern African countries." (2002), 1–108. "Strategies for Hope: Teaching AIDS at Low Cost" (TALC, P.O. Box 49, St Albans, Herts, AL1 5TX, UK) and www.stratshope.org.

23. G.A. Haughen, *Good News about Injustice—a witness of courage in a hurting world.* (Illinois and Leicster: InterVarsity Press, 2002), pp. 1–200.

Useful Websites:

Fanta Peoject – www.fanta.org

Population Council. www.popcouncil.org.

Source – www.asksource.info

Synergy Project – www.synergyaids.com

Tear Fund – www.tearfund.org

World Bank – www.worldbank.org

USAID – www.usaid.gov

UNIADS – www.unaids.org

UNICEF – www.unicef.org

PUBLIC AWARENESS FOR PREVENTING HIV/AIDS

A few years ago, my wife and two young children came across a homeless man and his dog at a grocery store. Feeling that they should do something, my family went home, grabbed some cans of food, and raced back to find him. The next day, my 5-year-old daughter was with some classmates and their mothers at a nearby restaurant. In walked the homeless man and his dog. With youthful innocence, my little girl leaped up to greet him. The mothers were appalled and dragged my daughter back. Her simple response was, "But he's my friend."

How often do we walk by people or causes? While most of us can relate to seeing a homeless man, many of us do not even know someone with HIV/AIDS. Do you? For many years, I did not. Jesus admonishes us in Matthew 25 that those who know him feed the hungry, visit the sick, and go to the prisoner. Do the hungry, sick, and imprisoned naturally enter your circle of relationships? Generally, the answer is no. To live out Jesus' command, we have to seek them out. We also must bring others.

How can you increase public awareness for HIV/AIDS prevention? We will look at the Why, Who, and How of advocacy and public awareness. I will conclude with what is different about Christian advocacy.

Clarifying the Terms

Merriam-Webster defines an *advocate* as someone who pleads or defends the cause of another. To *plead* is to make an earnest request. To *defend* denotes warding off actual or threatened attack. In some circles, advocacy is also understood as a specific strategy to influence decision and policymakers.

Public awareness is a specific strategy to influence the general public with a message. Public relations is generally considered a strategy for working with the media.

In this chapter, I use advocacy to refer to the general concept of one or more people speaking out on behalf of others—it connotes a state of *being*. Public awareness is the strategy, which includes relations with the media—it is related to *doing*.

Why Be an Advocate?

In our pursuit of justice and mercy for those infected and affected by HIV/AIDS, our first step is to understand from God's perspective why we should be advocates.

1. God clearly calls his people to be advocates.

This is reason enough. Isaiah 1:17 says, "Learn to do right! Seek justice, encourage the oppressed. Defend the cause of the fatherless, plead the case of the widow."

2. People are dying.

You know the horrific statistics. James 1:27 reminds us that pure religion is "to visit the orphans and widows" (NASB).

3. We need to see Jesus in order to know Jesus.

There are some things we will never know about Jesus until we follow in his footsteps. Until we look at him through the eyes of a sick person, such as an HIV/AIDS victim, we will not grow as we should.

Are advocacy and compassion happening in practice from followers of Jesus? A Barna Research poll shows that evangelical Christians are the least likely group to help AIDS victims in Africa; under 3 percent said they would financially help a Christian organization minister to an AIDS orphan.[1]

A primary reason for this lack of red-hot concern is confusion about God's perspective. Some Christians still think that people with HIV/AIDS are getting what they deserve—just like Sodom and Gomorrah. Do you know why God destroyed Sodom? Most people would say immorality. Ezekiel 16:49, however, says it was because of pride, fullness, and abundance that did not concern itself with the poor and needy.

The Who of Advocacy: You

In 1963, a then unknown 29-year-old attorney abandoned a conventional law practice in Hartford, Connecticut, and hitchhiked to Washington, D.C., to begin a long odyssey of professional citizenship. "I had one suitcase," he recalled. "I stayed in the YMCA. Walked across a little street and had a hot dog, my last." (A few years later he would expose the repulsive ingredients that go into hot dogs.) Taking a job as a consultant to the U.S. Department of Labor, he moonlighted as a freelance writer. He also acted as an unpaid adviser to a Senate subcommittee exploring auto safety. Who is he? Ralph Nader.[2]

Whether you agree with Nader and his causes or not, his humble beginnings point to an important point about advocacy. Beyond all the strategies and techniques, *you* are the agent of advocacy.

Micah 6:8 describes the same principle. It explains what is good from God's perspective: to do justly, love mercy, and walk humbly with your God. Ben Homan, president of Food for the Hungry United States, points out that this is not a three-step formula. Rather, doing, loving, and walking are intertwined. Indeed, the best advocates go beyond techniques to intertwine the Micah concepts of doing, loving, and walking.

The Hall of Fame of Advocacy

There are plenty of examples, both in the Bible and in modern times, of people who have gone way beyond lukewarm to live out the Micah model for advocacy. The Book of Esther tells of a young queen whose people, the Jews, were in danger of being wiped out because of an evil plot by Haman, a nobleman in the court of Esther's husband, King Xerxes. Esther agreed to risk her own life by going before the king uninvited to plead the cause of her people. She asked all Jews to fast and pray for three days, then boldly and tactfully presented the Jews' case. Xerxes spared the Jews and executed Haman. Esther's position as queen, her courage to be an advocate for others, and the earnest prayers of many saved a nation.

Esther's story has echoes in the life of Janet Museveni, who became first lady of Uganda in 1986, when nearly 30 percent of the nation's people were infected with HIV/AIDS. Back then nearly all African leaders sought to protect their tourism industries by denying the extent of the disease. At great political risk, President and Mrs. Museveni boldly and tactfully spoke up. He used his position to influence changes in discriminatory laws, policies, practices, and attitudes. She became the international spokeswoman for Uganda's anti-AIDS campaign, which was largely biblically based.

An outspoken Christian, Mrs. Museveni involved churches in heavily promoting abstinence, fidelity, and monogamy. She founded such organizations as the Uganda Women's Effort to Save Orphans and the International Youth Foundation's Global Action Council, which involved a select group of world leaders in advocating for the world's children and youth.

Uganda's success is legendary. The country's infection rate tentatively stands at about 6 percent. I say tentative because the number is still falling. This victory is largely due to brave and consistent advocacy.

While we won't have the access and connections of Janet Museveni, we too can make a difference. We will now look at some practical approaches to increase public awareness.

How to Increase Public Awareness

Uganda's airwaves, pulpits, and political channels were alive with a consistent message to prevent the disease through abstinence, being faithful, and using a condom when necessary (the ABC message). President and Mrs. Museveni exploited every opportunity to speak up and implement policies, laws, and programs. They raised the status of females in Ugandan society, spoke against discrimination of those affected by AIDS, relied heavily upon religious leaders, and offered free counseling and testing.

Paul Wetaka was a soldier in the Ugandan army and a bodyguard of President Museveni. "Every Ugandan became concerned about AIDS," said Wetaka of Museveni's bold public campaign. "No big person in government had ever come out about HIV."[3]

Uganda's advocacy campaign is notable in several ways.

- *It is contagious.* President and Mrs. Museveni's efforts mobilized people at a grassroots level, who work to mobilize those around them.

- *It involves speaking out.* The first couple stood alone to plead an unpopular cause.

- *It requires personal sacrifice.* President Museveni risked his political career, and this inspired people like Paul Wetaka to offer their own bodies for medical experimentation.

- *It relies on people being well informed.* Uganda's army trained Wetaka and others for over two years so that they would not only understand their role but also echo the right message to others. The same message was broadcast through every channel available.

- *It gains media attention.* Even outside of Uganda, the media has taken an interest. The Discovery Channel plans to air a documentary featuring President Museveni and his efforts to revitalize Uganda, including his HIV/AIDS programs.

We see the Uganda experience contained within four steps for effective advocacy promoted by the World Health Organization:

1. Documenting the situation.
2. Packaging the message.
3. Working with the media.
4. Mobilizing others.[4]

Let's look at each of these elements.

Documenting the Situation

The World Health Organization (WHO) states, "Good information and data lays the foundation for successful advocacy. Without credible research it is difficult to sustain an advocacy campaign. The most persuasive facts are those that are relevant to your target audience. Planning advocacy efforts involves assessing how to obtain facts and data (negative and positive trends). When vital information is unavailable the first most important advocacy step is to encourage research to collect data."[5]

Up to date information is critical. Nothing will lose an audience or the media quicker than giving outdated or inaccurate information. The Internet can help you avoid that mistake. Some particularly helpful sites are:

Source	Websites
Joint United Nations Program on HIV/AIDS	www.unaids.org
Unicef	www.unicefusa.org
World Vision	www.seekjustice.org
World Bank	www.worldbank.org/aids
World Health Organization	www.who.org

Give up to date information on the number of deaths and orphans. Make the statistics you use striking and personal. For example, let people know that life expectancy in a dozen African countries may drop by 17 years (64 to 47), or that the United States gives just 0.15 percent of its GDP for foreign assistance, the lowest among industrialized countries. Other important and timely facts include the financial burden placed on the society by the disease, costs for interventions and essential services, inequity of poverty, blockages in administrative and other systems, examples of effective interventions, mechanisms for raising investment, and needed policy reforms.

Packaging the Message

The first step in packaging the message is to know and understand your audience. Use language that is appropriate and meaningful. For example, politicians want public opinion on their side, and they want to show personal involvement in making a difference. Journalists want timeliness and hard news. Academics want new research. Corporations want to know the impact on their customers and stakeholders.

WHO recommends keeping the written message simple, with a few well-crafted facts rather than hundreds of cold statistics. WHO also recommends using powerful language with compelling words that create a sense of urgency. Personalize the statistics by attaching a human face to them. Keep the message visual and interesting, since images always have more impact on people than words alone.

Some of the key messages to get across include:

- HIV/AIDS is the plague of our generation;

- our generation will be judged by how it responds to HIV/AIDS;

- we need to mobilize and pray;

- we need to increase funding for faith-based initiatives;

- we need to urge partners and other nations to contribute their share to the Global Fund for HIV/AIDS;

- we need to promote the ABC approach (see "Statement of Conscience of the Evangelical Church"[6] for more details).

Working with the Media

The media plays a key role in public awareness. The media devours "massive amounts of content that must be replenished continually."[7] The intense competition for information is your opportunity to work with media in a positive way for HIV/AIDS.

It all begins with effective media relationships. Contact the media through advisories, news releases, and feature stories. Write for the media through opinion pieces and letters to the editor. Plan media events such as news conferences and press briefings (but only when you have something new or innovative to say). You can also meet with editorial boards and invite the media to photo opportunities.

When you get an interview, be prepared to get your message across factually, quickly, and from the heart. A simple rule of thumb is to say the bottom line first, and then explain. If you explain first, you probably will get cut off before you ever make your point. In this day and age of sound bites, you should be able to get a message across in less than 30 seconds. For television or radio, it should be down to 10 or 15 seconds. Radio news segments, for example, come in 10-second increments. "If you can't express what you want and why it's news worthy in ten seconds, you're off the phone," advises a news director for a major NBC affiliate.[8]

Some helpful media resources include:

Burrelles Media Directory	www.burrelles.com/indexmd.html
Media Finder	www.mediafinder.com
Online public relations	www.online-pr.com
Radio publicity	www.radiopublicity.com/gp

Mobilizing Others

The final step for effective advocacy is mobilizing others. Some target groups are policymakers, your circle of influence, arts and music, and the Internet.

We often assume that our letters to policymakers and decision makers have no impact. To the contrary, the Awake Project notes that "congressional offices often equate one hand-written letter with one hundred people that support that issue. Just 3 to 5 letters to a Representative's office will force . . . staff to address an issue and craft a response. Your letter will make a difference."[9]

Here are some simple tips. Letters should be one page. State the purpose at the beginning, be personal, name the action, and tell why it is important. Letters should be addressed as follows:

To a Senator:

The Honorable (full name)

___ (Rm. #)

___ (name of) Senate Office Building

United States Senate

Washington DC 20510

To a Representative:

The Honorable (full name)

___ (Rm. #)

___ (name of) House Office Building

United States House of Representatives

Washington DC 20515

Another key group is your circle of influence. The authors of *Guerilla Publicity* recommend when getting "on the map, start modestly. Don't think hemispheres, think townships, unincorporated villages, or little country lanes."[10]

A person who modeled this principle is John Wesley. This preacher in eighteenth century England does not fit the corporate image that we have for public awareness. Nevertheless, he created a grassroots movement that changed England not just spiritually, but socially. He is reported to have said, "Give me 100 men who hate nothing but sin and love God with all of their hearts and I will shake the world for Christ." Doing just that, there were 10,000 grassroots groups with 100,000 followers at the end of his life.

A sometimes-overlooked strategy of public awareness is the world of arts and music. Generally, artists and musicians lead cultural change in a nation. Songs can be a powerful way to communicate with common people. A song in a Food for the Hungry International HIV/AIDS project in Mozambique goes like this:

Health and Nutrition education has empowered us to fight against malnutrition.

HIV/AIDS awareness has empowered us to fight back against the pandemic.

We are empowered by hygiene education, diarrhea and malaria prevention education. Malnutrition is gone, cholera is gone, and child deaths are gone.

We are happy with FHI.

The final element of modern grassroots public awareness is the Internet. Different strategies include e-mail, creating a website, joining an Internet community, online newsletters, distribution services, and Web rings.

Each of the public awareness steps is good, but when put together, they are synergistically stronger. Integrated marketing communications (IMC), for example, became the dominant marketing concept of the 1990s. IMC creates a process based on the benefits of synergy and the assumption that the whole is greater than the sum of the parts.[11] This principle of synergism is also true in public awareness. World Vision experienced the benefits of synergism in a strategy called Hope City Tours. Ken Casey, senior vice president for HIV/AIDS initiatives, says that these two-to-three-day tours occurred in fifteen cities. After the first nine, technically 17,000 people participated. By saturating the areas, however, with integrated messages to churches, TV, radio and print, over 1.5 billion media impressions were made during the same period—touching many, many more people.

What is Different About Christian Advocacy?

Christian advocacy can include all of the above but with some major distinguishing elements: the example of Jesus Christ, prayer, a biblical worldview, the pulpit, and perseverance.

1. Jesus, the Ultimate Advocate

I once attended a conference that discussed what is different about Christian relief and development organizations. After much energetic dialogue, a Guatemalan man in the back of the room quietly raised his hand. He said the difference is "Jesus." Jesus Christ, who advocates for us day and night (Revelations 12:10), is our power, our goal, and our model.

Jesus, in his incarnational advocacy ministry, not only spoke on behalf of people, he lived among them. He experienced what we experience and is able to understand us (Hebrews 2:17–18). This is the truest form of advocacy, because it goes beyond techniques.

Jesus was drawn to the outcasts. Leprosy was the HIV/AIDS of his day. Rather than judge lepers and stay away from them, he seemed to be drawn to them, touching and healing them.

2. Prayer

If there were a hall of fame of advocacy, the late Mother Teresa would be in it. Like Wesley, she was not a stereotypical model of a media specialist. To the contrary, up until she was 60, hardly anyone knew of her work with the dying of Calcutta.

Nevertheless, she spoke at the United Nations. Many of the most powerful people on earth sought her out. She is often remembered for her effectiveness in seeking justice for the downtrodden through prayer. She once said, "When I was crossing into Gaza, I was asked at the checkpost whether I was carrying any weapons. I replied: 'Oh yes, my prayer books.'"[12]

Likewise, Uganda's key advocates also recognize the power of prayer. Janet Museveni says she finds strength in God and the solutions she needs by praying. She regularly calls for other Christians to do the same.

There is a church in New York City that mobilizes 2.5 million African Americans in an annual week of prayer for the healing of AIDS.[13] Founded in 1989, the Black Church Week of Prayer for the Healing of AIDS has been the catalyst for educating and mobilizing over 10,000 churches to provide AIDS education to their congregations and communities across the United States. It is the largest AIDS awareness program targeting the African American community.

3. Biblical Worldview

Darrow Miller defines worldview as a "set of assumptions held consciously or unconsciously in faith about the basic makeup of the world and how the world works.[14] A worldview determines our beliefs, our values, and ultimately how we act. Believing the truth of the Bible can set people free (John 8:31–32). Conversely, belief in lies can enslave a person and a nation.

Functioning from a biblical worldview significantly affects advocacy. Professor Dick Day of the University of Malawi notes that messages used successfully in Uganda have offered anything but a secular perspective. The secular perspective promotes condoms as the main strategy (big C), whereas abstinence and being faithful are secondary (small *a* and small *b*). President and Mrs. Museveni, using a biblical worldview, switched the order: a big A for abstinence, a big B for being faithful, and a small *c* for condoms only when necessary. And strategies based on a biblical worldview are having a dramatic impact.

4. The Pulpit

The Protestant work ethic largely emerged from preaching during the Reformation. John Wesley coined the phrase that became the rallying cry of the work ethic: "Work all you can, save all you can, give all you can."

We should encourage and help pastors to understand HIV/AIDS so they can preach about a Christian response. Food for the Hungry in Kenya, for example, provides pastors with sermons about HIV/AIDS.

5. Perseverance

Many people know William Wilberforce was mightily used to abolish slavery in the British Empire. But what is not well known is the personal cost he faced in his advocacy. He became a Member of Parliament at the young age of 21. Wilberforce was converted to Christianity in 1784–1785.

During the next few years, he struggled with his vocation. What was God's will for him? Should he be both a politician and a devout Christian? In 1787, he wrote in his diary the conviction that God had called him to labor for the abolition of the slave trade. In light of his divine call, as well as the righteousness of the issue, Wilberforce expected a quick and easy victory. He was sorely mistaken. Wilberforce began to express in Parliament the claims of slaves in 1787. He became ill, but was able to deliver his first parliamentary speech in 1789. In 1791, the issue came to a vote, but he was defeated. For the next 16 years he persevered in the fight but was repeatedly beaten. It was not until 1804 that Wilberforce won a victory in the Commons, only to be overthrown in the House of Lords. Finally, on February 23, 1807, abolition was secured. The House rose to its feet and broke out in cheers for Wilberforce. He was so overcome with emotion that he sat with his head in hand, tears streaming down his face.

Amazingly, Wilberforce did not rest long. He knew that while slavery was abolished, there were still men in chains. In spite of renewed criticism, threats on his life, and deep-seated prejudice against him, Wilberforce labored until July 26, 1833, when the Emancipation Bill passed. Three days later, Wilberforce died.[15]

Conclusion

HIV/AIDS is the plague of our time. If we continue at current rates, over 100 million people could be infected by 2012.[16] While it is a crisis, it is also a tremendous opportunity to show the love of Christ. Generations of Christians that came before us responded to similar crises with abandonment and love. The Emperor Julian reportedly said of Christians, "These atheists put us to shame. Not only do they take care of their poor, they take care of ours also." John Wesley, William Wilberforce, Mother Teresa, and others like them carried on the tradition of radical love.

Now it is our turn.

Let us stand in the gap first by *being* an advocate. With that as the basis, let us find every opportunity to make the public aware of HIV/AIDS and how to help before it is too late.

So I sought for a man among them who would make a wall, and stand in the gap before Me on behalf of the land. (Ezekiel 22:30)

Notes

1. http://www.worldvision.org/worldvision/pr.nsf/stable/new_barna

2. J.C. Levinson, R. Frishman, and J. Lublin, Guerrilla Publicity (Avon, Mass.: Adams Media Corporation, 2002), p. 2.

3. http://www.iavi.org/reports/233/Heroes_Ugandan1.htm

4. http://216.239.37.104/search?q=cache:IxJCfg7PCRYJ:www.who.int/entity/macrohealth/events/en/emro_advocacy.pdf+advocacy+success+statistics&hl=en&ie=UTF-8

5. Ibid.

6. http://www.worldvision.org/worldvision/wvususfo.nsf/stable/globalissues_aids_conscience

7. Guerrilla Publicity, p. 24.

8. Ibid., p. 11.

9. J. Eaton and K. Etue, *The aWAKE Project* (Nashville: W. Publishing Group), p. 234.

10. Guerrilla Publicity, p. 4.

11. C. L Caywood, *The Handbook of Strategic Relations and Integrated Communications* (New York: McGraw-Hill, 1997), p. 91.

12. http://www.spiritualityhealth.com/newsh/items/bookreview/item_2248.html

13. http://www.balmingilead.org/programs/weekofprayer2003.asp, www.who.org, and www.nader.org

14. Darrow Miller with Stan Guthrie, *Discipling Nations* (Seattle: YWAM Publishing, 1998), p. 36.

15. David J. Vaughn, *The Pillars of Leadership* (Nashville: Cumberland, 2000), pp. 71–76.

16. Eaton and Etue, p. 279.

PART THREE

BIBLICAL REFLECTIONS

CHAPTER 19
JOHN PIPER

███████

GUILT, GRACE, AND THE GLOBAL AIDS CRISIS

All sin comes with a price. And many pay the bill who never did the sin. This means that we must speak carefully about the cause of AIDS. If any epidemic ever spread because of disobedience to God's Word, it is AIDS. But millions are infected because of someone else's disobedience, not their own.

But be careful here. Even this way of saying it could lead to a simplistic, unbiblical response. The abused are not innocent. And the guilty are not hopeless.

We are all sinners, which means no one does not deserve AIDS. When the Bible says that "the creation was subjected to futility" by God (Romans 8:20), it means that a sin-permeated creation will be a suffering-permeated creation. God ordains that there be suitable signs in the physical world of the moral horror of sin. All of us are sinful. And all of us cry under the fall of creation. All of us groan in this "bondage to decay" as we wait for "the freedom of the glory of the children of God" (Romans 8:21 NRSV). Therefore, if we have AIDS because of a blood transfusion or a promiscuous spouse or a drug-using mother, we are not innocent.

But neither are the guilty hopeless. Mercifully, homosexual relations are made illicit by God. Few ancient texts are more stunning with modern relevance to AIDS than Romans 1:27: "Men, giving up natural intercourse with women, were consumed with passion for one another. Men committed shameless acts with men and received in their own persons the due penalty for their error" (NRSV). Mercifully, prostitution and every form of extramarital sex are forbidden by God: "Flee fornication" (1 Corinthians 6:18 KJV); "Thou shalt not commit adultery" (Exodus 20:14 KJV). Mercifully, God warns us against drug abuse: "Do not look at wine

243

when it is red, when it sparkles in the cup and goes down smoothly. At the last it bites like a serpent, and stings like an adder. Your eyes will see strange things, and your mind utter perverse things. (Proverbs 23:31–33 NRSV); "I will not be enslaved by anything" (1 Corinthians 6:12 NRSV).

But the mercy does not stop with divine prohibitions. God will hear the cry of the guilty who have brought misery upon themselves. Psalm 107:17–21 is mercifully relevant to AIDS in this regard:

> Some were sick through their sinful ways,
> and because of their iniquities suffered affliction;
> they loathed any kind of food,
> and they drew near to the gates of death.
> Then they cried to the LORD in their trouble,
> and he delivered them from their distress.
> he sent out his word and healed them,
> and delivered them from their destruction.
> Let them thank the LORD for his steadfast love,
> for his wondrous works to the sons of men! (RSV)

Self-inflicted misery does not put a person beyond hope. That is the only kind of guilt God forgives. It is the only kind of guilt there is. The fact that any of us is healthy after sinning is owing to Christ's mercy. Therefore, the fact that some are sick after sinning should bring out Christian mercy. And there is need for extraordinary mercy. Christians should pray and work toward research into cures, medical and hospice care, orphan ministries, education, moral challenges for abstinence and recovery, and above all, the spread of the gospel of Jesus Christ.

Today, 42 million people are living with HIV/AIDS. Of these, most are adults, with men and women infected in roughly equal numbers. The cumulative number of AIDS cases reported to the Centers for Disease Control in the United States was 816,149 through December 2001. (The number is surely higher now.) The Minneapolis *Star-Tribune* reported that the fastest growing HIV/AIDS epidemic is in Eastern Europe and Central Asia. Up to 90 percent of the known infections in Russia come from drug injections. Sub-Saharan Africa is the worst-affected region, with roughly

30 million people infected. In Botswana the HIV prevalence is 38.8 percent of adults. In Zimbabwe it is 33.7 percent.

The magnificent message of Christ is that there's hope—in this life for love, and in the life to come for new, pain-free bodies in fellowship with Jesus. My prayer and challenge to the Christian church is this:

> May the Lord raise up researchers, doctors, nurses, and tens of thousands of caring people to make the light of Christ shine through mercy. Freely we have received, O that we might freely give.

CHAPTER 20
RICHARD STEARNS

WIDOWS AND ORPHANS: THE HIDDEN FACES OF AIDS

Two thousand years after Jesus gave the church the parable of the Good Samaritan, we are still asking the question, "Who is my neighbor?" And we're still getting the answer wrong.

This simple-yet-most-profound parable speaks to the AIDS epidemic, a scourge that already has killed 25 million people, robbed 14 million children of parents, and turned 10 million wives into widows—many of them sick and desperate to find someone to care for their children when they die, too.

Jesus used this parable to challenge the religious establishment of his day. Today, the parable compels us to challenge our own community of faith, an American church that largely is ignoring the AIDS pandemic. We must respond with our heads, with our hearts, and with our hands in practical compassion.

The story begins in Luke 10:25 when an "expert in the law" challenges Jesus—attempting to engage in a battle of the mind, to expose Jesus' theology as defective. Jesus turned the encounter into an examination of the heart.

The scholar asks a theological question: "Teacher, what shall I do to inherit eternal life?"[1]

Jesus responds in kind, "What is written in the law?"[2]

The lawyer's answer was a conventional reference to the Old Testament law from Leviticus and Deuteronomy: "'You shall love the Lord your God with all your heart, with all your soul, with all your strength, and with all your mind,' and 'your neighbor as yourself.'"[3]

Jesus replies, "You have answered rightly; do this and you will live."[4]

Jesus brought the debate from the *thinking* to the *doing*. In other words, right thinking must be accompanied by right doing. The thought that he must change his behavior apparently troubled the man, so he asked a follow-up question: "And who is my neighbor?" [5]

This question is perhaps one of the most profound in all of Scripture. Even today, the answer defines truly Christian communities around the world.

Jesus' answer, in the form of the parable of the Good Samaritan, reverberates across the centuries as one of the most foundational and universal tenets of moral law, a lesson Jesus demonstrates through the actions of the four main characters: the victim, the priest, the Levite, and the Samaritan.

The Victim

The one thing that is clear is that he was in dire need: beaten, wounded, bleeding—and possibly dying. We're not certain of his ethnicity or nationality. We don't know why he was beaten. He may have been an "innocent" victim, unjustly attacked. He may have been a robber, beaten by fellow thieves. Perhaps he was engaged in some illicit activity and was beaten as a result. Or perhaps he was just careless and had traveled irresponsibly alone at night along a dangerous road. The point is that we do not know. Jesus did not feel that it was relevant whether the man who had been beaten was at fault.

Here I raise one of the critical moral questions with regard to the victims of AIDS: Should we distinguish between those who became victims because of sinful behavior and those who were innocent victims? I believe that one of the reasons the Christian community has not taken a leading role in the fight against AIDS is this issue of judgment. We distinguish between the "innocent" victims, such as children infected or orphaned by their parents, and the "guilty," such as prostitutes and the promiscuous.

In truth, we are bound by Scripture to respond to all those "beaten" and "left by the side of the road" by this devastating virus.

Scripture makes clear who has the right and the responsibility to judge: God, not us. Yet we judge people with AIDS. We conveniently forget that we all would be dead if we faced such a certain death for any of our sins—including indifference to those who are suffering.

That sin, of course, is the only one Jesus condemns in the story of the Good Samaritan, and is embodied in the next two characters in the drama.

The Priest and the Levite

They represent the religious establishment of the day. Today, they might be a pastor and a seminary professor, practitioners of the faith and well schooled in the law. They *saw* the man and yet passed by on the other side of the road, unwilling to help. They knew what was right, but they failed to act.

Peter Singer, an ethicist at Princeton University, holds some of the most radical views of any modern-day philosopher—views that are morally shocking to a Christian audience. Yet his writing challenges us to think through the ethical implications of our behavior, particularly where inconsistencies exist between our beliefs and our actions, between knowing and doing.

Using the issue of poverty, Singer tells a very similar parable to that of the Good Samaritan. We could just as easily substitute the problem of AIDS.

> The path from the library at my university to the humanities lecture theater passes a shallow ornamental pond. Suppose that on my way to give a lecture I notice that a small child has fallen in and is in danger of drowning. Would anyone deny that I ought to wade in and pull the child out?
>
> This will mean getting my clothes muddy and either canceling my lecture or delaying it until I can find something dry to change into; but compared with the avoidable death of a child this is insignificant.

A plausible principle that would support the judgment that I ought to pull the child out is this: if it is in my power to prevent something very bad from happening, without thereby sacrificing anything of comparable moral significance, we ought to so do it. This principle seems uncontroversial.

Singer goes on to suggest that failing to save the child is the moral equivalent of killing the child. But few of us will see a child drowning in a pond, or a man beaten by the side of the road. He continues:

Nevertheless, (this principle). . . is deceptive. If it were taken seriously and acted upon, our lives and our world would be fundamentally changed.

For the principle applies, not just to rare situations in which one can save a child from a pond, but to the everyday situation in which we can assist those living in absolute poverty. . . . Not to help would be wrong, whether or not it is intrinsically equivalent to killing.[6]

Peter Singer wrestles with the question, "Who is my neighbor?" He also faces the logical follow-up question, "What is my responsibility toward him?" He is advocating the same radical thought as Jesus: Walking by on the other side of the road is wrong. To Christians, this connection of belief to action seems obvious. Singer is not saying anything new. But, too often, beliefs fail to translate into action.

In 2001, World Vision commissioned a study through the Barna Research Group to determine the willingness of the Christian community to get involved in fighting the AIDS epidemic. When evangelical Christians were asked whether they would be willing to donate money to help children orphaned by AIDS, only 7 percent answered that they definitely would. More than half said that they probably or definitely would *not* help. Evangelicals were even less likely to support *education* efforts to help prevent AIDS.[7]

The survey found that by many measures, non-Christians were more inclined to help than those who claim to be followers of Jesus, in both spirit and word.

Here again is the gap between knowing and doing. My pastor, Gary Gulbranson,[8] said one Sunday, "It's not what you believe that counts. It's what you believe enough to do." The priest and the Levite had the right beliefs, but they were unwilling to do what those beliefs logically dictated.

The book of James says it eloquently and succinctly: "But be doers of the word, and not hearers only, deceiving yourselves."[9] A chapter later, James is more explicit when he says:

> What does it profit, my brethren, if someone says he has faith but does not have works? Can faith save him? If a brother or sister is naked and destitute of daily food, and one of you says to them, "Depart in peace, be warmed and filled," but you do not give them the things which are needed for the body, what does it profit? Thus also faith by itself, if it does not have works, is dead.[10]

In light of this, how should the Christian community respond to the victims of HIV/AIDS? The fourth character of Jesus' parable shows us.

The Samaritan

The Jews despised the Samaritans. They were considered heretical and unclean. Jews would not associate with them. Jesus' introduction of the Samaritan into this parable would have been shocking to the expert in the law, and the contrast between the compassion of the unclean Samaritan and the "righteous" priest and Levite scandalous.

This Samaritan saw the man at the side of the road "and took pity on him." He bandaged his wounds and poured oil and wine upon them as a salve. He put the man on his own donkey, transported him to an inn, and left money for his care. And he promised to return to check up on the man. It was not a minimal response. Rather, it was a complete engagement.

The Samaritan had compassion, which translated into action. Jesus turns the question back on the expert in the law, asking, "So which of these three do you think was neighbor to him who fell among the thieves?"[11]

The man could not even bring himself to say the word "Samaritan," and answers instead, "He who showed mercy on him."[12]

The Samaritans of the AIDS crisis seem just as unlikely to today's religious establishment. They include individuals from groups including:

- The homosexual community

- Hollywood

- Political liberals

- The U.S. government

- The United Nations

- Secular humanitarian organizations

- The Bill and Melinda Gates Foundation

And who would expect a rock star to be leading the charge? Bono, lead singer of the group U2, may be doing more to address the AIDS crisis than any other single person in the world. When addressing a group of Christians in Washington, Bono asked, "Will American Christians stand by as an entire continent dies for 'small money'?"

The Lesson for the Church

Years from now, the AIDS pandemic will be judged as one of those crossroads in human history. Every generation struggles with events and crises that ultimately define it. Every generation has its sins—of commission and omission. The lens of history can be brutally honest in its judgment.

How could American pioneers justify their treatment of Native Americans? How could pre-Civil-War America have tolerated slavery? How could churches in America have turned a blind eye to racial discrimination in the 1940s and 1950s? These are the kinds of questions that history asks, and the questions that children and grandchildren ask of their parents and grandparents. "Why didn't you act? How could you remain silent?"

No one can predict the outcome of the AIDS crisis with certainty— whether vaccines will be found or whether the epidemic will be somehow stopped 10, 50, or 100 years from today. No one can predict how many men, women, and children will die, or how many orphans and widows will suffer in obscurity. No one can predict how this generation will be viewed through that lens of history. But I know that we cannot remain silent, and I am certain of what Jesus would have us do.

A Call to Action

I am certain about God's expectations of his people. I am certain that God sees these widows and orphans as our neighbors, lying beaten and bleeding on the side of the road, needing our help. And I am certain that he calls us to stop, show compassion, comfort them, bind up their wounds, and see that they and their children are cared for.

Matthew 25 describes the spectacular scene at the last judgment when all of the nations will be gathered before the Master and we hear these remarkable words:

> "Come, you blessed of My Father, inherit the kingdom prepared for you from the foundation of the world: for I was hungry and you gave Me food; I was thirsty and you gave Me drink; I was a stranger and you took Me in; I was naked and you clothed Me; I was sick and you visited Me; I was in prison and you came to Me." Then the righteous will answer Him, saying, "Lord, when did we see You hungry and feed You, or thirsty and give You drink? When did we see You a stranger and take You in, or naked and clothe You? Or when did we see You sick, or in prison, and come to You?" And the King will answer and say to them, "Assuredly, I say to you, inasmuch as you did it to one of the least of these My brethren, you did it to Me." [13]

Mother Teresa saw Christ in every dying beggar or leper she served. She once said this of these broken and forgotten souls: "I see the face of Jesus in disguise—sometimes a most distressing disguise." She understood that in serving the "least of these," she was not serving the loathsome and despicable, but Jesus himself.

Henry Nouwen, a priest, professor and philosopher, pointed out: "God rejoices. Not because the problems of the world have been solved, not because all human pain and suffering have come to an end, nor because thousands of people have been converted and are now praising Him for His goodness. No, God rejoices because one of His children who was lost has been found."[14]

We can reach out to the one: the one widow, the one orphan, the one father, the one mother. We can demonstrate the love of Christ to these dear children who have lost their parents. We can encourage right behaviors so they can avoid their parents' fate. We can come alongside grandparents, aunts, and uncles trying to raise these orphaned children. And we can comfort the sick and dying and offer them hope for a new life in Christ. We can reach out to the "least of these."

How? By advocating for right theology in our churches and right policies by our government. By praying for people with AIDS, for the children they leave behind, and for their caregivers. By volunteering with local organizations serving people affected by HIV/AIDS. And by supporting our brothers and sisters in Africa and elsewhere in their efforts to stop this epidemic and care for those whose lives already have been shattered.

Jesus ends the parable of the Good Samaritan with a powerful challenge. When he asked the expert in the law which of the three men had been a neighbor to the man who fell into the hands of robbers, he answers with a new understanding: "The one who had mercy on him."

Jesus then looks at this man and concludes what is perhaps the most powerful moral teaching in all of history with a command of just four words. These four words declare Christ's expectation for every Christian. These four words have the power to change the world.

"Go and do likewise."[15]

Notes

1. Luke 10:25 NKJV
2. Luke 10:26 NKJV
3. Luke 10:27 NKJV
4. Luke 10:28 NKJV
5. Luke 10: 29 NKJV
6. Peter Singer, *Practical Ethics* (Cambridge: Cambridge University Press, 1993).

7. "Americans' Interest in Assisting the International AIDS Crisis," national survey of U.S. adults conducted by Barna Research Group, Ltd., Ventura, California, January 2001.

8. Gary Gulbranson, Senior Pastor, Westminster Chapel, Bellevue, Washington.

9. James 1:22 NKJV

10. James 2: 14–17 NKJV

11. Luke 10:36 NKJV

12. Luke 10:37 NKJV

13. Luke 25:34–40 NKJV

14. Phillip Yancey, *What's So Amazing About Grace?* (Grand Rapids: Zondervan, 1997).

15. Luke 10:37 NKJV

CHAPTER 21
TOM CORRELL

HIV/AIDS: A CHURCH-SIZED PROBLEM

The evangelical community is becoming increasingly aware of the terrible disaster wrought by HIV/AIDS. The numbers tell the story of an unparalleled tragedy. In just 20 years, HIV/AIDS has directly touched 1 percent of the world's population. Some 25 million have died from AIDS or its complications. Another 42 million are HIV-positive or living with AIDS. Of these, approximately 70 percent are in sub-Saharan Africa.

Every 10 seconds, one person dies of AIDS and another two are infected. And HIV/AIDS is increasingly a malady of women and children. Over half of all those infected today are women or girls. Children 15 years old and younger represent 15 percent of all new infections and 20 percent of all deaths from AIDS. This has also resulted in more than 15 million AIDS orphans—a number that is estimated to grow to 40 million by 2010.[1]

The tragedy doesn't stop there. Millions of elderly are left with no means of support because the children they expected to support them in their declining years are dead from AIDS. These elderly are left as the sole supporters of multiple grandchildren. The current famine in southern Africa (with upwards of 15 million people facing starvation) is due as much to lack of agricultural workers from HIV/AIDS as from drought. A recent United States government study warns that HIV/AIDS could seriously harm the economies of Russia, China, and India in the next 20 years.[2] Most global economic models assume these nations will be driving forces in the world economy. In other words, HIV/AIDS has the potential of bringing about global economic depression.

HIV/AIDS, unchecked, could have repercussions of apocalyptic proportions. (See Revelation 6:5–8.) In early 2002, I took a six-week sabbatical to Africa. I wanted to look at the impact of HIV/AIDS and answer the question, "How should our church minister to those affected by HIV/AIDS?" I expected to find some ministry—perhaps an orphanage, a school, or a clinic and say, "That one's ours. We'll help fund this project." However, it became apparent that we needed a massive grass-roots movement. Then, as I observed the limited public infrastructure in Africa, I became convinced that the tragedy of HIV/AIDS is a church-sized problem.

The HIV/AIDS pandemic presents, perhaps, the greatest opportunity for the global church to rise up and be the incarnation of Jesus Christ in a dying world. There are three reasons. First, the church uniquely has the *mandate* to take the lead in combating HIV/AIDS. Second, only the church has the *presence* to serve those impacted by HIV/AIDS. Finally, the church has the *precedent* for successfully changing the course of history.

A God-Given Mandate

When challenged by a teacher of the law to name the greatest commandment, Jesus gave the following answer:

> Love the Lord your God with all your heart and with all your soul and with all your mind. This is the first and greatest commandment. And the second is like it: Love your neighbor as yourself. All the Law and the prophets hang on these two commandments. (Matthew 22:37–40)

We can look at this mandate in a number of scriptural ways.

1. The Prophetic Mandate.

To address HIV/AIDS, the church needs to speak out prophetically against sinful behavior. HIV/AIDS is a terrible portrayal of the moral failure of humanity. Two keys are to reduce the number of sexual partners that an individual has—Christians refer to it as faithfulness in marriage— and increase the age of first sexual activity—abstinence before marriage. The church needs to call its people and the world to God's standard of sexuality.

Yet the church slights its prophetic task simply by preaching, "Just Say No." It must confront underlying worldview and cultural attitudes that encourage high-risk behavior. There remains, in parts of the world and Africa in particular, a lingering polygamous worldview that says that a man's power is demonstrated in the number of women he possesses. Even though formal polygamy may be illegal or socially unacceptable, men of power and prestige continue to flaunt their "women on the side." Such societies assert that men of strength, power, and virility have virtually unlimited sexual need, and that no one woman can satisfy that need. Thus, multiple partners are a necessity.

This attitude of sexual entitlement for men all accompanies the attitude that the primary role of a woman is to satisfy the needs of a man. In the face of these attitudes the church must proclaim—first to its own people and then to the wider society—that a husband is to love his wife as Christ loves the church. First, of course, church leaders must model this lifestyle. They in turn need to teach it to other men and boys from elementary age up. They need to teach and show that rather than taking, a Christian man gives. A Christian man can exercise discipline in sexual matters as well as in other areas of life. Followers of Jesus need to demonstrate that a husband puts the needs of his wife before his own—including his sexual needs or desires (Ephesians 5:22–31).

Churches thus need to be at the forefront of proclaiming and demonstrating the dignity of women, that they too are created in the image of God. Women and girls—even very young girls—need to know they have the right to protect themselves. Women also must have the right to protect their children, especially young girls, from predatory sexual practices. Finally, they need to know they have rights in the face of unfaithful husbands (Matthew 19:9), including spousal support and the means to earn a livelihood for themselves and their children. Christians who have historically championed the rights and dignity of women must reclaim that role in the face of HIV/AIDS.

The church also needs to address the issue of circumcision, for both males and females. There has been a great deal of appropriate focus in secular circles about the tragedy of female mutilation. The church needs to lend its support to this cause by teaching young girls—and their parents—that their bodies are a gift from God, that they are wondrously and gloriously created, and that self-control comes from within.

The church, unfortunately, too frequently has overlooked male circumcision practices. This ceremony traditionally marks the onset of adulthood. It usually concludes by encouraging young men to go out and "prove their manhood." In contrast, a large church in Nairobi has given an altogether new meaning to this rite. Church leaders take all their 13-year-old boys on a weekend "Adulthood Retreat." There they frankly and openly teach these young men about their sexuality, but from a Christian perspective. These young men learn that a strong man doesn't prove his strength in conquest, but rather in self-control. They also learn that young women are to be treated with dignity and respect. As part of this weekend, they hear about the causes and risks of HIV/AIDS.

We in the Western church also need to speak against the morality, or more explicitly the immorality, that the popular media proclaims throughout the world. Western ideas and culture attract young people, especially in the developing world. The media incessantly hammer home the message that immodest dress and immoral behavior are cool. We need to not only speak up against this kind of material, but also demonstrate a contrasting lifestyle.

People will notice when Westerners take a stand for decency. Recently a team of young singles from our church visited a Muslim area for a week. One of the local leaders told us, "You people are different. You are not immoral, your women dress modestly, and your men do not pursue our women." We must teach in word and action that immorality is not "normal" for Christians.

Yes, the church needs to speak out strongly against unbiblical sexual conduct, and live out the biblical standard of purity. But we will not succeed in getting the message across if we ignore the underlying cultural values that encourage such conduct.

Other cultural issues remain for the church to address. Stigmatization of those infected with HIV/AIDS is almost universal. In Africa, I witnessed case after case of women who, when they admitted that they were HIV-positive, were cast out of their homes—though in all likelihood they got the disease from their husbands. They ended up on the street. They could not return to their family of origin because relatives either assumed these women were immoral, or family members were unable to pay back the bride price they had received from the husband's family at the time of marriage.

Churches, too, may not be free from stigmatization. At a Prescription for Hope Conference sponsored by Samaritan's Purse in early 2002, a highly educated, professional woman told of confronting her husband for immoral behavior. When she asked for a clean HIV test from him as a precondition for reconciliation, he refused. Instead, he brought the leaders of their church to instruct her to "submit to her husband." She stood her ground to the point of eventual divorce—in the face of stern rebuke from her husband's family, her family, and her church. Within six months of their divorce, the former husband was dead from AIDS. Because of her stand, her three young children still have a mother to care for them.

In yet another tragic cultural practice, widows whose husbands have died from AIDS must often forfeit homes, land, and property to the husband's relatives. These unfortunate women then have no means of providing for their children and are often vulnerable to sexual exploitation. The church needs to take a prophetic stand—speaking for proper sexual conduct and condemning predatory practices that make AIDS all the more painful.

In Uganda, church leaders are speaking out, and the number of new AIDS infections has plummeted (see chapter 6). Christ Presbyterian Church in Edina, Minnesota, working with the International Justice Mission, has opened an office in Uganda to provide legal aid for women who have had their property expropriated illegally by relatives of their deceased husbands. Secular media and government are now speaking strongly about the dangers of HIV and AIDS.

Yet the church uniquely can speak from the perspective of obedience to God's command. Where secular society can speak only of "safe sex" and dangerous behavior, the church can talk in terms of love of and obedience to God, who created us and gave his Son that we might have eternal life and the Spirit's indwelling power to enable right behavior.

2. The Pastoral Mandate.

If love of God mandates us to speak out prophetically, love of neighbor drives us to care pastorally for those affected by AIDS. Eighty percent of all hospital beds in southern Africa are filled with those suffering from AIDS, yet most people die at home—often alone. Thirty-five percent of girls in Swaziland drop out of school to care for a parent who has AIDS. In South Africa, I visited a church that had a team of volunteers who visit the homes of the so-called "chronically ill" to see that they have proper nutrition, rest, and hygiene. These volunteers saw small children trying to dress open wounds on infected parents.

Then there are the orphans and the elderly. You simply cannot build orphanages for 40 million children—even if orphanages made sense. These orphans will either find housing with families and neighbors, or they will become members of terrorizing street gangs.

Social security and pensions for the elderly do not exist in much of Africa, where adult children provide care for their parents. I visited an elderly woman in a Nairobi slum. Rather than being supported by her children, she was the sole provider for her five orphaned grandchildren. She represents a vast number of people in the same predicament. Love of neighbor says we *must* care for the sick, the dying, the orphans, and the widows. Thankfully, churches are increasingly providing care for those like her. Sometimes these churches encourage an elderly person, typically a widow, to provide a home for orphaned children. In turn the children, when trained by a knowledgeable adult, provide for her needs through farming. Then the church provides a stipend. This arrangement allows children to receive the nurture and support of a family environment.

3. The Priestly Mandate.

Finally, the church needs to act in a *priestly* manner. God, and only God, can change the worldview of those engaging in sexual practices that spread HIV/AIDS. God can heal disease. God can change the evolution of the virus that causes AIDS. God can give insight to researchers seeking a vaccine or cure. God can encourage the hearts of donors to provide the medicines to extend life, to reduce the likelihood of mother-to-child transmission, or to cure opportunistic diseases, such as tuberculosis. God can cause governments to allocate resources to the fight against HIV/ AIDS. (As an American I thank God for the recent federal commitment to fighting AIDS in Africa and the Caribbean and pray that the money will be appropriated and distributed.) God can raise up courageous governmental leaders like President Museveni of Uganda, who has made HIV/AIDS his government's number one agenda item.

When God called Moses to confront Pharaoh, he said, "I have seen the misery of my people. . . . I have heard their crying out. . . and I am concerned about their suffering." Is God any less concerned about those afflicted by HIV/AIDS than those suffering from slavery in Egypt? We must pray for our brothers and sisters afflicted by AIDS.

A Providential Presence

When challenging Queen Esther to confront the Persian King, Mordecai said she may have been brought into the king's court at just that time so that she could save the Jewish people from destruction. For the last century, we in the developed world have come to expect government to provide the infrastructure and services needed when calamity strikes. Tragically, this infrastructure does not exist in most poor countries. There are no government offices, hospitals, or social service offices in much of Africa, India, or Southeast Asia. Tragically, many Third World governments have neither the will nor the resources to deal with the AIDS pandemic.

Yet, in God's wisdom, he has planted his church throughout sub-Saharan Africa and in many other areas. God has put his people in place for "just such a time as this." Today, churches are near most African HIV/AIDS sufferers. This would not have been true 50 years ago. The numbers associated with HIV/AIDS mean that the church must take the lead. You simply cannot build hospitals for 28 million AIDS patients. They must receive home care. Who will provide caregivers? Only the churches have the vast numbers of potential volunteers. Likewise, you cannot build orphanages for 40 million children. Only the church has the human resources. But first we must repent of unbiblical cultural practices that spread HIV/AIDS and limit care, set aside cultural and theological differences that limit cooperation, and "ask the Lord of the harvest . . . to send out workers into his harvest field" (Matthew 9:38).

A Precedent in History

In *The Rise of Christianity,*[3] sociologist Rodney Stark noted that Constantine didn't declare the Roman Empire to be Christian. He merely acknowledged that the empire had already become Christian. Stark showed mathematically that even with a 4 to 5 percent annual growth rate from the time of Jesus, the majority of the empire's population could have become Christian by year A.D. 300.

Stark listed four traits of the Christians of those days that parallel the situation in Africa today. (1) The early Christians practiced a high degree of morality without being judgmental. They demonstrated a lifestyle that was an attractive contrast. (2) In a time when infanticide was rampant, when pagans often left girl babies beside the streams to be killed by exposure or wild animals, each morning Christians took these babies into their homes. (3) When plagues hit cities, residents would flee for the relative safety of the mountains. Christians, on the other hand stayed to care for the sick and dying. Eventually non-Christian writers began to ask why only Christians showed compassion. (4) In an era in which women were treated merely as property, Christians gave them dignity.

These actions by God's people literally changed the direction of an empire. Could they not do the same today?

Throughout history, followers of Jesus Christ have served their neighbors. During the Middle Ages, monasteries were places of healing and refuge for the poor as well as places of prayer, meditation, and study. During the Industrial Revolution, Sunday schools, the Salvation Army, the YMCA, and the YWCA helped those left behind economically. In our era, relief and development organizations such as World Vision and World Relief have provided a hand up to the needy in the name of Jesus Christ. God's people have wonderful precedents of serving those in need. Today, HIV/AIDS presents perhaps the greatest opportunity for service that the church will face—and the greatest potential for positive impact.

North America's Role

African churches need to take the lead in dealing with HIV/AIDS, and they are doing so. I have witnessed God's caring people in South Africa, Mozambique, Malawi, Uganda, Rwanda, Nigeria, and other countries. Yet many, if not most, are tragically poor. The per-capita income of two-thirds of those living in Africa is less than two dollars per day.

To the parents who will welcome three foster children into their home and feed them, can we not provide the $5 per month per child for school fees? For the volunteers who will care for the sick, can we not provide aspirin and supplies? For those too ill to work, or who have no one to provide for them, can we not provide food? For those pastors and teachers who will teach morality and call for appropriate behavioral change, can we not provide teaching materials?

HIV/AIDS isn't just an African problem; it's a global problem. We North American Christians need to walk beside our brothers and sisters in Africa and other areas devastated by HIV/AIDS. We also need to encourage our government to provide aid for those countries most devastated by HIV/AIDS and to continue research into medical care.

Believing that HIV/AIDS presents a unique challenge to the church both in Africa and in North America, four churches—Mars Hill Bible Church of Grand Rapids, Michigan, Perimeter Church of Atlanta, Georgia, Mariners Church of Irvine, California, and Wooddale Church of Eden Prairie, Minnesota—have formed what we call the Africa AIDS Initiative (AAI). The vision statement of AAI is: *A movement of churches working together for hope and wholeness in the face of AIDS.* Its mission is *engaging North American churches to join with African churches in collaborative initiatives that transform communities devastated by AIDS.*

We are recruiting additional church partners. In the meantime, we are working to identify African structures and networks that can facilitate partnership from the African side. North American and African indigenous NGOs understand best ministry practice and often have the experience to bridge the cultural differences. We are concerned that working partnerships be both culturally and missiologically sound. We do not want North American churches investing in ministries that are not valid or effective; nor do we want these partnerships to foster dependence or economic imperialism.

A Unique Opportunity

At the Prescription for Hope Conference, I spoke with a veteran church planter who had worked for 30 years in Thailand. Most recently he had been teaching church leaders how to help people impacted by HIV/AIDS. He told me, "As the church in Thailand has begun to serve those suffering with AIDS, it has learned compassion. As it has demonstrated compassion, people have started coming to Christ. Perhaps this [lack of compassion] is why we've been there for 150 years and have only 1 percent of the population."

Two hours later, I had lunch with a woman representing a medical ministry from a mainline church. She said, "HIV/AIDS has changed the very foundation of how we do ministry. Everyone we serve is going to die—within days or weeks. We cannot just give them medicine and a cup of water and tell them that we love them; we must offer them hope."

At this same conference, apologist Ravi Zacharias said, "If the church of Jesus Christ rises to the challenge of HIV/AIDS, it will be the greatest apologetic the world has ever seen."

We as the church have this God-given opportunity. And if we don't take it, who will?

Notes

1. www.unaids.org.

2. "The Next Wave of HIV/AIDS: Nigeria, Ethiopia, Russia, India and China," National Intelligence Council ICA 2002–04D, September 2002.

3. Rodney Stark, *The Rise of Christianity: How the Obscure, Marginal Jesus Movement Became the Dominant Religious Force in the Western World in a Few Centuries,* (Princeton, N.J.: Princeton University Press, 1996).

CHAPTER 22

HIV: A WORLDVIEW PROBLEM

Roger Maluka (a pseudonym) was a competent medical assistant in the Congo. He had directed a rural health center for several years. We then promoted him to be supervisor of a network of six such centers. However, in September 1982 he came to our large rural hospital complaining of low-grade fever, fatigue, and an intensely pruritic fungal skin infection, all of which he had battled for more than a month.

We could find no cause for his fever. Local and systemic antifungal preparations had no impact on his rash. A widespread lymphadenopathy did not respond to anti-tuberculosis treatment, and general measures of good nutrition and care did not improve his condition. After some months, he went to the University Hospital in Kinshasa for further diagnosis and treatment. He died there the following spring. His family informed us that a blood specimen sent to Belgium for analysis showed that he died of a "new white man's disease." This was subsequently confirmed as being GRID: Gay Related Immune Deficiency. This made no sense to us, for Roger was certainly not involved in the homosexual lifestyle.

In the meantime, we were caring for others with this "new disease," which soon came to be known as HIV infection and AIDS. Reading early reports of the epidemic and through increasing contacts with colleagues serving in Uganda and Kenya, we saw that networks of multipartner sexual relationships were the principal reason for the rapid spread of the infection in many parts of the world. These unhealthy sexual relationships were also responsible for infecting blood supplies and mothers of unborn children.

Current evidence suggests that HIV entered human history in the middle of the twentieth century. From an unknown entity in 1980, it developed in just two decades into a global pandemic that has now affected the lives of 1 percent of the world's population. I believe a *fundamental worldview problem* is behind the explosive and destructive spread of this infection. A change at this deep level will enormously help the medical community's efforts to prevent the spread of HIV.

The Worldview Problem

A worldview is a set of assumptions or presuppositions about the basic makeup of the world around us. It is what we take for granted about reality. The worldview problem underlying the explosive HIV pandemic is ignorance or rejection of God's view of human life and of sexual behavior.

Questions about spirituality and personal identity are at the core of a person's worldview.

1. Is there a personal God and, if so, what is God like?

2. Who am I?

3. For what purpose was I born?

4. What is my ultimate destiny?

5. What has gone wrong with the world and with my life?

6. How am I to live?

7. How can I distinguish right from wrong?

Let's look at these questions in light of the HIV pandemic.

Who is God?

The Bible says there is indeed a personal and knowable God. He is the Creator of all things: the physical world, humankind, and the unseen spiritual powers of the universe; and he is the author and sustainer of life.

What is God like?

In the Bible God has given us specific names for himself, each one revealing insights about his nature. Genesis 1:1 says, "In the beginning, [Elohim] created the heavens and the earth." The Hebrew name *Elohim* means "the strong God who binds himself by the oaths he has made to himself." In other words, God is internally consistent, faithful, never changing, and absolutely trustworthy. God is the truth for he cannot lie, deceive, or take advantage of anyone. As bearers of God's image, we represent God and must be trustworthy and faithful, exploiting no one.

Elohim likewise implies that God is completely whole, yet also a multidimensional unity. Applied to us, this means we also are multidimensional whole beings, most notably body, mind, feelings, spirit, and social relationships, all in an interdependent and inseparable unity. What happens in one dimension, or whatever we do in one dimension of our life, affects all the others. We cannot separate our physical behavior from our emotional or spiritual nature. Sexual activity therefore engages us as whole persons: spiritually, emotionally, socially, and physically.

In Genesis 2, God calls himself Jehovah, the God who communicates. God communicates within the Godhead and with those in whom God has put his image. This means that God is personal and knowable, a God with whom we can speak and to whom we can listen. This raises human communication—nonverbal as well as verbal—to a high level of responsibility, for as we communicate with others, we mimic God's communication. Every communication that comes from us, be it about love, sexual activity, or anything else, should conform to God's standard.

God is love. This means God cares for the creation and gives himself for the good of all he has created, including us. He wants us to have life, health, and right relationships with him, with others, and with the world in which we live.

Who am I?

God has created us in his image so that we can have a personal relationship with him. Men and women alike bear the image of God. This image is stamped into our personalities from the moment of conception.

As bearers of the image of God, we represent God, whoever and wherever we are.

We have a spiritual nature because God, who has put his image within us, is Spirit. We can relate to God and to the spiritual world in which we live via our spirits. Our spirit is likewise the seat of our will and where we determine our answers to the worldview questions listed above. Because we bear God's image, we have infinite value and an eternal destiny, regardless of gender, ethnicity, or religious faith.

God also created us as sexual beings, masculine and feminine. Our masculinity and femininity come from God and are therefore good. God has separated these attributes in us for a purpose. When sexual union occurs according to God's plan, the spiritual and emotional unity between man and woman becomes an illustration of the kind of intimate spiritual relationship God wants the church to have with him.

These beliefs have important consequences for my relationships. If I use another person for my personal pleasure and satisfaction, abuse another person in any way whatsoever, or treat anyone else as an object to gratify my own needs, then I am defacing the image of God in that person and will be held responsible before God. I am also defacing the image of God within me because I am acting selfishly rather than acting as God does for the good of others.

For what purpose was I born?

Belief in the transcendent strongly influences human behavior, individual and collective. Jehovah is faithful and self-giving, the model for our lives. Because Jehovah has given us freedom of choice, we can decide how to live. We are responsible to our Creator for these choices, but he will empower us to glorify him with our lifestyles, behaviors, and relationships. Because God is faithful, I must not lie, deceive, or take advantage of anyone. I can live as God wants me to if I am empowered by the Spirit of God living within me.

Our spirituality shapes our physical behavior. Genesis 2:7 says that God took the dust of the earth and formed a human body. Amazing design and complexity are encompassed within that terse statement. God designed every organ, tissue, cell, and liquid, put them into their proper places, and joined them in harmony with every other part of the body. Even a cursory study of anatomy and physiology leads us to exclaim in awe with David: "Behold, I am fearfully and wonderfully made."

The Bible clearly states that we are stewards, not owners, of our bodies. The purpose of the body is twofold: to be a house where God can live by his Spirit, and to be the physical means of serving God by serving other people. We are to subordinate our personal desires to serve God and others. Our bodies are sacred. We have no ultimate rights to our bodies or to use the bodies of others.

In contrast, secular humanism considers man to be an intelligent animal devoid of an eternal spirit and ultimate worth. According to this worldview, a person's behavior is his own affair, and he is accountable only to himself. Sexual behavior is presumed to be an individual matter, not a moral issue. (This is in spite of the obvious social nature of sexual behavior and the consequences of individual behavior on others— including the spread of sexually transmitted diseases.)

Secular humanism is a fatalistic or deterministic worldview. Supposedly man has appeared in the universe by chance, and each person is the sum of the chance arrangements of DNA—I was born this way and therefore I am not responsible for my behavior. However, the scientific evidence for this belief is weak at best. Although inherited DNA does in some ways predispose us to certain lifestyles, the major determinants come from environmental influences and how we respond to them. According to the Bible we are responsible to God and to others for how we respond.

What went wrong?

God created the human body and breathed into it mind, soul, and spirit. He wanted our will, in subjection to his Spirit, to rule over the needs and desires of our human nature, controlling the potent urges of body and mind. However, our ancestors, in their freedom of choice, rejected this submissive relationship to God and chose to submit to the evil spiritual powers of the universe. This misuse of our freedom has been passed on to all subsequent generations, and by our own choice unredeemed humanity now lives in alienation from God and the control of his Spirit. In our alienated human condition, the powerful needs and desires of our body and mind control our thoughts and behavior. In no sphere of life is this more evident than in our sexual behavior.

God, however, has not abandoned us. Through Jesus Christ God made possible reconciliation and a new relationship with him. When we choose to live in relationship with God by faith, his indwelling Spirit empowers us to live as God wants in all our relationships, including our sexuality. Romans 8 says that if we are filled with the Spirit of Christ, our will can once again rule over the desires of our body and mind, resulting in life. Without the Spirit of Christ within us, however, the will does not have the power to rule over body and mind. Their desires rule over our will, and this leads to death.

How am I to live?

God has revealed the patterns of behavior that bring life and health. In Leviticus 18, a chapter that could rightly be called the HIV chapter of the Bible, he commands us to follow these patterns for two reasons.

1. Primarily, we are to obey His laws *because He is God* and has created us in his image. Repeatedly in the chapter he says, "I am the Lord."

2. Secondarily, we are to obey his laws because they are good for us. Leviticus 18:5 says, "Follow the practices and laws I give you; *you will save your life by doing so.*" (GNT, italics mine). The chapter then continues with many proscriptions about sexual relationships, including incest, child abuse, adultery, homosexual behavior, and bestiality. These proscriptions, if obeyed, will preserve health and life, but, if disobeyed, can lead to disease and death. Could anything be clearer than this?

For life, health, and the greatest personal fulfillment as God's image bearer, I am to live according to the patterns God, my Creator, has established. This includes my sexual behavior as well as all other social relationships. Under my own control, I will most likely fail. However, if the Spirit of God lives in me, God can provide the power to live and relate to others according to his will. As I do this, I become able to model this pattern for others and teach them healthy patterns of relationships, including sexual behavior.

Worldview Education

Behavior is the outward expression of our inward disposition. We do what we do because of our values, beliefs, and worldview. Bringing about lasting change in behavior requires changing our beliefs and assumptions. Effective education for change in health-related behavior must therefore begin with worldview issues. That is a difficult, long-term process. Above all, it requires building the kind of relationships that permit interchange at a deep level. The process of helping people adopt the biblical pattern of healthy sexual behavior must begin with us.

Self control

1. We ourselves must thoroughly understand God's plan for human life and sexual behavior as revealed in the Bible.

2. We can submit to God's plan for our lives only if God's Spirit lives in us. Powerful spiritual forces of immorality pervade our world, operating through human institutions, social structures, and the media. Without our conscious choice to critique these structures, reject these powers, and submit to God's control, we fall quickly into the patterns set by these spiritual powers of immorality.

3. As we submit to God, his Spirit within us enables us to model the life of God in our conversations, behavior, and relationships and to obey his directives, especially in our sexual behavior and in marriage.

Sharing God's plan with others

1. Conveying an understanding of God's ways and the desire to follow them requires building relationships of trust with people. We can gain their hearing only as we gain their trust.

2. On this foundation of trust, we begin by telling the story of God from the beginning—who he is, what he is like, who we are, what has gone wrong, and what God requires for our lives. At the center of the story we come to Jesus, God in human flesh. Jesus modeled the life God wants us to live and, by his death and resurrection, made possible our reconciliation with God.

3. Then comes the warm invitation to others to enter the kingdom of God. This occurs when people ask Jesus to enter their lives and empower them by his Spirit to obey his will and laws. Without the Spirit of God within, the human will has insufficient power to rule over the desires and urges of body and mind.

4. We must also clearly teach what the Bible says about God's plan for healthy sexual relationships. We do this through our own lifestyle, through acts of compassionate service, and through interactive communication such as dialogue, story telling, drama, music, and so on.

5. Our real battle is against the evil powers of immorality, deception, and the exploitation of the weak by the strong. The basic goal is to convince people to choose God rather than to follow these destructive powers. Educational efforts are essential to clarify the choices.

6. Fervent prayer must accompany all of this. In prayer our spirit cooperates with God, who alone can draw people to choose God's way and be set free from destructive evil powers.

The apostle Paul sums up how inner transformation by the Spirit of God makes possible changes in outward lifestyle and behavior, including sexual behavior. "Because sin lives in me, the good things I want to do I am not able to do. The evil things I want to avoid, I do. Who can rescue me from this body that is taking me to death? Thanks be to God who does this through our Lord Jesus Christ!" (Romans 7: 17–15, my paraphrase)

Motivating healthy sexual behavior patterns through a worldview-based educational process is an immense task requiring time, effort, and relational skills. We can do this only as the Spirit of God empowers us.

Note: Workshops on biblically based worldview education for HIV prevention are available at King College in Bristol, Tennessee. For information, visit www.king.edu/academics/PeekeSchool/GlobalHealth.

CHAPTER 23
KEN CASEY

BIBLICAL REFLECTIONS ON HIV/AIDS

The HIV/AIDS pandemic is the greatest human crisis of our time—possibly of all time. It has left a path of devastation for individuals, families, and communities. As of December 2002, over 64 million people had been infected with the incurable HIV/AIDS virus. Of these, 25 million people had already died. Most of the other 42 million know they are harboring a virus that will eventually kill them. Fourteen million children have already lost one or both parents to AIDS. While we sleep, all of these numbers continue to grow. No corner of the earth has been spared from the onslaught of HIV/AIDS.

Where is God in the midst of such tragedy? How can we begin to grasp the HIV/AIDS epidemic in light of Scripture and our understanding of God and the world he created?

Three Lenses

One quickly realizes that many difficult questions arise in the face of HIV/AIDS. These are a few basic questions.

- Why does God allow such pain and suffering?

- Does having HIV affect God's love for someone?

- Is HIV/AIDS God's judgment for sinful behavior?

- What is Christian hope in the context of HIV/AIDS?

- What does God expect followers of Jesus to do in the midst of this tragedy?

Let's look at these questions through three lenses: (1) God's ideal world, (2) the real world we live in, and (3) God's desire to renew and redeem.

1. *God's ideal world.* The Bible is clear that God created the world and all its inhabitants for his own delight and glory. All men and women have been formed in the image of God and have infinite value and dignity. God's ideal plan was to commune together in perfect harmony with all creation.

There would be no pain and suffering. Sickness, death, anguish, and fear would have no part in this ideal world. Instead, all would rest in the continual embrace of an infinitely loving God and find constant joy in singing his praises.

2. *The real world we live in.* But the Bible also tells us that God gave man a choice, and our first parents chose to seek their own will instead of God's. Disobedience led to estrangement from God and to the proliferation of sin. Instead of seeking to glorify God in all that we do, we seek to glorify ourselves and disobey or disregard the God who created us. None has escaped this temptation, and we have all sinned and fallen short of the glory of God.

One consequence of our collective disobedience and sin is a world unlike God's ideal. Sin has tarnished both our spiritual relationships with God as well as our own physical well-being. Sickness and death abound. Half the earth's population lives in poverty. Greed, corruption, disease, famine, abuse, and pain are common companions.

3. *God's desire to renew and redeem.* But the Bible is also clear that God has provided a plan to renew and redeem his creation. Central to his plan was sending Jesus to bear the price of sin and disobedience so that all who place their trust in him are restored to their intended relationship with God. As believers in Jesus, we are redeemed, transformed by the renewing of our minds. As new creatures in Christ, all things become new. We receive the confident certainty that we will enjoy an eternity restored to our rightful relationship with our Creator. We can live with hope and joy—even though we continue to live in a real world that bears the consequences of sin and disobedience.

In God's ideal world, HIV/AIDS, along with murder, lying, sickness, and anger, would not exist. HIV/AIDS needs to be seen as one consequence, among many, of a world estranged from God.

How to Approach HIV/AIDS

Let's examine the issue by answering some common questions.

Why does God allow such pain and suffering?

Pain and suffering are not part of God's ideal world. Isaiah tells us that in the new earth, "the sound of weeping and of crying will be heard in it no more" (Isaiah 65:19). Revelation promises, "He will wipe every tear from their eyes. There will be no more death or mourning or crying or pain, for the old order of things has passed away" (21:4).

But in the present, God allows pain and suffering—not because he chooses it but because we, by our collective disobedience, have chosen it.

Does having HIV affect God's love for someone?

God's love for every human being is immeasurable. This love persuaded him to sacrifice his own Son on our behalf. The Scriptures are clear: God has an infinite love for each of us. This includes those who are HIV-positive.

Is HIV/AIDS God's judgment for sinful behavior?

There is no simple answer to this question. Clearly, the HIV virus has been spread, in part, by sexual behavior that violates God's word. In God's ideal world, sex is to be enjoyed within the context of marriage. Those who are married are to be faithful to their spouses. Those who are not married are to practice abstinence until they become married.

But many people have chosen not to follow God's instructions, unleashing horrific consequences. Many do not enjoy the full richness of marriage and family. Divorce is rampant. Children grow up without mothers and fathers. Sexually transmitted diseases—including HIV/AIDS—proliferate.

However, it is equally true that many who are suffering from the consequences of HIV/AIDS (either directly or indirectly) have done nothing to violate God's commands for sexual purity. Unfaithful partners have infected faithful spouses. Children have borne the pain and fear of losing parents through no fault of their own. Thus, one cannot conclude that those who are infected or affected have sinned, nor that those who are not suffering have not sinned.

God's word cautions us against trying to tie specific consequences to specific sins. It is not our role to judge (James 4:12). Instead, our challenge is to encourage people to follow God's law regarding sexual behavior and to enjoy the benefits of sexual purity and God-honoring lifestyles.

Many are promoting the use of condoms as one means of reducing the transmission of the HIV virus. Won't that also promote sexual promiscuity?

Condoms, when used consistently and correctly, can significantly reduce transmission of HIV. Obviously, the Bible does not address condom use, but biblical principles do shed some light on this question.

As mentioned above, the Bible gives us clear instructions to be faithful within marriage and abstinent outside of marriage. Marriage is a God-designed relationship. We should do everything we can to promote choices and lifestyles that conform to God's ideal.

God's word also talks about the sanctity of life. Life is sacred. We are not to take life away. We must do all we can to protect and preserve life.

The promotion of condom use seems to create a tension between these two ideals. Condoms can protect lives by keeping people from being infected with the HIV virus. However, some people might also misuse the availability of condoms to engage in sexual behavior that violates God's desire for sexual purity and the sanctity of marriage.

Which to choose? In order to honor both the sanctity of marriage and the sanctity of life, we should clearly promote fidelity within marriage and abstinence outside of marriage as God's desire for sexual behavior. At the same time, we should support the use of condoms as a means to protect life. They have a track record as a reliable barrier to the transmission of the deadly HIV virus.

What is Christian hope in the context of HIV/AIDS?

Hope is one of the pinnacles of our faith: "And now these three remain: faith, hope and love" (1 Corinthians 13:13). God wants us to overflow with hope (Romans 15:13). It delights our God when we put our hope in his unfailing love (Psalm 147:11).

But how do we bring hope to those affected by HIV/AIDS? How do you offer hope to a young mother who has already lost her husband to AIDS and is herself dying, knowing that her young children will have no one to care for them? What does hope feel like for a child of twelve who lives alone with his younger siblings in a meager house next to the two piles of rocks covering the graves of their mother and father? How would you describe hope to a young man in the prime of his life who realizes that he will likely never see his twenty-fifth birthday?

The ultimate hope comes through a renewed relationship with God through faith in Jesus Christ. As believers, we can enjoy a new hope, both for the future and the present: the future, because we know we will share eternity with God; the present, because we have new meaning in life. As Paul prayed for the believers in Rome, "May the God of hope fill you with all joy and peace as you trust in him, so that you may overflow with hope by the power of the Holy Spirit" (Romans 15:13).

The blessing of a new life in Christ also helps us put the *real world* in perspective. Paul writes that "our light and momentary troubles are achieving for us an eternal glory that far outweighs them all" (2 Corinthians 4:17).

Thus, the ultimate answer to the question of hope for those affected by HIV/AIDS is to renew their relationship with God with faith in Jesus Christ. This is the central message of the Bible, and we have the privilege of sharing it.

At the same time, not all will choose to respond to Jesus' invitation. They still need hope. How can we respond? Hope and encouragement can come in a number of ways. Simply being available during difficult times is a conduit for hope.

I met a poor family in a village in eastern Africa. The father had died of AIDS a few months before. The mother was extremely ill with AIDS-related illnesses and would probably not live long. Seated with us in their very dilapidated mud home were seven of her eight children. I have been in these situations many times. In most cases, a cloud of sadness and discouragement hangs over the home.

But while the pain of loss was very real, there was something different about these children. Instead of drawn faces with eyes focused sadly at their feet, these children had smiles and a glimmer in their eyes. When I asked the oldest son about his hopes for the future, he said he wanted to be a computer engineer. I was startled at his ambitions. I asked the next oldest child; she wanted to be a nurse. I went down the line and was told teacher, doctor, nurse, auto mechanic, and (from the youngest) "manager."

How could they have such hope and vision in the midst of such painful circumstances? I found the answer as I met another lady who had been sitting quietly in the room while we talked. Her name was Marie Christine, a friend of the family.

A few months earlier, as AIDS was ravaging the village, she asked her pastor what she could do. Since she had no resources or assets of her own, the pastor suggested that she care for those affected. She chose this family, which lived relatively close to her home.

She became a daily fixture as she dropped in to see how they were doing and to help them with their routines. The mother and her children all spoke of how important Marie Christine's presence had been in bringing them comfort, encouragement, and support. Tears welled in their eyes as they reflected on the strength that her hugs and listening ear had brought. To them, she was an angel of hope. She brought nothing in the form of material goods. She had no degree in grief counseling or psychology. All she gave was her time and love. The result was a family filled with hope—even in the midst of very trying circumstances.

God has called us to be instruments of hope. We can do this by helping people understand and embrace the good news of the gospel. We can also do this by reaching out in practical ways to help people who are struggling.

What does God expect his followers to do in the midst of this tragedy?

On September 15, 2002, I attended a large church in Kampala, Uganda. To the best of my knowledge I was the only American in the church that morning. I had dropped in unannounced, so no one knew I was coming.

Shortly into the service the pastor announced that in recognition of the first anniversary of September 11, the church would pay a special tribute to those children orphaned by the terrorist attacks in New York, Washington, D.C., and Pennsylvania. A small choir of 10 children—all orphaned by AIDS—walked in, wearing T-shirts with an American flag and the words "One Nation Under God." Together they sang "America the Beautiful"—all three verses.

Tears flowed from my eyes. In a country of 22 million people, where AIDS has orphaned 1.7 million children, they cared enough about the children in a land far away to express their sympathy.

What does God expect us to do in the face of the AIDS pandemic? Nothing less than to show the compassion and concern that those children orphaned by AIDS demonstrated on that Sunday morning.

God's instructions to his children are clear. He wants us to love our neighbors as ourselves. He wants us to give special attention to the poor, the orphans, the widows, and those who are disadvantaged. Jesus modeled this love and compassion. We should show the same love and compassion. As much as we do this for the least of these, we are doing it for him (Matthew 25:40).

Suggestions

Break the patterns of silence, denial, stigma, and discrimination

Unfortunately, many churches have responded to the first 20 years of the pandemic with silence, stigma, and discrimination. Church leaders have been reluctant to speak out about HIV/AIDS. It is much easier to pretend that it does not exist.

As a result, prevention messages have not gone out. Churches have shunned people who have needed help. Other people have avoided getting tested for fear that the church will turn them away if they are HIV-positive. Thus, the virus has continued to spread undetected, affecting countless more lives.

As believers and, particularly, as church leaders, we should boldly address this pandemic and demonstrate the love of Christ. The church should be the first place people turn for support, care, and encouragement.

Promote prevention

HIV/AIDS is preventable. Proper knowledge and behavior choices can significantly reduce the likelihood of contracting the virus. Since sexual activity is one of the main transmission routes, the church should speak out clearly on issues of abstinence and faithfulness. Who else has the moral authority to speak up about sexual purity?

Parents must ensure that children know about HIV/AIDS and are equipped to make proper choices. Studies show that many people still do not understand how HIV spreads. We must make sure people have both the knowledge and capacity to protect themselves.

Promoting prevention is hard. When people look healthy and there is little sign of the disease, we are tempted to invest our time and energies elsewhere. However, our short history with the pandemic shows that in the absence of concentrated prevention efforts, the virus will spread silently and effectively.

We need to emulate Noah. Although he could not see the rain coming, "By faith, Noah, when warned of things not yet seen, in holy fear built an ark to save his family" (Hebrews 11:7). Our "ark" is prevention. And, we should be exercising the same degree of commitment to the task.

Provide care

With millions of people infected and millions more affected, there is a tremendous need for compassionate care and encouragement. People's needs range from simply knowing someone cares for them, to having their everyday physical, emotional, and spiritual requirements met. We have an abundance of opportunities to help.

This is especially true in developing countries, where over 90 percent of those infected and affected by HIV/AIDS live. Those of us with much should support those with little. Even something as simple as providing medications to relieve the impact of opportunistic diseases that take advantage of weakened immune systems can greatly improve the quality of life for people who are HIV-positive.

Children have tremendous needs. Already more than 14 million of them have lost one or both parents to AIDS. That number is projected to grow to 25 million by 2010. In addition, there are probably at least that many children who are highly vulnerable because their parents are chronically ill or because family resources that would have been available for their schooling, nutrition, or healthcare are instead going to cousins and other children who have lost their parents.

These orphans and vulnerable children desperately need a reasonable chance of realizing their God-given potentials. Jesus gave us numerous examples of the importance of caring for children—particularly orphans.

Be a voice for the voiceless

Governments and international agencies need to implement policies and programs to help people infected and affected by HIV/AIDS and to prevent the spread of the virus. Wealthier countries have an obligation to assist those who lack sufficient resources. As Christians, we should speak truth to those in power to ensure that those policies and programs receive approval and funding.

When faced with HIV/AIDS, we are all too quick to judge and condemn. But God has called us to be instruments of his love, bearers of burdens, and servants to those in need. It is God's role to judge, not ours. Our response to those affected by HIV/AIDS should be compassionate, caring, and full of God's love.

Some have likened today's HIV/AIDS pandemic to the leprosy that existed in Jesus' day. Indeed, there are many similarities between how people then reacted to lepers and how people today respond to those affected by HIV/AIDS. One day a leper came to Jesus, fell to his knees, and begged, "If you are willing, You can make me clean" (Mark 1:41 NASB).

While there is no vaccine or cure yet, we can do much to significantly enhance the lives of those affected by HIV/AIDS, if we are willing. I picture those affected by HIV/AIDS on their knees, crying out to us, "If you are willing, you can ease my suffering, console me, care for my children, tend to my needs."

Are we willing? Jesus was.

God has called us to be salt and light. Salt preserves. Light illumines. In the face of HIV/AIDS, we have a unique opportunity to preserve and enrich the lives of those affected by HIV/AIDS. We also have an extraordinary opportunity to be God's light in a darkened world. Through our loving response, people may just find hope, their eyes opened to the loving beauty of the God we serve. May God give us the grace to faithfully steward this sacred opportunity.

CHAPTER 24

TOKUNBOH ADEYEMO

███████

THE CHURCH'S STRATEGIC ROLE

Acquired Immune Deficiency Syndrome (AIDS) has been variously described as a global nightmare, an international tragedy, an epidemic with pandemic proportions, a silent killer with no known cure, a ravaging plague, a human disaster. Like a restless locust of the apocalypse, it ruthlessly devastates nations and decimates their populations. With a very short medical history, the colossal damage caused by AIDS defies logic.

It began in the early 1980s with a handful of cases in a minority community. Today, over 42 million people globally are living with HIV/AIDS. Three-fourths of them (29.1 million) live in Africa. More than 21 million Africans have died from AIDS, while the average life expectancy in sub-Saharan Africa has dropped from 62 years to 47 years. More than 15 million children have become AIDS orphans. Friends, we are in a *crisis* more catastrophic than global terrorism. Jeremiah's lamentation comes to mind:

Is it nothing to you, all you who pass by?
　Look around and see.
Is any suffering like [AIDS suffering]?
(Lamentations 1:12)

The harvest is past,
　the summer has ended,
　and we are not saved.
Since my people are crushed, I am crushed;
　I mourn, and horror grips me.
Is there no balm in Gilead?
　Is there no physician there?
Why then is there no healing for the wound of my people?
(Jeremiah 8:20–22)

If philosophers, politicians, and physicians cannot solve the AIDS problem, what about the church? Unfortunately, the church has been part of the problem over the years. In the 1980s, the church was largely silent about AIDS. It was a period of ignorance and denial. In the early 1990s, the church stigmatized those infected with AIDS and dismissed them as sinners.[1] However, this period of indifference and discrimination was short-lived. In the middle of the decade, well-placed church members (including clergy) confessed to being infected. At this point, HIV/AIDS ceased being "their problem" and became "our problem." That was a significant breakthrough in attitude.

Yet it doesn't mean an end to the war against AIDS. On the contrary, the battle has intensified as the epidemic, like a hydra, has sprouted two new heads—feminization and commercialization. This is dangerous. The number of AIDS-related nongovernmental organizations and ministries that has sprung up in the last three to five years is staggering.

Historically, God has always come through for humanity whenever we have been in crisis. The supreme example of this is the cross. To be alienated from God is more serious and deadly than to have AIDS. Yet God in love sacrificed on the cross his one and only Son, Jesus our Lord, so that whoever believes in him may not perish (John 3:16–17).

What is God saying and doing regarding the AIDS pandemic today? And as we answer that question, what should be the church's action plan? Our strategic role must derive from what God is saying and doing (and not what UNAIDS is saying and doing, good as that may be). Following God takes vision.

- Where sight sees problems, vision sees potentials.

- Where sight sees plight of man, vision sees power of God.

- Where sight sees barriers, vision sees bearings.

- Where sight sees dead ends, vision sees divided highways.

- Where sight sees despair, vision sees hope.

What then is the Spirit saying to the church?

1. God is calling for prophets.

In biblical history, in times of national or global crisis, God usually raised up a class of leaders known as prophets. God is calling for such people today. Prophets are unusual men and women who live above board. They are nonconformists who never settle for the status quo. They represent God, speak on his behalf, and perform superhuman acts. They articulate God's moral standards, starting often with the phrase, "Thus says the Lord." They exemplify uprightness, holiness, and integrity of character and conduct. They are bold, courageous, daring, and decisive. They fear no man: presidents, priests, or philosophers. Prophets command an incredible authority and power.

Imagine a young man, Elisha, telling a military general, Naaman, to go wash himself seven times in the River Jordan in order to be healed of a leprosy (2 Kings 5:1–19). Or consider the case of his mentor, Elijah, telling King Ahab to his face: "As the LORD, the God of Israel, lives, whom I serve, there will be neither dew nor rain in the next few years except at my word" (1 Kings 17:1). Both events happened as the prophets said. Leprosy was cured and heaven ceased to give rain for three and half years.

Critical moments demand radical discipleship, in Bible times and today. We cannot say the church will fulfill a prophetic role unless it also demonstrates the kind of prophetic anointing seen in the Scriptures. We must not think of prophets as a bunch of religious bigots. Rather, they are social-political activists, moral and ethical reformers, popular movers and shakers. They are risk takers, always ready to pay the ultimate price for any cause they believe in.

As a class of leaders and change agents, prophets are found among administrators and judges such as Daniel and Deborah, among liberators and politicians such as Moses and Nehemiah, among royal dignitaries such as David and Esther, among military generals such as Joshua and Gideon, and among missionaries, including Paul, Peter, and Luke, the physician. In every instance, God raises them up and fills them with his Holy Spirit to do great exploits. They wield tremendous power. Satan and his demons fear them; sicknesses and diseases obey their command; and they solve crises of famine, drought, war, and epidemics. (Remember Pharaoh on his knees before Moses in Exodus 4:12?)

Medical experts generally agree that prevention—i.e., behavior change—is the most effective way to stem the tide of HIV/AIDS. No parliaments in the world can legislate a change of behavior. But when prophets proclaim God's word with power, nations fall to their knees in repentance. Remember Jonah in Nineveh or John the Baptist in Judea (Jonah 3; Luke 3)? For the church to make a difference and regain her apostolic credibility, she must give birth to prophets, not puppets.

Historian J.C. Ryle tells of gross immorality in eighteenth-century England. Corruption, dishonesty, and mismanagement in public offices were the order of the day. All classes of people participated in bribery in broad daylight. Factories were few and primitive. The nation itself was small and weak, and many of the people were drunkards. But by the beginning of the nineteenth-century, this trend had dramatically changed. England became a great power that stood against Napoleon as he brought the whole European continent under his feet. At the same time England began to spread its influence to Africa, Canada, Australia, India, and China.

How did it happen? Ryle said when England was at its lowest, God sent a handful of anointed preachers—including Whitefield, Grimshaw, and the Wesley brothers. These prophetic preachers drew large crowds all over the country. Under their powerful preaching, God poured out fires of revival, lives changed, and a new England was born.

Friends, this is what the church in Africa needs. We must put an end to the proverb that says: "The church is one mile long but one inch deep." My heart breaks that the region of the world with the fastest church growth (i.e., sub-Saharan Africa) is also home for 75 percent of the world's AIDS cases. Something is wrong. We need prophets; we need powerful preaching of the Word; we need revival; we need social and cultural transformation!

2. God is calling for pray-ers.

Pray-ers are human representatives before God. While prophets prophesy, pray-ers plead with God to stay his anger and wrath. While some call them priests or intercessors, I simply call them pray-ers. They are the righteous ones that God is always looking for when foundations are being destroyed (Psalm 11:3). They do not seek a platform but a closet. Their lives are marked by solidarity with the people, sensitivity both to the Spirit and to the people, sincerity in service and in love, and tenacity. They understand the human predicament and bear people's pain. They know what it means to be poor and weak by agonizing in prayers with fasting.

God calls for this caliber of men and women, who humble themselves before God and pray, who seek his face and plead for mercy on behalf of the infected and the affected. In Ezekiel 22 the Lord couldn't find even one such person among the priests (verse 26), nor among the civil leaders (verse 27), nor even among the prophets (verse 28). Today God is still looking for those who will build up the walls and bridge the gaps, that he might not destroy the land.

I will participate in a UNAIDS-sponsored scenario building project for HIV/AIDS in Africa for the next 25 years. I have attended several workshops, consultations, and conferences on HIV/AIDS in the past 10 years. The latest one was the thirteenth International Conference on AIDS and Sexually Transmitted Diseases in Africa, which took place in Nairobi, September 21–26, 2003, attended by over 7,000 delegates. At all of these meetings I have witnessed demonstrations and protests, but not a single prayer meeting. God is left out of the crisis. What a tragedy!

This awesome prayer responsibility is for the church.

- Prayer destroyed plagues before (Exodus 8:1–30), and it can do it again.

- Prayer cured epidemics before (2 Kings 2), and it can do it again.

- Prayer healed the sick before (Matthew 8), and it can do it again.

- Prayer raised the dead before (John 11), and it can do it again.

Prayer can do what God can do, and HIV/AIDS is not beyond God. Our Champion, Jesus Christ, has all authority and power. And he has delegated the same to his church to drive out evil spirits and to heal every disease and sickness (see Matthew 10:1).

The scientists say there is no cure for AIDS. What does the church say? The story of Sarah Timarwa is telling. Sarah is a Ugandan attorney, a Christian, and an advocate. Her husband, also a lawyer, died of AIDS in 1995. Sarah's first test revealed that she was HIV-positive. She cried unto the Lord and called on her Christian friends (especially women from PACWA, a prominent Christian group) to pray. Two subsequent tests showed her to be HIV-negative. God answered her prayers and reversed her condition. Today, Sarah is alive and well. She has already shared her testimony over BBC Radio. She also told it in Kampala, Uganda, during the premier African AIDS Initiative Conference (September 4–6, 2003).

While God is calling for prophets, he is also looking to the church to rebuild the ruins, repair the broken walls, and restore hope to the millions of people living with HIV/AIDS. While the prophets major on prevention and behavior change, pray-ers provide support and hope. But there is also the pastoral responsibility of the church.

3. God is saying: Shepherd the flock.

Our track record shows that

- where people are bruised, the church supplies the balm;

- where people are battered, the church restores human dignity;

- where people are broken, the church bandages the wounds;

- where people are buffeted, the church soothes;

- where people are bereaved, the church comforts;

- where people are banished from society, the church provides a home.

Well done, church. In 1991, 15 percent of the population of Uganda had HIV/AIDS. Different denominations worked together in partnership with the civil society, the government, and other faith-based communities in a nationwide campaign. In 10 years, the level of infection has fallen by as much as 50 percent, and the prevalence rate is down to about 3 percent. The main reasons as follows:

1. *Leadership commitment:* From the president to the local community leaders, the fight against AIDS has been top priority.

2. *The involvement of churches and the faith-based community:* Churches and mosques became primary delivery channels for awareness, education, prevention, and care.

3. *Personal touch:* The ABC message was delivered in person to young people, students, prostitutes, truck drivers, and others by people who play significant roles in their lives such as Sunday School teachers, pastors, and community leaders.

The church took God's love to the marketplace, to the grassroots where people are suffering. It was a visible replay of Jesus' ministry as described in Acts 10:38:

> God anointed Jesus of Nazareth with the Holy Spirit and power, and how He went around doing good and healing all who were under the power of the devil, because God was with Him.

Likewise, the pastoral ministry of the church to the AIDS-infected and affected must bear these two trademarks: *agape* love and the power of the Holy Spirit. Let's shut our doors and pray in our closets until the ground shakes and the heavens open before stepping out to minister to the needy in Jesus' name.

The massive presence of the church globally and, in particular, in Africa must proclaim and practice the unadulterated good news with heaven's anointing. God seeks to raise up prophets, pray-ers, and shepherds to society. These servants will:

- *Push* AIDS out;

- *Press* for change in behavior and in social structures; and

- *Persevere* with God until he acts in mercy.

For these are the expected acts of righteousness in every generation. They have produced spiritual and social "vaccines" in the past, and they can do it again. So let it be, Lord, in Jesus' name. Amen.

Notes

1. Two statements made by two church world bodies are illustrative:
"When we have raised our voices in the past, it has been too often a voice of condemnation."

Anglican Primates on HIV/AIDS (Nov. 2001).

"We (the church) confess that sometimes our words and deeds have been harmful and have denied the dignity of each person. We preach the good news 'that all may have life,' and yet we fear that we have contributed to death." World Council of Churches (Nov. 2001).

DAVID DAGEFORDE AND TINA BRUNER

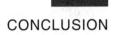

CONCLUSION

During the first century, lepers were the outcasts of society, yet Jesus healed them. During the fourth century, Christians treated patients infected by the plague with compassion and dignity. Christians also took babies who were targeted for infanticide into their homes. The challenge for Christians in the twenty-first-century is similar. We must develop a godly attitude toward today's outcasts and help the worldwide church help those who are considered by many to be outcasts of society today: those affected by the HIV/AIDS crisis.

The contributors to this book have addressed Christian responses to the crisis. In this conclusion we will briefly examine four major themes: (1) the devastation that the crisis visits on millions of people around the world; (2) God's clear instruction to Christians to help; (3) the response of the worldwide church to the crisis; (4) and the challenge to the Western church to respond.

Devastating Impact

The numbers infected and dying with HIV/AIDS around the world are well documented in this book. However, the contributors have also recorded how the poor are unable to acquire resources to care for themselves, which locks them into the devastation of poverty. The HIV/AIDS crisis has a specific impact on the individual, the community, and the church.

Impact on individuals and families:

Individuals can become carriers of HIV, can experience debilitating consequences from the disease, or can die from AIDS. Often they cannot afford or comply with complicated treatment regimens. Families can lose income when they lose the labor of those infected. Extended family members become widows and orphans. Often grandparents either must take care of the surviving children, or the surviving children must take care of the grandparents. As a result of the 20–30 percent transfer rate of HIV from mother to newborn, or the 15 percent transfer rate caused by breast-feeding, many newborns are infected. To intensify their suffering, the stigma associated with the disease results in families being shamed and ostracized by their communities.

Impact on communities:

HIV/AIDS devastates not only individuals and their families, but also entire communities. Most of the impact stems from the decimation of the work force, especially in the 15 to 49 year age group. This loss of the most productive age group leads to multiple other economic and social problems. With the death of food workers and farmers comes a loss of food security. Additionally, AIDS causes a shortage of teachers in schools. Students with HIV-positive parents must leave the classroom to earn money for their own families. Governments usually cannot provide adequate treatment facilities and pay for associated costs. Communities in India, China, Ethiopia, Nigeria, and Russia are currently facing a rapid expansion of the epidemic that will continue to threaten their communities with economic and social distress.

Impact on the church:

HIV/AIDS impacts the local churches in these communities. False doctrines have spread about why individuals become infected. Christians emphasize their sin as being more offensive to God than the sins committed by other church members. Some churches have hesitated to discuss the real problems behind the crisis and how churches should respond. Finally, many downplay the use of condoms in the "ABC" prevention approach in their perfectly understandable attempts to support abstinence and being faithful. However, condoms do have a role in protecting individuals with multiple sex partners and with people whose spouses are HIV-positive.

God's Word

The Bible teaches us about our responsibility to help individuals and families affected by HIV/AIDS. God created all things (Genesis 1:31). We are created in his image (Genesis 1:27). We all sin and fall short of the glory of God (Romans 3:23). Some of these sins include homosexual acts (Romans 1:27), sexual immorality (1 Corinthians 6:18), adultery (Exodus 20:14), and being mastered by things not of God (1 Corinthians 6:12).

Sin, which results from seeking our own glory instead of God's, affects the entire world's population. Half of the world's people live in poverty because of sin and the greed, corruption, famine, and disease that run rampant in our world.

But in Christ there is hope. People need to repent (Matthew 5:14–17), but God's compassion and grace are always available (Psalm 103:13; 2 Corinthians 12:9–10). Christians have been given new birth into a living hope through the resurrection of Jesus Christ from the dead (1 Peter 1:3). God commands us to love him and to love our neighbors as ourselves (Matthew 22:37–40; Luke 10:25–37; 1 Corinthians 13:13). We know that serving others means serving Christ (Matthew 25:31–46).

Once saved, we are transformed by the renewal of our minds and commanded to follow God's will. Jesus, the most powerful moral teacher ever, calls us to demonstrate Christlike love, compassion, and grace to those individuals and their families suffering with HIV/AIDS; spreading the gospel to them, praying for the victims and their families, and ensuring proper teaching in our churches about HIV/AIDS.

We should not judge people caught in this epidemic, regardless of the reasons they have the disease. We must remember that God is the judge. We should not distinguish between victims of HIV/AIDS and seek to help only those who acquired the disease innocently. After all, we are also sinners and God has not dealt with us in the manner our sins deserve. Finally, we need to overcome the stigma that confronts the infected.

The Response of the Worldwide Church

Contributors to this book have described different church responses around the world. Often such responses involve a combination of secular and Christian goals, with an emphasis on ministering in local communities. Many secular and Christian organizations recognize that the local church is the primary or only grass roots organization for most poor communities.

Secular goals the worldwide church seeks to follow or integrate into its program include the following:

1. Implementing the UNAIDS Good Practice campaign: integrating and promoting prevention and care activities to reduce the patient's vulnerability to infection, and alleviating negative social and economic impact on victims and their families;

2. Working to prevent communities from reaching the 5 percent prevalence threshold, which is the critical mass of HIV-infected people from whom the disease can rapidly spread;

3. Eliminating unsafe medical practices that hurt HIV/AIDS patients and their families;

4. Identifying and treating sexually transmitted diseases, which increase the likelihood of becoming infected with HIV;

5. Promoting an aggressive prevention campaign;

6. Working to decrease the stigma of HIV-positive patients;

7. Placing a greater emphasis on prevention for women and children in the Two-Thirds World.

Christian goals the worldwide church seeks to follow or integrate into its program include the following:

1. Admitting the need to work as a family to both care for HIV/AIDS patients and to prevent more cases within each community;

2. Working with faith-based organizations to promote ABC prevention of HIV/AIDS, emphasizing abstinence and fidelity in marriage, yet realizing there is a limited role for condoms in prevention within church community programs;

3. Promoting anti-AIDS clubs, especially for the 15–24 age group, to teach the facts about HIV/AIDS and to encourage people to make wise Christian choices;

4. Using biblically holistic programs where the main purpose is to lead people to a personal relationship with Jesus Christ, but also to provide compassionate medical, social, psychological, and spiritual care;

5. Providing quality home care programs, including food and shelter for HIV victims and/or their displaced family members, counseling and behavioral modification, school fee support, intense prayer support for all affected family members, loans or other income-generating projects, literacy programs, and rehabilitation and training programs.

The Challenge to the Western Church

With fewer people infected in the United States, the rich American church has more resources to deal with this crisis than does most of the worldwide church. We need to respond to the victims of this deadly disease with compassionate care, whether they live in the United States or in places where the impact is even more devastating.

As we do so, we must avoid indulging ourselves in stereotypes. While it is right and good to disapprove of any sexual behavior outside of marriage, we must not label those who do so as being "more sinful" and "more guilty." We are sinners as well, saved only by the grace of God. And while HIV spreads largely because of sinful disobedience to God's word about sexual relationships, we need to remember the millions of people who are infected because of someone else's disobedience to God's word.

Squarely facing some statistics showing the American church's slowness to respond to the crisis, we need to challenge our congregations to do more. We need to challenge our leaders to move beyond teaching and preaching to Christ-inspired servanthood. We need to teach about the magnitude of the crisis and the need for ABC prevention. The church must understand the needs of those affected by this crisis and respond with compassionate care.

The financial resources of the American church far outweigh the resources of the churches that serve in the neighborhoods of the world most affected by HIV/AIDS. In the vast majority of those communities, families earn less than two dollars per day, not enough to sustain their own families—let alone contribute to the HIV/AIDS effort in their churches and communities. The American church must respond to this worldwide crisis by giving of its considerable financial resources, its people, and its time.

However, we must give with our eyes wide open. One major moral and ethical dilemma for both the American and the worldwide church is the role of the church in providing anti-retroviral (ARV) treatment to individuals in their communities, understanding that preventive measures are more effective at hindering the spread of the disease and are more cost-effective when compared to ARV treatment. But ARV treatment does provide both compassionate care and decreases suffering for those who are infected with HIV/AIDS.

At the Global Missions Health Conference in November 2003, Tokunboh Adeyemo explained three reasons why Christian professionals in African churches often do not want to pursue ARV treatment:

1. personal spiritual strongholds (beliefs that override their science-based conclusions about the need for ARV medicines);

2. cultural reasons (the ethical dilemma that faces the entire African continent when some individuals receive treatment and some individuals don't); and

3. financial reasons (realizing the cost barriers that face a massive treatment program and knowing that all Africans who suffer from HIV/AIDS will not receive ARV treatment).

Western Christians also face many questions regarding ARV treatment. How affordable is ARV treatment for the millions of infected individuals around the world? How can so much be spent on ARVs when current treatment programs for many of the less expensive infectious diseases are underfunded? How do we ensure patients stick with the complicated treatment regimens and avoid introducing drug-resistant HIV strains? How do we sustain lifelong ARV treatment programs? Both secular and Christian organizations raise these important questions that have far-reaching implications for millions of individuals around the world. Those questions cannot be answered easily, and they require intense prayer for wisdom.

After telling the parable of the Good Samaritan, Jesus told the expert in the law, "Go and do likewise." He commands us to do the same for victims of the HIV/AIDS crisis. He also reminds us in Matthew 25 that when we care for the sick, the poor, and the needy, we are caring for him.

APPENDIXES

AVENUES OF INVOLVEMENT FOR THE CHURCH

An African proverb says,
"The best time to plant a tree is 20 years
ago; the next best time is today."

Two-hundred delegates gathered in Louisville, Kentucky, a day prior to the Global Missions Health Conference to explore "The Church and the HIV/AIDS Crisis: Providing Leadership and Hope." Workshops held on HIV/AIDS later in the main conference, attended by 1,600 people, were full. Our hosts at Southeast Christian Church demonstrated attitudes of *humility*, *service*, and *involvement*, watchwords for the church in these days.

An Attitude of Humility through Repentance

The church, particularly the church in the West, has been slow to become involved in the HIV/AIDS pandemic. Apparently forgetting that Christ lived a life of compassion and did not question the source of a person's illness, many in the church have seen AIDS as God's judgment being rained down upon those who engage in the sins of homosexuality, intravenous drug use, and prostitution. While showing some sympathy for those affected by tainted blood transfusion and transmission from mother to unborn child, the church has been slow to acknowledge that in the majority of the world's HIV/AIDS comes from heterosexual activity, the same sort of activity that is daily promoted around the world by the Western media and entertainment industry.

Since the number of those with HIV/AIDS is highest in Africa and Asia, Westerners have for too long turned a blind eye to their suffering.

Even in the West, those suffering from AIDS have been stigmatized and forgotten by the church. Many have faced death alone and uncomforted.

Many Christians, because of their belief that the advocacy of condom use encourages a higher rate of premarital sex, have refused to acknowledge that condoms, when used correctly and consistently, are 90 percent effective against the spread of HIV/AIDS.

HIV/AIDS is no respecter of persons. Believers and unbelievers alike are affected. Research has indicated that, tragically, evangelical Christians are some of the least likely to become involved in the battle against AIDS or to contribute to the needs of those orphaned by AIDS.

The church today must repent and seek forgiveness from God for our sins of apathy, indifference, despair, condemnation, and lack of compassion for those suffering from this horrible disease.

An Attitude of Service through Compassion

We of the household of faith must in loving service join hands with those who are suffering. Like believers confronting those suffering from the Black Death during the Middle Ages, we must run to the sick rather than from them.

The church has a worldwide reach. Situated close to 90 percent of the world's poor, it can easily connect with the grassroots. Ten million children a year die from diseases such as pneumonia, diarrhea, and malaria, each of which is preventable for a few cents a day for each child. Many of these children are infected with HIV. Bringing resources to these problems—as well as health issues such as sexually transmitted diseases, nutrition, and clean water—will result in significant life extension. A longer life will provide time to get more data about anti-retroviral (ARV) drugs, to develop the infrastructure so that ARV medication is affordable and available, and to develop a cure. Since faith-based organizations carry out more than 50 percent of the health care in many African countries, the church needs to show compassion by increasing giving to such organizations.

The Bible instructs us to care for widows and orphans. The HIV/AIDS crisis and its effects will be with us well into the future. Entire generations are being decimated, including teachers, health workers, public servants, and church leaders. The number of AIDS orphans in different areas peaks approximately 10 years after the number of AIDS deaths has peaked.

When facing the growing number of AIDS orphans, the church must not make decisions based on guilt or a naive belief that there are quick and easy solutions. Building orphanages to house and care for orphans should be an option only after all other alternatives have been considered. In addition to issues of social dislocation, research from Africa indicates that the annual cost to care for an orphan in an institution is $1,000—versus $150 for foster care.

Those suffering from AIDS need our compassion. We need to visit them, talk with them of our eternal hope, and embrace them in the name of Christ.

An Attitude of Involvement through Ministry

An African proverb says, "The best time to plant a tree is 20 years ago; the next best time is today." Though it is late, Christians must now take the lead in increasing public awareness about AIDS and AIDS prevention. We need educational efforts at all levels and through all means. After we become educated about HIV/AIDS, we can educate others. We need articles, bulletin inserts, letters to the editor, campaigns, stories, sermons, dramas, art, and public presentations. We should provide money for a wide variety of educational endeavors all over the world.

The HIV/AIDS disease spreads primarily by sexual behavior, which in turn emerges from personal and cultural values. The church can speak about values in ways that others cannot or will not. Two-thirds of those who become affected with HIV/AIDS are 15 to 24 years old. Instruction about risk reduction must begin at an early age. Almost one-third of the world's population is 15 years or younger. The vast majority of them are AIDS-free. Along with the church, parents must be equipped to teach their children about AIDS. Children, the abstinent, and those who remain faithful to their marriage partners do not need messages about condoms. However, those involved in multiple-partner liaisons do.

The church must mobilize. Almost all local congregations in the West have members in medicine. They can teach, share experiences, and go on short-term medical trips. A Western church can "adopt" a church or a community from Africa, Asia, or the former Soviet Union and share resources to help its partner address AIDS issues in an appropriate manner.

A cell-church of 8,000 members in Kampala, Uganda, determined that each of its cell groups would care for one orphan or for one family whose head of household had died due to AIDS. Can we who have so much more do less?

Action Steps

The crisis affords the church the opportunity to demonstrate Christ's concern for the suffering. How we respond will be the church's defining issue for the next 50 years.

We should take the following five steps immediately:

1. Encourage your church (local congregation and denomination) to commit a minimum of 1–3 percent of its resources annually—people, pulpit time, and finances—to HIV/AIDS awareness and involvement.

2. Encourage your church (local congregation and denomination) to empower an AIDS task force to research and educate, then allocate and evaluate where to use these congregational resources.

3. Advocate, either directly or through appropriate agencies, that regional and national government bodies set aside additional resources to address HIV/AIDS.

4. Uphold through prayer those who are suffering from HIV/AIDS and those who are involved at all levels in addressing and combating HIV/AIDS.

5. Boldly promote the A–B–C strategy: A = Abstinence from sexual intercourse until marriage; B = Being faithful to one partner; and (when A and B are not being followed), C = Correct and consistent use of condoms.

APPENDIX B
EVVY HAY CAMPBELL

FURTHER RECOMMENDED READING

Beine, David K. (2003). *Ensnared by AIDS: Cultural Contexts of HIV/ AIDS in Nepal.* **Kathmandu, Nepal: Mandala Book Point. 411 pp.**

Christian anthropologist David Beine illuminates an indigenous understanding of AIDS, newly emerging in Nepal, by exploring illness beliefs and practices in the rural Gorkha District of central Nepal. He then draws on 30 texts collected from persons with AIDS in Kathmandu to identify diverse views of this emerging illness. An important cultural study.

Bender, David L. et al. (1998). *AIDS: Opposing Viewpoints.* **San Diego: Greenhaven Press. 203 pp.**

A unique juxtaposition of opposing viewpoints on numerous controversial issues surrounding HIV/AIDS: routine versus mandatory testing, the value of combination drug treatments, the use of condoms, and needle exchange programs. Writers present different points of view on these issues, stimulating critical thinking and a nuanced understanding.

Dixon, Patrick. (1994). *The Truth About AIDS.* **Eastbourne, England: Kingsway Publications. 479 pp.**

Founder of AIDS Care Education and Training (ACET), an international AIDS agency, Dixon provides a classic text with an overview of HIV/ AIDS and then focuses on moral issues, the response of the church, and issues faced by poorer nations. Appendices deal with setting up community programs, providing home care, and dealing with burnout among AIDS care workers.

Dortzbach, Debbie (Ed.). (1996). *AIDS in Africa: The Church's Opportunity.* **Nairobi, Kenya: MAP International. 43 pp.**

This challenge to the church in Africa arose out of *The All Africa Church and AIDS Consultation* held in Kampala, Uganda, in April 1994. It contains an important declaration by the church in Africa and deals with the mission of the church in AIDS, pastoral care and counseling, sexuality, family, orphans, and the interrelationship of belief and behavior. An important primary document of the response of the church in 28 countries.

Dortzbach, Karl and Ndunge Kiiti. (1996). *Helpers for a Healing Community: A Pastoral Counseling Manual for AIDS,* **2nd Edition. Nairobi, Kenya: MAP International. 51 pp.**

Using a case study methodology, this helpful publication considers a counselor's role, strategies for beginning a session, and guidelines on how to respond to AIDS. It provides principles to encourage those living with AIDS, suggestions for facing deep needs, and responses to important issues related to death and dying. The book also considers follow-up strategies and suggestions for mobilizing the church.

Farmer, Paul. (1999). *Infections and Inequalities: The Modern Plagues.* **Berkeley, Calif.: University of California Press. 375 pp.**

Written while Farmer served as director of the Program in Infectious Disease and Social Change at Harvard Medical School, *Infections and Inequalities* explores the impact of AIDS and tuberculosis in Peru and Haiti. As a physician-anthropologist with 15 years of field experience, Farmer explores the relationship of emerging infectious diseases and poverty, challenging many commonly held assumptions and provoking needed reflection.

Fountain, Daniel E. (1995). *Care of Persons with AIDS in a Christian Hospital.* **Vanga, Democratic Republic of Congo: Vanga Hospital. 15 pp.**

Describes the Vanga Evangelical Hospital initiative in caring for persons with HIV/AIDS. The program has five aspects: an open welcome for those with HIV/AIDS, appropriate medical care, social support, pastoral care, and a ministry of prayer. A physician at Vanga for 36 years, Fountain stresses the importance of whole-person care.

Garland, C. Jean. (2003). *AIDS Is Real and It's In Our Church.* **Bukuru, Nigeria: Africa Christian Textbooks. 268 pp.**

Written to encourage a Christian response to AIDS in Nigeria, the book mingles straightforward information about AIDS with deeply moving stories of those who contracted the disease. Considers the nature of the virus, testing, transmission of the infection, the place of condoms, ways to avoid AIDS, home care, counseling, and the church's role. The publishers invite reproduction and translation for noncommercial purposes.

Gifford, Allen L., Kate Lorig, Diana Laurent, and Virginia González, (2000). *Living Well with HIV and AIDS,* **2nd Edition. Palo Alto, Calif.: Bull Publishing. 245 pp.**

Practical and clearly written, this book for people with HIV/AIDS and their caregivers is full of counsel for managing symptoms, medical treatment, personal issues (such as talking with family and friends), exercise, and diet. Flow charts, sidebars, and a question and answer format provide numerous helpful tools for those seeking to live well with a profoundly limiting disease.

Granich, Reuben and Jonathan Mermin. (1999). *HIV, Health, and Your Community: A Guide for Action.* **Stanford, Calif.: Stanford University Press. 245 pp.**

Written for community health workers, this text includes a discussion of the biology and epidemiology of AIDS, as well as a global overview of the disease, counseling strategies, information on HIV tests, and recommendations for training other health workers. Contains ideas for designing programs and writing grant proposals. A helpful and practical guide.

Green, Edward C. (2003). *Rethinking AIDS Prevention: Learning from Successes in Developing Countries.* **Greenwood, CT: Praeger Publishers, 2003. 392 pp.**

The author provides convincing evidence to show that the largely medical solutions funded by major donors (condoms, drugs) have had little impact in Africa. Instead, relatively simple, low-cost behavioral change programs stressing increased monogamy and delayed sexual activity for young people have made the greatest headway in preventing the spread of HIV. Uganda pioneered these simple, sustainable interventions and achieved significant results. Faith-based organizations played a key role in promotion of abstinence and faithfulness in all successful countries. The book argues for a much stronger role for FBOs in future programs.

Ilori, Joseph A. (2002). *Faith-based AIDS Awareness Manual for Teaching Human Sexuality and HIV/AIDS from a Christian Perspective in Secondary Schools.* **Jos, Nigeria: Faith-based AIDS Awareness Initiative, University of Jos. 80 pp.**

Beginning with a biblical exploration of human sexuality, this manual goes on to deal with HIV/AIDS and a Christian response. Appendices deal with the art of lesson preparation and include a sample lesson plan. Text lessons incorporate a variety of methodologies: story, debate, question and answer, drama, and discussion. Assignments for students, supplementary readings, definitions of key words, and content summaries round out the excellent lesson plans.

Landau-Stanton, Judith and Colleen Clements. (1993). *AIDS, Health, and Mental Health: A Primary Sourcebook.* **New York: Brunner/ Mazel Publishers. 343 pp.**

The authors thoughtfully consider an integrated approach to AIDS using systems theory both for prevention and clinical management. They use case studies to explore the multiple levels at which persons with HIV/ AIDS function. They explore spiritual, cultural, and community systems that share the burden of care as a therapist's best allies.

Levy, Jay. A. (1994). *HIV and the Pathogenesis of AIDS.* **Washington, D.C.: American Society for Microbiology. 359 pp.**

A systematic and comprehensive treatment of HIV/AIDS, this thorough discussion covers the discovery and nature of HIV, features of transmission and infection, and the effect of HIV on tissues and organ systems in the host. Includes treatment therapies. An excellent scientific overview of HIV/AIDS written by a leading physician in the field.

Life at the CrossRoads: Life Skills for Character Development, 2nd Edition. (2001). Orlando, Fla.: New Life World Aid, Inc. 538 pp.

An outstanding update of the 1995 *Life at the CrossRoads* curriculum through which 1,000,000 students were trained by 15,000 teachers in 40 countries and 16 languages in Central and South America, Western and Eastern Europe, Africa, and Asia. Developed in response to global AIDS, it applies to teaching students age twelve through secondary school. The curriculum focuses on character building, biblical sexuality, and making right choices in life. The text is only available as part of the program.

Powell, Josh. (1996). *AIDS and HIV-Related Diseases: An Educational Guide for Professionals and the Public.* **New York: Insight Books. 246 pp.**

This text summarizes, describes, and illustrates the clinical manifestations of HIV/AIDS. It suggests strategies for educating and informing people about HIV/AIDS and provides laypersons with an understanding of what is known about transmission, HIV testing, causes, and treatments.

Robinson, Paul, et. al. (Eds.) (1996). *Choosing Hope: The Christian Response to the HIV/AIDS Epidemic.* **Nariobi, Kenya: MAP International. 109 pp.**

Contains curriculum models for theological and pastoral training institutions. Modules include facts about HIV/AIDS, biblical foundations for responding to AIDS, mobilizing the church to involvement, changing feelings and attitudes about AIDS, pastoral counseling, giving hope to parents and youth for AIDS-free living, and home-based care. A helpful tool for training pastors for their role in the pandemic.

Rubenstein, William B., Ruth Eisenberg, and Lawrence Gostin. (1996). *The Rights of People Who Are HIV Positive.* **Carbondale, Ill.: Southern Illinois University Press. 384 pp.**

This American Civil Liberties Union guide provides detailed information on the health, insurance, education, prison, employment, and immigration laws that relate to persons with HIV/AIDS. Written in a question and answer format, it is a useful tool for those facing legal issues regarding HIV/AIDS.

Schoub, Barry D. (1999). *AIDS and HIV in Perspective: A Guide to Understanding the Virus and Its Consequences*, 2nd **Edition. Cambridge: Cambridge University Press. pp. 274.**

Scholarly and thorough, Schoub writes as both head of the Department of Virology of the University of the Witwatersrand, South Africa and as director of the regional Medical Research Council's AIDS Virus Research Unit. Detailed yet readable, the text illuminates the nature of the virus, disease mechanisms of HIV, transmission of HIV, anti-AIDS drugs, the quest for a vaccine, and ethical issues.

Shilts, Randy. (1987). *And the Band Played On: Politics, People, and the AIDS Epidemic*. **New York: St. Martins Press. 630 pp.**

An extraordinarily well-documented account of the early days of the pandemic. Published the same year that award-winning *San Francisco Chronicle* journalist Randy Shilts learned he had AIDS, *And the Band Played On* contains poignantly written vignettes culled from 900 interviews in 12 nations. Material from government documents underscores the human tragedy and social complexity of the epidemic.

World Relief HIV/AIDS Team. (2000). *Hope at Home: Caring for Family with AIDS*. **Kigali, Rwanda. World Relief. 60 pp.**

A guide for family members caring for those who have AIDS, this manual written for Rwandans underscores the deep need of families to be together in illness, gives suggestions on providing comfort, and identifies numerous practical aspects of giving care. Illustrated with both photos and drawings, it is a helpful tool of hope.

APPENDIX C

MICHAEL J. KANE

███████

THE ROLE OF TECHNOLOGY IN COMBATING HIV/AIDS

The information technology revolution of the past 25 years has created unprecedented access to knowledge and information that can dramatically improve people's quality of life. However, the last mile of the worldwide information highway is yet to be paved for many—especially in the African nations hit hardest by the HIV/AIDS pandemic. If information is power, we must first understand the barriers facing those seeking to provide this power through technological solutions.

AIDS and the Digital Divide

"Digital divide" describes the gap between those who have access to information and technology and those who do not. Given the rapidly advancing state of technology, the benefits derived from access to the latest information have not reached most of the people most affected by HIV/AIDS.

A few statistics confirm this gap:

- An estimated 429 million people are online globally. Forty-one percent reside in North America, compared with only 4 percent in South America. These 429 million people represent only 7 percent of the world's population.

- In the United States, over 190 million people, or approximately two-thirds of the population, have cellular telephones. In the 11 countries targeted by President Bush's AIDS Initiative, cell phone usage is estimated at 8.8 million users, or just 2 percent of the total population.

- The United States has more personal computers than the rest of the world combined.

- The cost of a personal computer in the United States represents only 3 percent of annual per-capita Gross Domestic Product. In most African nations, it is 100 percent or more on a purchasing power parity basis.

Infrastructure and Cultural Barriers to the "Last Mile"

Infrastructure is a major barrier to the use of information technology in rural areas. The prerequisite electrical and telecommunication pathways simply do not exist. Recently I came across a newsletter for a nonprofit that proudly displayed a picture of a new information center in one rural African village. The photo showed a dozen brand new personal computers in small room where children were seated and ready to work. The report went on to say that electricity had not yet reached the village. Unfortunately, even areas with the requisite infrastructure often lack the stability to reliably transfer critical information.

Simple economics inhibit access to life-saving and life-changing information technology. Compounding the problem is the fact that telecommunications infrastructure is a major source of hard currency for many developing countries. Making it widely available to the masses would cut down on government profits. Rates for telecommunication services still remain extremely high when compared to countries that have a low rate of AIDS.

Many discussions of the barriers to deployment of information technology focus on economics and infrastructure. There are other factors, however. The international research firm Ipsos-Reid found that the biggest reason for those not going online was the lack of perceived need (40 percent). This was followed by no computer (33 percent); no interest (25 percent); and lack of knowledge for use (25 percent). Interestingly, only 16 percent of the respondents cited cost as the reason they did not have access to the Internet.

Information technology has value only if a person can use it in an application he or she deems important or necessary. We need to ask not only what applications will best contribute in the battle against HIV/AIDS, but also what indigenous users will adopt.

Orality as a Barrier to Deployment of Information Technology

The term orality is increasingly used to distinguish the literate world from the non-literate. Of the more than 10,000 languages spoken in world history, only about 100 have ever been written down. While literacy is an important tool in providing critical prevention and care information, most of the world communicates orally. Consider these facts:

- There are more non-literate people in the world today than at any time in history.

- Illiteracy is not in the process of being wiped out. The number of non-literate adults steadily increased during the twentieth century. This is particularly true among women.

- Thirty to fifty million people are added to the illiteracy numbers each year. By 2050 the world's non-literate population could exceed the total world population of 2003.

This is not only a developing country problem. According to the International National Adult Literacy Survey, 15–20 percent of people living in 12 Organization of Economic Cooperation and Development member nations, including the United States (20.7 percent), are Level 1, functionally illiterate. Exhibit 1 presents a segmentation of the world population based on five categories of orality.

Exhibit 1: Orality Segmentation of the World Population

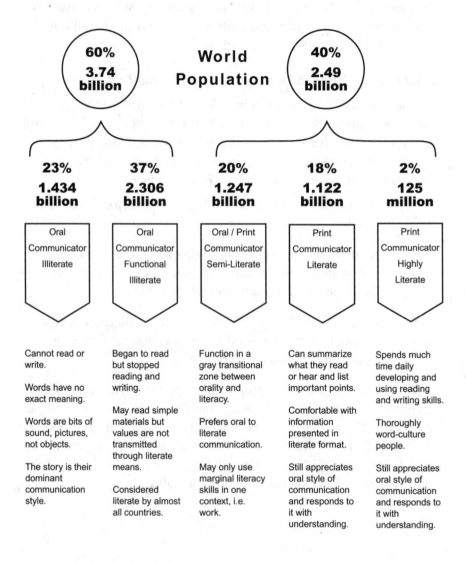

As Exhibit 1 indicates, the world's population consists primarily of oral communicators. As much as 80 percent of the world prefers to receive information in an oral rather than in a literate form. We should recognize that literate-based information presented in an audio format is not the same as oral-based information. Oral-based information must accommodate the cultural context in which information is created, disseminated, and consumed. This is opposite to the manner in which the Internet and much of the developed world's technology operate.

In the battle against HIV/AIDS, information technology must overcome the economic, infrastructure, and orality barriers that prevent the flow of critical life-saving and life-changing information. Any deployment of information technology must address the issues of cost, environment, and orality.

Critical Success Factors

Information technology can play a key role in the HIV/AIDS pandemic. Whether it is disseminating prevention messages, providing treatment instructions, or filling the void of training a rapidly depleting and inexperienced army of medical personnel, access to information is a critical need.

AIDS applications must consider the cost to the user of any technology platform, the need for solar power and rugged designs for rural and harsh environments, and the critical interface between the oral culture and the technology.

The cost of most information technology is out of reach for those most affected by AIDS. We must develop technology with a cost structure commensurate with the economics of the country where the technology is deployed. It cannot be seen as source of cash or barter, or redirected for other uses, such as entertainment.

The environment plays another factor in deployment. Information technology tools must be water-resistant, dust-resistant, and rugged as needed in harsh rural environments. They must accommodate the lack of electricity and reliability of power.

Finally, we cannot overlook the context of orality among the poor and rural victims of HIV/AIDS. Oral communicators are relational. They share and accept information in a group setting. Information must be presented and shared in a manner conducive to non-literate cultures.

Information technology deployed in the battle against HIV/AIDS can have a significant impact if we carefully incorporate these factors.

To order copies of this and other fine books
or for a complete catalog, please contact:

- STL, Inc.
  ordersusa@stl.org
  129 Mobilization Drive, Waynesboro, GA 30830
  1-8MORE-BOOKS or fax 706-554-7444

- amazon.com

- authenticbooks.com

Authentic
MEDIA

Also available from Authentic Media

Power of Generosity

How to Transform Yourself and Your World

David Toycen

An intimate journey down the road of giving, *The Power of Generosity* will strike a chord with all who want to fulfill a vital part of their humanity—the need to give.

Dave Toycen, President and CEO of World Vision Canada, believes generosity can save lives—both the benefactor's and the recipient's. The act of giving without an ulterior motive inherently nurtures a need human's have for significance. During three decades of traveling to the poorest and most desperate countries, Dave has seen and met individuals who have been freed by acts of generosity.

What is generosity? What motivates a person toward benevolence? *The Power of Generosity* is a practical guide to developing a spirit of generosity, providing thoughtful answers and encouragement for all those looking for ways to be more giving in their lives.

Authentic
MEDIA

The Skeptics Guide to the Global AIDS Crisis

Tough Questions, Direct Answers

Dale Hanson Bourke

Despite almost weekly coverage in media outlets, many people are unclear and uncertain as to what the HIV/AIDS crisis is all about. *The Skeptics Guide to the Global AIDS Crisis* presents the information in a very friendly but candid question and answer fashion.

Investigating both popular and seemingly unpopular solutions and with careful regard to the balance of the arguments, the author answers questions people often have but are too intimidated to ask. Sample questions include:

- In the United States, everyone panicked when AIDS was first reported, but now things don't seem so bad. Isn't it possible that we are overstating the problem?

- What about Magic Johnson? Wasn't he diagnosed with AIDS, but is still fine?

- What about charities? Aren't many of them concentrating on fighting AIDS?

- How is HIV/AIDS spread in different parts of the world?

- Do condoms really stop the transmission of sexually transmitted diseases?

Authentic
MEDIA